ARE YA RIGHT, MATE?

A walk around Australia

Woodslane Press Pty Ltd
10 Apollo Street
Warriewood, NSW 2102
Email: info@woodslane.com.au
Tel: 02 8445 2300 Website: www.woodslanepress.com.au

First published in Australia in 2024 by Woodslane Press

NATIONAL LIBRARY OF AUSTRALIA
A catalogue record for this book is available from the National Library of Australia

FSC www.fsc.org
MIX
Paper | Supporting responsible forestry
FSC® C136333

Printed in China by Asia Pacific Offset Ltd
Book design by Luke Harris

ARE YA RIGHT, MATE?

A walk around Australia

TERRA ROAM

WOODSLANE PRESS

CONTENTS

AN ACKNOWLEDGEMENT

I acknowledge the Aboriginal and Torres Strait Islander people as the First Nations of this continent and its islands.

I respect the elders, storytellers, healers and my friends who have helped enrich my understanding of their countries, landscapes, lore, spirits, food, medicine and culture.

I celebrate First Nations ancestors as the first explorers, astronomers, farmers, merchants, scientists and inventors on this continent.

I recognise the sovereignty of Aboriginal and Torres Strait Islander nations; it always was and always will be their land.

Traditional Aboriginal names, nations or language groups are used in this book. Where I could, I have sourced information from locals, online and literature at the time of writing. As more language and knowledge is saved and reclaimed some of these might change with new editions.

The Indigenous knowledge and experiences shared in this book have been approved to share with you, either while writing, during the walk or from public learning platforms. Nothing is shared without prior consent; we have already taken enough without taking the traditions and stories too.

If you are Aboriginal or a Torres Strait Islander reading something in this book which needs to be changed, removed or added, please let me know. As knowledge is passed on, permissions change and awareness increases. I hope this book stays current and helps others.

PREFACE (AND DISCLAIMER)

This is an adventure book full of stories from my 17,200-kilometre walk around Australia for suicide prevention.

I sincerely believe that everyone who feels that death is the only escape from their pain can find healing and new happiness in their lives. If this is you, I know your pain and understand exactly how you feel. I see you, your struggle and your fight.

When I was sick, cliches didn't help, they felt impersonal and irrelevant to the lonely, dark place I was in, so I have tried to avoid using them. I will share my personal experiences with you instead and hopefully some of you will relate and find hope and healing in these pages.

Together we will dive deep into difficult topics, including uncomfortable stories which may confront you. To avoid being triggered by these please make sure you are in a safe head space and can talk to someone if you need to work through how it makes you feel. It is important to have someone who can listen and support you when you are trying to survive mental illness, trauma and loss. It is much healthier to talk about it than to stay silent.

If any of my experiences upset you, please put the book down or bookmark it, go for a walk or ride, listen to some music, call a friend, journal and/or do some of the other exercises suggested by your therapist. Your mental wellbeing comes first.

In Australia we have some very good crisis hotlines, please use these if you need help.

1300 224 636	Beyond Blue 24/7
1300 659 467	Suicide Call Back Service 24/7
1800 011 046	Open Arms–Veterans and Families 24/7
1800 551 800	Kids Helpline–5-25yrs 24/7
1300 726 306	PANDA–Perinatal Anxiety and Depression 9am-7.30pm AEST Mon-Fri
1300 789 978	MensLine Australia 24/7
1800 424 287	Friendline 7 days
1300 308 699	Autism Connect 8am-7pm AEST Mon-Fri
1800 737 732	1800RESPECT SMS 0458 737 732–Sexual Assault and Domestic Violence 24/7
139 276	13YARN–Aboriginal and Torres Strait Islander Support 24/7
131 114	Lifeline 24/7

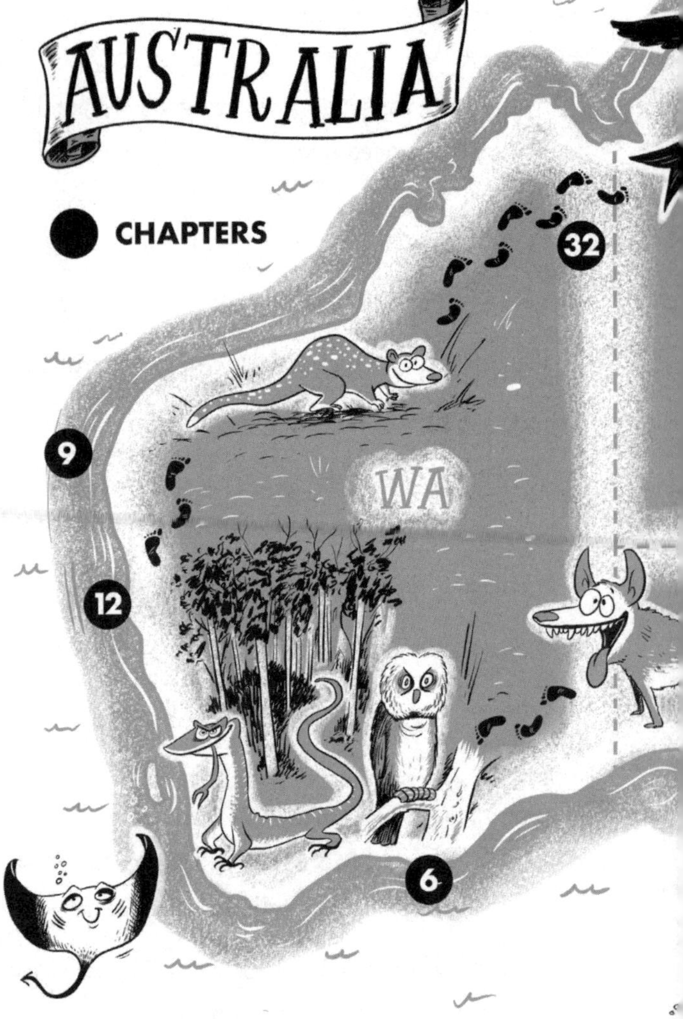
AUSTRALIA
CHAPTERS
32
9
WA
12
6

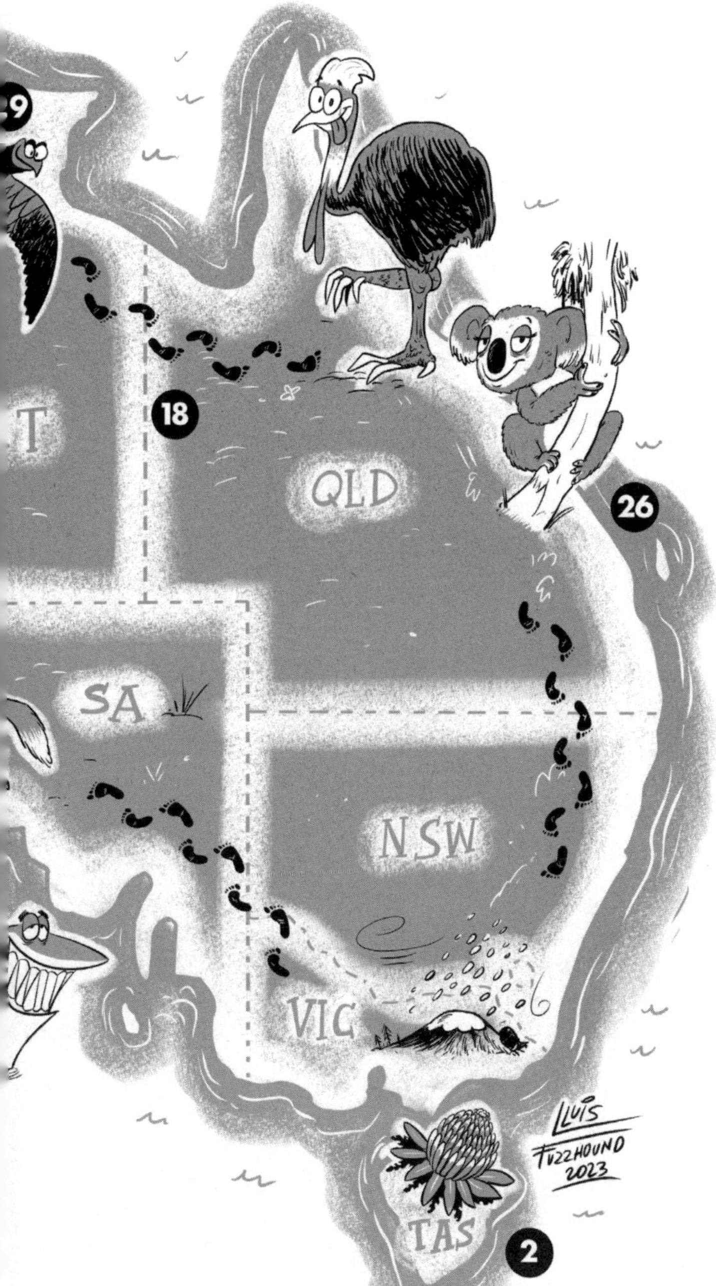
9
18
T
QLD
26
SA
NSW
VIC
TAS
2
LLUIS
FUZZHOUND
2023

Good, better, best.
Never let it rest.
When your good is better,
make your better best.

~ anonymous

CHAPTER 1

GO FOR A WALK

When my psychologist Bronnie told me to go for a walk every day, I don't think she had an entire lap of the country in mind.

Okay, let's jump right in. This is a story about walking around Australia, but it is also the story of how I helped myself recover from suicide. An adventure story with a survivalist backbone. You're going to read edge-of-the-seat exciting action, tips, tricks and anecdotes for your next adventure, as well as my first-hand experiences of mental health, trauma and recovery. Some of this will be confronting. Please remember every care plan is individually designed, this story is not your care plan, but it might help you or someone you know.

In our first therapy session, I immediately felt at ease with Bronnie and knew we would be able to do a lot of good work together. She saw through the appearance of calm and found the painful places in need of repair. I'm glad she had a box of tissues handy; the peaceful demeanour was the smooth façade covering a secret portal into a maelstrom of untreated, undiagnosed and misdiagnosed mental illnesses.

In our second therapy session Bronnie gave me some

homework, she asked me to draw a timeline and write the best memories above and worst memories below. It was a confronting exercise, many people with depression and post-traumatic stress disorder (PTSD) unconsciously focus on the bad stuff and have trouble remembering the good stuff. My timeline was bottom-heavy, as expected, but Bronnie had explained this would happen and gave me instructions to sit with the timeline each day and try focusing on the positives. Gradually, over two weeks, I kept adding more above the line until those memories started returning easier than the bad ones.

In the next session we sat on the floor together and reviewed my homework. I had made a very long timeline. We looked at how most of the best memories were in nature: the outdoors, bushland, mountains, snow, ocean, mountain bike riding, sailing, snorkeling and kayaking, but mostly walking for days, weeks, even months, alone through wild places. It gave me some of the most useful insights into my life, how I had unconsciously been applying survival techniques from my infancy through to my childhood, teens and adulthood, and how these had changed to adapt to working and relationship environments.

Since childhood I had used solitude in nature as my safe place, refuge, sanctuary and escape from a cruel world which I didn't understand and which couldn't understand me. The times I became sick correlated with limited access to the outdoors. Bronnie pointed out how effective nature was for my mental health and the importance of freedom in the outdoors.

However, I had made a series of choices that took me away from the safety of nature to a very dark place where I saw suicide as my only escape. I was not a stranger to suicidal thoughts.

My first memories of suicide are of being way back in primary school, at only eight years old.* I would come home from school, get changed into play clothes, grab a piece of fruit and go outside to the tree swing. Sitting there, looking down the hill, across the paddocks to the lake, I'd recall the day and rework scenarios to better endings. As an autistic child I was acutely self-aware, even though I was not aware until much later of the autism itself.

Usually, I'd end up sitting there crying, hating the world, despising the church and wishing I was dead. There were too many rules, and it was exhausting perpetually living against my nature, pretending to be someone I was not.

The only thing which changed through the years was the crying part; I stopped feeling sorry for myself and became angry at the world instead. Death was logical. In my head it was a natural solution to the emotional and psychological agony I was experiencing. At the age of eight, I had no concept of fear of death or the repercussions for family, nor did I know how to go about it. How does a healthy eight-year-old die?

As I headed into my teens, twenties and thirties the notion was never far away, but the drive to make change in a broken world was always a little bit stronger than leaving. I just needed to complete one more campaign to wake up the world and then I could leave. I went through this over and over. It was my duty to protect nature which kept me here longer than I intended, a strange nature/nurture symbiosis fraught

---

* For the full trauma backstory check Appendix I.

with human shame. The more I campaigned for awareness and change, the more humanity's ignorance and apathy eroded my mental health. It felt like I was walking a tight rope, about to fall into the darkness if I lost momentum. But the darkness was a destination where I would eventually find peace, constantly pulling at me, reminding me of the hell I lived in and the trauma I carried.

In between these campaigns, I would decompress by packing for treks alone through wild places* in the Australian Alps or through coastal national parks. There was no need for official tracks, I could confidently link national parks, conservation parks, reserves, beaches, 4WD tracks and swim across rivers to make my own adventures.† All I needed was a good kit, enough food and bush food knowledge, a clean water source, topographic maps and a compass.

Nature was an unconscious survival strategy, until Bronnie helped me see consciously how important intentional nature and solitude would become as my path to mental health recovery hit rough patches. My homework between therapy sessions was "go for a walk every day". It didn't need

---

* I avoid thinking of any place as wilderness if it has been altered by us with tracks, clearing, dams, mines and air/water/soil pollution. Wilderness, from my point of view, bears no trace of humans: places we have passed through without leaving evidence or are yet to explore. It is a controversial stance given we are a natural animal species of Earth, spread across every continent, even Antarctica, intentionally changing our environment for survival and functionality, much the same as most species of animals, just (unfortunately) far more destructively. So let's use the term "wild places" to describe where I trek.

† Note, not all national parks allow off-track travel: always check before venturing off formal paths.

to be far or for too long, around the block or down a country lane, so long as it was outside, breathing fresh air, getting sun on my skin and watching nature. But from this seed, a much greater idea grew, and four and half years later I arrived in Newcastle, as the first female to walk solo and unsupported around Australia.

CHAPTER 2

SNOW FALLING ON WARATAHS

The clanging bell of a currawong's call,
high in the fragrant flowering eucalypt.
Fairy wrens hopping around the soft dirt,
foraging for morsels of protein.
Rustling undergrowth as a black tiger snake
turns and glides away.
The little blonde echidna burrowing into the grass
as it feels someone approaching.
A line of bubbles leading to a slick platypus
coming up for air in the waterfall's pool.

The big walk began with a 1,280-kilometre lap around lutruwita/Tasmania.* This was the shake-down for gear and to see if I was physically strong enough. Other circumambulations and traverses of Australia had missed walking in lutruwita, and so I decided to start there. I had been there many times, lived there twice while studying, and I keep returning because the lush forests, mountains,

* A glossary of place names can be found at the end of the book.

endangered wildlife and fierce coastlines call me back to explore more.

Before starting I had to catch the ferry over, from Naarm/Melbourne to limilinaturi/Devonport. After a rough and expensive night, it was good to disembark in limilinaturi early. My tent, poles, pegs and boots were returned to me, but not the dehydrated vacuum sealed food, which was confiscated by a quarantine officer. First stop was the Dockside Café for a hot breakfast and coffee. The owner was there and asked where I was off too with such a big pack. After telling him about the big walk for suicide prevention he kindly gave me free breakfast, some homemade snacks, a toasted sandwich, $20 cash and wished me lots of luck. That helped change my mood after losing a week of meals, and I was able to carry his enthusiasm all the way through the day.

I took a really big pack, two in fact. This was my first big mistake but let me explain. It was near impossible to find information about walking around Australia without support vehicles. I was able to send a few messages to other long-distance hikers walking around Australia at the time, Scott Loxley (*Storming Australia*) and Mike Pauley (*Climate Action Now*), and they were very generous with their time and advice. I wanted more information about the places I had not walked before, particularly the more remote back roads, and the seasons I planned to walk in, so I became a lifetime member of ExploreOz. It was a great online forum for people travelling in Australia, mostly 4WD enthusiasts and the *Adventure Before Dementia* crowd, very helpful and mostly supportive. Most people were pretty cool about what

I planned and respectful of the experience and survival skills I had already accumulated.

One of the most popular of my forum threads was the question about gear, something like: "In your experienced opinion, what do you think I will need to pack to walk around Australia?" I had already opened a can of worms when I introduced myself and the walk plans; the trolls came out for a frolic.

Oh, my gods! A woman! Alone! Without a vehicle! Are you stupid? You'll die, you'll be raped. There were a lot of detailed explanations of exactly what would be done to me if I tried. They assumed I was not from Australia and had no idea, completely dismissing my solo and survival training. Some even went as far as abusing me for wasting the time of rescuers who will inevitably need to risk their lives to save mine. That was my introduction to the small percentage of males who harass females who dare step out of their societal boundaries.

The gear lists from other travellers were amazing! A lot of great ideas! To be beyond criticism I subconsciously overcompensated in gear, training and learning local knowledge. That was why I had a 20-litre front pack weighing 12 kilograms and an 80-litre expedition backpack weighing 31 kilograms, including food and water. I nearly fell over every time I put them on. What the Hels did I have in there?!? It turned out that it included a whole lotta stuff I didn't need in lutruwita.*

It was spring and the weather was perfect: sunny, warm, not too windy or wet as I set out along the north coast on

* Refer to Appendices for gear lists.

the first week of walking to kanamaluka/River Tamar. Some beaches were soft sand or pebbles, so I tried to stay on the dunes, grass or beside the coastal roads and rail when the tides came in. The air was salty and energising, the sound of the waves washing over the pebbly beaches made a hissing rattling sound as the stones jostled against each other. The sunscreen melted off my face with the sweat pouring out as I laboured under the heavy packs. Each day ended with blistered feet, sunburn and aching muscles but I felt fantastic.

The extra exertion under the weight played tricks on my mind. I had difficulty keeping track of the distance I had walked, thinking I had made much more progress than the short spurts I could barely manage. Looking at the map each time I rested only made me feel frustrated and more exhausted. My planned schedule for lutruwita was abandoned and I had to just take one day at a time, and for some of those days, one step at a time.

It didn't take long before I met with more of lutruwita's legendary hospitality. People would meet me as I walked through their town or village and offer a place to sleep or camp, to fill my water bottles and give me fruit. Walking past roadside fruit and vegetable markets I was offered free produce. It didn't happen all the time but when it did happen, I was immensely grateful. It lifted my spirits and lightened the load.

Eventually, after 400 kilometres, the ridiculous weight of the pack began taking a toll on my hips. On the back roads of larapuna/Binalong Bay the pain in my hips became unbearable. Amongst white beaches, granite boulders covered in red lichen, turquoise blue water, thick tall ash forests, mirror reflective lagoons and quiet bays, I tamped down the pain by absorbing the beauty. I had to walk a few kilometres then rest for half an hour, walk, rest, walk, rest, slowing down my progress significantly and causing more mental and physical fatigue than I could handle (and I have a superhuman pain threshold, it's an autism spectrum thing). During a forced ten-day recovery break, I completely changed my heavy gear for ultralight everything. Best decision ever! I had tried a pack full of everything recommended for health and safety, now it was time to return to my sensible multi-day bushwalking roots: lightweight and enjoyable.

This shakedown section around lutruwita helped set me up for smoother problem solving later. I tried out familiar and new packing, camping, eating and sleeping systems, tweaking some and moving on from others. Deciding not to pander to the critics was a necessary step to take.

Many times after lutruwita I had to remind myself, "This is my walk, I'll do it the best way I know how and I'll learn from my own mistakes." It was a pretty safe bet there were a few more lessons to learn; only a few people who had attempted to walk across or around Australia were willing to talk about it.

Late each evening in larapuna, flotillas of little penguins return to their chicks in dune burrows, after a big day of fishing. One night I wandered down across the lagoon to sit in the dunes and wait. It was a densely dark night without any moon, and I didn't bring a torch. Nocturnal animals are very sensitive to light and shining our phone torches or headlamps on them can temporarily blind and disorientate them, not to mention making them visible to predators. I sat in the cooling air, mozzies buzzing and biting, listening to the tell-tale sound of excited hungry chicks calling out to their parents. Then it happened; a ruckus picked up in the grass and scrub around me and I could just pick out the faint white ghosts of little penguins waddling over the beach, disappearing into the dune vegetation. I was startled as one ran over my hand!

By 11pm it was over, and my mozzies had sent invitations to their friends. It was time to walk back. I stood up, turned around and was stunned by the sight of a southern aurora filling the sky with a white curtain of light. I could just make out the faint tint of yellow and pink. I had never seen anything like it with the naked eye. At first I couldn't believe it, had I fallen asleep, was this a dream? I turned back to the beach to see if anyone was there to share the moment with but what met me was the crown of natural wonders. The bay was filling with glowing bioluminescence. Each wave came to life with a blue-white fire. I turned back to the aurora and then the glowing water, I shook my head, stunned.

You would think that with all the beauty surrounding me in lutruwita, it would be the most ideal place to continue, even fast-track, my mental health recovery. This was not the case. For a while I was in denial and kept pushing on, wearing The Happy Walk* mask, until I hit the wall and had a breakdown in Bicheno. I booked four nights in a motel; the owners helped by offering a generous discount and booked me in to see the doctor. As soon I was safe in the room I fell apart on the inside. I now had the added pressure of the walk on top of managing depression and PTSD. I didn't cope. To

* The walk was called The Happy Walk.

be honest, I felt like a hypocrite, not able to walk the talk, living in a big lie I had woven around me like a safety cocoon.

The doctor was compassionate and very matter-of-fact. It was depression, I needed to rest and be with friends. She encouraged me to keep walking to Hobart where I could stop and stay with friends, but to take a lot of rest days on the way because my mind was not handling the physical fatigue. Her diagnosis was devastating. I had thought after two years of intensive therapy that I was finally on top of it all, but her prescription for self-care, slowing down, hanging out with friends, was spot on.

Taking advantage of the slower pace, I stopped in some ideal locations. A bed and breakfast donated two nights of accommodation near Freycinet National Park; in the evening I walked down to puthimiluna/Anna Bay and spent a day walking in Freycinet. I saw the huge middens of the palawa paredarerme people, a patina/tiger snake, an echidna and some cheeky roos. On the way back a massive storm chased me, changing the iconic vivid blue water of Freycinet into dark moody green, indigo and grey.

The spellbinding turquoise beach and white sands,
Deceiving to the sweaty bushwalker seeking a dip,
As the chill of the Southern Ocean catches the breath.
Track rights negotiated with a patina sun baking,
As mayaluwarana rises.

I mentioned earlier how I had lived in lutruwita while studying. I also lived on a ship moored in nipaluna/Hobart, but it was only for six weeks so it doesn't count. The first time, I lived in Smithton for a year in 1991, hometown of one of Australia's living treasures, Hannah Gadsby. For a young conservationist, living in Smithton was a mind-expanding experience, learning to see the world through very different perspectives whilst strengthening my moral resistance. It was a metaphorical primordial swamp from which emerged my rebellion against the prejudices of the Christian world. That year in Smithton was at a missionary college from which I was nearly expelled several times, each an ultimatum: go to bible college or come back home.

One great thing came out of 1991: long-term friends who had moved to nipaluna welcomed me back into their lives unconditionally for as long as I needed to recover. I played tourist, walking up kunanyi/Mount Wellington, going to the beach, visiting Harbour Lights Café (which was a favourite haunt when I lived on the water), Salamanca Market, brunches and dinners with friends in the city, until it was time to keep going.

I highly recommend walking up kunanyi at least once in your life, when you're still fit. It was a highlight for me. The steep elevation from sea level to over 1,200 metres takes you through multifarious layers of various ecosystems, habitat and volcanic geology. The views from the top on a sunny day are worth every step. Public safety warning: do not go up in blizzard conditions, it can and has killed people.

Later in lutruwita I had to take three weeks off to recover from pneumonia and bronchitis. It was horrible and I had to go through it alone without help. I was in Strahan and feeling very tired, so I spoilt myself with a nice hotel room to rest for two nights. It was a place I had been looking forward to visiting since I started planning the big lap. Unfortunately, I had only one day of energy left to walk around and spent that time trying to find a doctor. It quickly went into the lungs, and I could barely breath. Each morning I managed to crawl into the ensuite bathroom, fill the water bottles I forced myself to drink through the day, and look at my grey face and blue lips before coughing up blood. I didn't end up seeing much of Strahan and spent a small fortune staying in the room for a week. No doctors could see me, and I had no supporters to help get me out of there.

It was a shock that nobody in Strahan would help me, not even the hotel staff. I guess I was asking the wrong people. It didn't occur to me to phone friends or an ambulance, naturally assuming each day I would feel better tomorrow. Eight days later I had to check out of the hotel because I was about to run out of money. Taking a double dose of pain medication and eating lozenges like lollies I managed to hitchhike out of Strahan to Hobart, organise a small loan and catch the buses north to pick up the walk at Marrawah. I tried walking again, but my lungs were still struggling to get air and I was still coughing up blood. In Smithton I used the loan to pay for another two weeks of hotels until I could breathe without pain and wheezing. This was one of the lowest parts of the entire walk. My body failed me, I had to skip a section I had been looking forward to so much, funds had disappeared before finishing the shake down, my lungs were now scarred and would cause another bout of pneumonia a few years later. What was I doing?

I decided not to do the 88-kilometre South Coast Track around the bottom of lutruwita, I didn't want to get caught out into the middle of such a wild landscape without a safety net if my health took another turn. Instead, I walked down to putalina/Oyster Cove, caught the ferry over to lunawuni/ Bruny Island and walked the 130-kilometre length (and a bit more) to Cape Bruny Lighthouse and kaparati/Adventure Bay. I love lighthouses, the architecture of them, haunted stairs and keepers' cabins, the insanely remote places where they perch on top of dangerous hazards, warning seafarers to stay away. Many a lighthouse keeper was driven to madness. This is the real metaphor for the lighthouse, not a beacon of safety and hope: it says stay away or you'll die.

Lunawuni was a good choice: wildlife, wild ocean, waves smashing on the geometric cliffs of hexagons and tunnels falling into the sea. Being spring, flowers were in bloom everywhere and the birdlife was prolific. I even saw and heard the endangered forty-spotted pardalote and the albino wallabies, thanks to locals letting me in on some of their secret places.

White gum manna feeding the flitting spots, pardalotes
White shrub blossoms covering windy headlands, fairy wrens
Nuts and fruit falling from the canopy, green rosellas
Roaring forties ocean pounding the sea cliffs, albatross
Protected shoals stretching across wide bays, pelicans

I spent a couple of days with one of my favourite hardcore adventurers, Cynthia (aka Lady McGuyver), learning about the natural habitats, animals, plants of and conservation threats to the west coast, takayna/Tarkine and mountains, in Peerapper and Toogee country. A lot of lutruwita is logged; there is not much old growth forest left, and what is still there is being logged, mined and dammed. This is what makes lutruwita a place of contradictions: the natural beauty which brings in millions of tourist dollars, the billions of dollars of carbon capture value of the native forests, home of the world's tallest flowering tree and 650 species of threatened animals and plants, against governments who want to take everything they possibly can before the island is destroyed by progress.

Lutruwita is one of the most beautiful states of Australia, but it is also the most environmentally ravaged. There has been a war for more than half a century between conservationists, environmentalists, bushwalkers, tourist operators, wildlife carers, climate scientists and the governments, mining companies, hydro companies, loggers and communities employed by them. Only a small percentage of planet saving actions make it to the news.

There have been wars here since convicts and colonisers arrived 200 years ago. When I lived here the first time in 1991, locals in Circular Head told me "the Aboriginals no longer exist". This claim was repeated over and over in local stories, history and schools. IT IS WRONG! Yes, they were hunted down and killed by troops and mercenaries, led by black trackers; yes there were wars and genocide; thousands of palawa people were shot, poisoned and caught diseases they had no immunity against. The few who were left were forcefully taken to truwana/Cape Barron Island, northeast lutruwita. However, since then, many palawa Aboriginal peoples have returned to lutruwita, and those on truwana also returned.

These lies have continued into this century, even as the palawa nations reclaimed their culture, stories, language and land. It is not my story, but this one and many similarly atrocious stories are told by many Aboriginal and Torres Strait Islander people across the land and sea. The fight for acknowledgement, respect, equality, health, housing, access to clean water, education, land rights and Treaty is ongoing.

A child of about 12 years asked about the Aboriginal sticker on my water bottle while I took a rest stop at a small general store. I said I was an ally and would be walking through many Aboriginal countries. Until then we were having a pleasant chat about school and her next holidays, but her whole demeanour changed as she puffed up her chest saying, "There are no Aboriginals in Tasmania, we wiped them out." I asked where she had heard that, and she told me it was from her teacher and her dad.

This is one of the reasons I am an active ally of Aboriginal and Torres Strait Islander peoples and proactively anti-racist. My white privilege is even more reason to stand up for the traditional owners wherever I travel. The consequences for me to speak out are nothing compared to what Aboriginals have endured for centuries.

Apart from a tornado, waterspout and a huge hailstorm, the weather gods were being kind to me: a perfect spring. The Derwent Bridge day was a 32-kilometre hike up into the mountains, with a stop at the Wood Carving Museum and lunch with an unexpected visitor. A young blonde echidna trundled over top of my feet, oblivious to the fact I was another animal. They have bad eyesight and rely almost entirely on scent, hearing and vibrations. It began raining on and off through the afternoon. The sun warmed everything, then the rain cooled it; when the sun came back out everything steamed. As I gained altitude the temperature quickly dropped until it was below 0°C. Luckily there was no wind.

The landscape and birdlife had changed dramatically since the day began, from flat expanses of dammed lakes and denuded farmland to dark, fragrant mountain ash, gold alpine tussock grass, fens, bogs of bright green sphagnum moss, colourful flowering heath and snow gums painted by the rain.

And then it snowed, just a little at first, a few snowflakes falling on my jacket sleeves. The ground was too wet and warm for it to settle but as it fell heavier it started collecting on the grass and in the heath creating a nice contrast to the dark overcast bushland. A small breeze was beginning to rise. My eyes had adjusted to the low light while watching glossy ravens and currawongs playing in the snow, landing on top of shrubs and boulders, walking about on the flowers as clumps of snow tumbled down. They were having a great time, as was I.

Then something caught my eye, a flash of bright red in the dark green and white. It looked like a banksia flower, but different to anything I had seen before. It was only about 20 metres off the road, so I dropped my pack, grabbed my camera and carefully picked a path through the thick tundra. The heath was higher than my head. I began spotting more flashes of red and soon I saw the flower in detail. I was surrounded by a small grove of the iconic Tasmanian waratahs. I could hardly believe my eyes. I had hoped to see these but thought it was too early in the season. The waratah produces a large bulbous bunch of flowers, about the size of a fist, made up of flower head tubes, each with its own stigma. The bunch is surrounded by a circle of red petals and green scalloped leaves.

Standing there in a bright red rain jacket, completely hidden in the thick bush, with fully formed flakes falling on my face and salty tears of joy wetting my lips, I gazed up at the snow falling on waratahs.

CHAPTER 3

THE SOUTH

We live on an island continent full of diverse and sublime beauty. Even at walking speed, the landscape changes every day, whether it be the terrain, the wildlife, the plants or the season. Each day gave me something new to look at and listen to.

In lutruwita/Tasmania I experienced the coastal wild places, mountains, islands, lakes, heatwaves, snow, tornado, hail and giant double blizzard rainbows. Currawongs and crows followed me through their foraging grounds, pademelons and wallabies came into my camps, the last of the spring flowers and first of their fruits caught the eye like jewels in magic forests.

While traversing the south, from Boorloo/Perth to Canberra, I saw a completely different set of landscapes. Heading south to Cape Leeuwin I visited idyllic sandy coves, patted stingrays, and explored caves while being buzzed by bats. The forests were like the cathedrals of giants, full of towering karri trees (*Eucalyptus diversicolor*), the second tallest flowering tree on Earth, growing some 70 metres high and living for up to 600 years. In the forest floor, covered in ferns, moss, orchids, I could imagine pixies and faeries.

Standing on rugged Cape Leeuwin at the lighthouse, with the Indian Ocean on one side and the Southern Ocean on the other, the south-westerly wind roared, surf crashed, salt water sprayed over me. It was the day the southern wet season arrived, like clockwork, with waves of storms rolling over the southwest, watering the newly sown crops of wheat and canola. All the coastal plants, from the succulent pig face, ruby berry and saltbush, to the gnarly leptospermums, were stunted and everything grew at an angle, sculpted by the wind.

Recherche Bay is one of the most beautiful places in the world and home to award winning beaches. The water is emerald blue, washing onto white sandy beaches. The granite rocks are red and gold from lichen. Pods of dolphins surf the waves and big water dragons sun themselves on the walking paths. I arrived in this little paradise in pouring rain and gale force winds, soaked to the skin, even with all my wet weather gear.

I was welcomed to Esperance by Marli and Banjo and shared their cottage. Marli made excellent coffee and had the fire going in the living room. For the next two days I washed and dried all my gear, attempted to swim in the achingly cold Southern Ocean and spent hours sitting by the water, absorbing all the colours, relaxing and re-energising. I like to think of Recherche Bay, the beaches and islands and people, as the gem encrusted slippers of Western Australia.

Back in 2003, I hitchhiked the 4WD Old Balladonia Track with three Dutch backpackers in a camper Land Cruiser. I had picked up a couple of weeks of work at the Condingup Pub, cleaning dishes and childminding over the Christmas season. When it was time to go, a local recommended the track. It was the most hilarious trip, with bumps and potholes, dipping from one side to the other, swinging around corners. Two of them had the front seats and I shared the double mattress in the back with the other. It was a cushy rollercoaster ride. We hit the ceiling a few dozen times and rolled into each other enough to be good friends by the time we reached Balladonia.

As far as I'm aware, the track is now closed to public access to help protect the Great Western Woodlands. Back then, and when I walked through the protected reserve and national park, it was clearly a significant place. The Great Western Woodlands are bigger than England in size, home to more than half of the southern hemisphere's flowering plant species and more than 300 eucalyptus species. It is a world biodiversity hotspot with 440 rare and threatened species of plants and 32 endangered species of animals. The 4WD enthusiasts might be disappointed to have their tracks closed but it is an essential part of conservation in such an important woodland, that and keeping the mines out, plus halting deforestation by farm expansion.

I have been lucky to have seen endangered mallee fowl, Carnaby's black cockatoos, pink cockatoos, pygmy possums and a honey possum in the Woodlands reserves. Plans are in place to create a 1000-kilometre corridor of forests and woodlands across southwest Western Australia, called the Gondwana Link, to help protect the vulnerable and endangered species of animals and plants, tens of thousands of years of Aboriginal history and unique geology. Hopefully, this will be fire-managed by traditional owners, as it is very susceptible to the wrong kind of fire.

Having already been on the old track, and wanting to get away from the rain, I changed my plan and walked from Esperance to Norseman instead, through the salmon gum forests, past the natural spring in Gibson, filling up with water from their soak, past the little salty pink lakes, to the groovy retro art Railway Motel and Woodlands Guesthouse. There was not much bushland along that stretch of road as most of it was farmland. I stopped here for a couple of days before again changing plans. Instead of turning right onto Eyre Highway for the Nullarbor I caught the coach to Kalgoorlie and walked back to Norseman, to see a part of Australia I had only previously passed at night.

I was keen to visit a 24-hour brothel or titty bar: for the outback cultural experience, you understand. It is a part of Kalgoorlie's commercial infrastructure. Unfortunately, it was like a ghost town. When I arrived Australia's iron ore exports were at an all-time low and mines had laid off thousands of workers. The sex industry must have also been laid low with less clientele.

I walked past the poo farm, through the botanic garden, visited the lookout to see the big hole and left. The walk down the highway back to Norseman was much more interesting. There was a hot pink toilet on top of a mound of dirt; a kettle tree filled with old broken electric kettles; the hard hat tree where miners hang their hats when they leave, signed by their mates; and some ruins beside the road with a set of bone china teacups and a teapot glued to the old red brickwork.

In Kambalda I stayed in the hotel. I'm pretty sure some of the sex workers had found employment there; I had to listen to them through the walls all night. One of my old school friends, Neridah, was living in Widgiemooltha; her ex-partner collected the gold ore rocks beside the highway, which fell off overloaded trucks. She asked me, "If you find some good ones, pick them up for his collection."

Widgiemooltha had a population of about eight. Most of them collected rocks and were planning to build a smelter to extract their own gold. I saw a rock fall off a truck, picked it up and was shocked by how heavy it was—gold is heavy—so I put it into my barrow. A bit further down, I found another, the same size. It was heavier, so I replaced the first one. Then I found another and another. After a day of rock collecting, I realised the barrow was getting pretty heavy; I must have had rocks in my head to agree to this.

Ultimately, I carried three good, heavy rocks of iron ore distributed evenly inside the barrow. I could see the gold dust in them when the sun hit just right. It was a relief to reach Widgie and offload them. Apparently, after inspection, I had picked up about $600 worth of gold. They gave me a fossicker's magnifier as a thank you, showing me how to spot gold and fossils. It was a great gift, and I used it mostly to look at insects, feathers, shells and plants.

Walking past the wide red clay pans of Lake Lefroy, Lake Cowan and across the Nullarbor, I had a lot of fun identifying animal tracks left after rain, when the dry cracked ground turned to mud. There were goanna, emu, camel and kangaroo tracks heading in all directions, and dingo tracks following them. Some of the lakes along the Coolgardie Highway had sculptures made from recycled engines and rusted corrugated roofing. One notable thing missing on this crossing were the iron stone deposits in some of the pans. The first time

I crossed, hitchhiking, we would stop to fossick in them, some of these were 50 metres across with nuggets of solid iron, layered stones, bowls and hollow rings like big knobbly chocolate donuts. They have all been bulldozed out since. Nothing, not a pebble, was left in any of the iron stone pans. I had also learnt they can hold opals and when the striped ironstone is polished it is collectable, so I guess it isn't surprising in a remote, unregulated area to steal what belongs to the traditional owners. I bet it was valued by them too; those places may even have had dreamtime stories attached to them.

On the South Australian side of the border, the further east I walked the more I was surrounded by agricultural and industrial landscapes, and the more locals shared their polarised views of them. I kept my thoughts to myself and listened as people groaned about insecticides and pesticides and the farmers groaned about the government banning the more dangerous chemicals. I heard complaints about how ugly the solar farm was going to be while standing next to half a mountain covered in dust and yellow trucks like industrious ants; the other half had been removed by mining companies.

Whyalla was confronting. The people were so welcoming, green gardens and paths filled the public spaces, and the view out over the gulf was gorgeous, but turn your head north and the hulking old rusty, dusty steelworks dominates the landscape. Many people would like to see it shut down, while many more work there and need to feed their families. When I was studying conservation ecology at university, Whyalla and Goordnada/Port Augusta were used as examples of diversifying and retraining to encourage the closure of dirty industries and opening up renewables. It didn't work in practice. In Tarparrie/Port Pirie I helped out the wonderful team at the Lifeline Headquarters clothing warehouse, sorting donations, making rags and bagging specialty items for women in developing countries. It was an honour to work alongside such amazing people.

I knew I risked being caught in the first heat waves as I crossed the top of Spencer Gulf in September and October, but had no idea how intense they were going to be. I spent more days hiding in cheap dodgy hotel rooms with noisy air conditioning than I did walking. Stepping out of the room at 6am in the morning I would be met by a blast of what felt like air from a furnace. The days between heat waves were still too hot for a full day's walking. I walked from port to port, making sure I could sit beside the water each afternoon, waiting for the wind to change and come in from the south.

Previously, I had been on a road trip around Spencer Gulf with my friend Sarah. We visited every little coastal village and port and walked along all the jetties. If there was a jetty, we had to walk to the end of it. I returned to each of these towns and walked all the jetties again, sitting out on the ends to watch the sunset and feel the cooling breeze. A lot of marine life can be seen underneath jetties: turtles, stingrays, sharks, seals, dolphins, nudibranchs, sea cucumbers, crabs, all kinds of colourful and flashy fish. One day I saw an endangered leafy sea dragon floating weightlessly in the seaweed growing on a jetty pylon.

CHAPTER 4

THE NULLARBOR

"There's nothing out there."

I heard this repeated many times by travellers, even from people who had taken the journey across. Don't believe it, it's simply not true. It is a landscape full of life and history. Most people driving across the Nullarbor calculate their travel time according to the distance and fuel stops, crossing too fast to appreciate its variety and vibrancy. Even a couple of extra travel days will reveal its secrets and surprises.

The 1,200-kilometre stretch of the Eyre Highway, between Norseman in the west and Ceduna in the east, is commonly called The Nullarbor. One section of 147 kilometres is completely straight, without any bends. Eleven roadhouses and villages break up the journey, at intervals between 10 and 180 kilometres, so the furthest you need to walk between roadhouses is 180 kilometres: Norseman to Balladonia. And even then, there is a camping ground a few kilometres off the highway between them. For the seasoned winter walker, the distance is not challenging with so many pitstops along the way. Don't even think about trying it in summer though, it's too hot for safety.

The only leg of the walk I did counterclockwise was from Boorloo/Perth to Tarparrie/Port Pirie, to make the most of the southwesterly winter winds. It was supposed to be all the way to Naarm, but it took too long, and I was caught in the first two heat waves in spring, with temperatures above 40°C, and ended up with ligament damage requiring rest.

The Nullarbor was my favourite part of the traverse across the bottom of Australia. There was so much to see, the landscapes and wildlife changed almost every day.

It wasn't my first time on the Nullarbor. In the summer of 2004-05, I hitchhiked across three times with truckies and in an old bus, and caught the Indian Pacific train once, in the economy 'sitting sleeper'. The first trip over was for my first long solo unsupported expedition, following the coastline 450 kilometres from Esperance to Israelite Bay. This was inspired by the Bedouin nomads I met in the Moroccan Sahara and learning about Wudjari, Ngatjumay and Mirning Aboriginal food and water migration paths. I had even invented a nifty little saltwater distiller for the trip.

As a result of that journey, and the contacts I made for resupplies, I worked a couple of weeks as a short order cook at a roadhouse, leading up to New Year. I was not good at that job but just after New Year, Eyre Bird Observatory, on the Great Australian Bight, asked me to fill in as emergency caretaker for a month. The three-times-daily routine of reporting to the Bureau of Meteorology, taking records of bird counts in the bushland and on the beach, hosting guests and maintenance was one of the best months of my life. I was in my element.

Regardless of already being familiar with the Nullarbor,

it was a new experience to be walking it. It was very useful already having an understanding of what it would be like.

In Norseman I stayed with an ecologist who shared her knowledge about the first 300 kilometres of bushland I would be walking through, part of the Great Western Woodlands, which is home to more than 3,300 species of flowers and twice the size of lutruwita. The section I was about to pass through was mostly gimlet eucalyptus woodland, the soil of which is extensively covered by a protective fragile crust, or skin, of lichen and moss. The contrasts of dry red soil, salmon-coloured trees, blue saltbush, and yellow wattle flowers in winter was spectacular, even more so at sunrise and sunset. It felt like walking through a faerie land.

Each evening I carefully left the road and gently trod a path to flat ground, trying not to crush the soil cover, walking around camp in my own footprints to minimise the area I disturbed. If I sat quietly enough, the birds would forget I was there and come closer to camp. Each morning my alarm was a raucous cacophony of noise as nature woke around me. If I was lucky, I would spot a mallee fowl running through the undergrowth. I had to be very cautious when cooking on the small stove—the Great Western Woodlands are dry, but they do not like fire. Some of the trees, like the gimlet, take 100 years to grow back.

Coming to the end of the woodlands, the terrain became undulating, long slopes slowly rising and falling, for 100 kilometres. Rocky outcrops started to show the closer I was to the escarpment, plus huge dark red bowls of dry cracked mud, and the vegetation opened up with more grassland, pungent native herbs and less trees. The birdlife also changed from sweet little tree birds to emus, raptors and ground nesters.

Nearer the escarpment the ground flattened out before falling away to the flat sandy plains below Madura Pass. The escarpment is a rain catcher and in amongst the rocks can be found hidden glens of lush soft mosses, ferns, orchids, colourful wildflowers and small springs tumbling over the rocks.

It was while crossing the Nullarbor that the difference between radio transmission and phone towers was more apparent than anywhere else. Radio transmission towers pass radio waves, the transmitter is usually a disc or cone shape, and are important for farmers and truckies who use radio communications with each other and their homesteads. Phone towers pass microwaves, and the transmitter/receiver is usually a rectangular shape. From a distance, on the horizon, I would see a tower and get excited, turning on my phone only to find it's just a radio tower. There were plenty of phone towers out there, about one every 100 kilometres, close to the roadhouses, shared with large farms, depending on who was subsidising the cost of it, but not all of them were in sensible places. The phone tower above Madura Roadhouse was well placed for distance across the escarpment and plains but left the roadhouse, tucked snug into the bottom of the escarpment, in the shadow zone. To get phone range in Madura you needed to walk back up to the top of the escarpment, which is where I sat for half a day to update my blog and social media. At the time, approximately a fifth of the highway had phone coverage.

On the plains the trees were growing more lithe, concentrated mostly under the shelter of the escarpment.

There were very few opportunities to get close to the cliffs, so one of my favourite rest areas, an official free camping area with toilet and picnic tables, was Moodini Bluff, with plenty of trees and the most superb sunrise lighting up the cliffs. That place, although beautiful, had a strange feel to it, and I wondered what old story there must be attached to it.

The only water available on the highway for travellers is bore water or bottled water. The bore water was disgusting when warmed up inside my barrow under the sun all day. A few times it was sulphuric, but it was mostly a thick powdery lime taste which caused my throat to constrict when trying to swallow it. It was fine cold but at an ambient or warm temperature my body refused it. Bottled water on the Nullarbor was the most expensive I have ever seen anywhere; I ended up spending over $900 on water.

One day a lovely couple who had camped near me offered to fill my water bottles from their jerry cans. I took 20 litres. The next morning, I barely had time to run behind a bush to empty my bowels. I had the sweats and felt so weak. Checking the water, I found floaties, so I sterilised it. For the next 10 kilometres I had the runs. It wasn't even 9am when I pulled up and made camp, barely off the road, just inside a fence which led to a cattle station above the escarpment. The next roadhouse was only 78 kilometres away. I had phone range from a tower on the escarpment about 15 kilometres away so I called the roadhouse and asked if they could possibly send a ute out so I could have a few days rest before returning to continue. They were unhelpful, refusing to drive out, telling me to call the ambulance (hundreds of kilometres away, hundreds more to the nearest nursing outpost and about $20,000 in costs) if it was so bad I couldn't walk. It was very disappointing. Even more frustrating was knowing they had a Royal Flying Doctor kit for travellers who needed help: it was part of their job. In my first aid kit I had water purifiers, Imodium, glucose, electrolytes and vitamins. Using them I crawled into the tent and slept all day and night, waking only to rehydrate. The next day I was still weak but packed up, continued walking and stopped regularly. When I reached the roadhouse, I had a very frank chat with the owner. Apparently, they get people trying to walk across the Nullarbor "all the time", and if they help one they will be expected to help all. I knew that actually only a handful of people attempt it each year. I bought more water and kept going. Their attitude was jarring but thankfully not shared by all the roadhouses.

Halfway is Mundrabilla Roadhouse, the cheapest fuel on the Nullarbor. I had worked there a decade earlier and the same owners were still tough as nails. It felt weird being there as a customer although they didn't remember me. I stayed a couple of nights and did an interview on the public phone with ABC radio Mid North Coast. It was nice to relax and recover for a day and wander around, remembering that career mistake with an amusement only time can bring. What was I thinking! A roadhouse cook! The pay wasn't even any good.

The next day was my biggest walking day ever...

Looking at the map the night before, I had two choices: break up the distance to Eucla into two short 32-kilometre days, with a rest area in the middle; or see how I felt when I reached it—if I had enough energy and time I could push on. Eucla had already offered to donate a couple of nights in the Nullarbor Nymph Hotel, and it didn't matter if I arrived that day or the next, so I had some flexibility, but a soft bed, and hot shower called. Leaving before sunrise meant I reached the halfway rest area for lunch; it was a no-brainer to keep going. After a two-hour break, avocado and tomato sandwiches and a litre of lemon electrolytes I marched into the next 32 kilometres with lots of spare energy.

At sunset I mounted a white strobe light and flashing amber lights on the barrow, put on my headlamp and turned on the flashing red LEDs in my reflective safety vest, it was a pretty groovy vest. I did a lot of night walking across the Nullarbor as I was pushing out 50+ kilometre days: it was essential to be seen by the trucks, although I imagine there were some interesting alien stories as a result. The trucks, all lit up at night, often looked like UFOs themselves from 10-15 kilometres away, silently making their way over the distant horizon.

It wasn't until my usual stop time came and went that the fatigue set in. First it was the feet, the muscles and tendons starting to ache, then it slowly worked its way up through the body into my back and shoulders. The mental fatigue took longer. At the other end of the escarpment, where the road winds back up to the plateau, a huge crucifix is mounted at a lookout. Lit up, glowing at night, it can be seen from the plain for more than 20 kilometres and until you're only a few kilometres away it feels as though you are never getting any closer. That did my head in. At 60 kilometres my feet were cramping up badly with every step and it felt like walking on raw stumps, but by then the crucifix was looming close. Only a few more kilometres and I would be collapsing into a bed or curled into a foetal position under the shower.

Those last few kilometres were slow and painful, shuffling along trying to keep momentum. It took an hour to push the barrow the final two kilometres up the escarpment. The first place I saw was the Eucla Hotel, but I had booked into the Nullarbor Nymph Hotel, or so I thought. I had to muster up a bit more strength and keep going. I walked through the village of Eucla, and out the other side, back down the Highway, looking for my hotel. Were the lights out? I couldn't find it, so I walked another circuit. It seemed like everyone was asleep, garden lights were on, a few dogs barked, but the houses were dark. I pulled out my phone to check the map more carefully. It was 11pm! No wonder the village was so peaceful.

There was only one place which looked like an hotel, the Eucla Hotel, so I went back. When I had decided to walk on after lunch, I had called ahead to confirm my arrival and room. Everything was supposed to be ready: if I arrived after reception closed, they would put my key in room 11. I parked my barrow near the rooms and had a little explore. There it was! My room! With the key in the door, and a lovely welcome note. It was a rather fancy room too. I was caked in layers of sunscreen, my hair and clothes were crusted with sweat crystals, and my feet stank pretty bad, so I chose the high road and had a shower instead of dirtying the crisp fresh sheets. Ah! That felt good. Well-earned after 67 kilometres (two of which were unnecessary: the hotel name had changed years before but not on Google maps). To this day it is still my personal distance record. I ended up staying for three luxurious nights and explored the area, climbed the dunes and looked at all the pretty things on the beach, even took a sneaky little skinny dip in the ocean.

That damned tormenting crucifix has saved people's lives: the ones travelling across the country leaving behind everything, lost love, failed careers, homes and farms foreclosed by banks, with seemingly nothing ahead. Eyre Highway is also known as *The Blue's Highway*, I called it the Broken Hearts Highway. I met many men travelling across who needed someone to listen to their stories of sadness, despair and seeking redemption. Some had heard my interviews on the radio, or people talking in roadhouses about the walker for suicide prevention, so there were many who stopped to share their stories of recovery, rehabilitation and starting anew. For some of the people who stopped, I was the first person they had ever shared their struggles with. I became the 'roadside counsellor', listening, reassuring, guiding them onto a path of recovery. So I also helped save lives, which made even the most painful day worth every step.

Nulla arbor: Latin for no trees. As I have already mentioned the trees, you might wonder where the name comes from. The Eyre Highway passes through the Nullarbor protected areas, a remarkable limestone area extending over 1000 kilometres wide and 300 kilometres across, with cave systems underground which might go even further. The actual 'treeless plain' you pass on the South Australian side of the highway is only 20 kilometres wide. Blink and you miss it! If you're walking, you get to enjoy it for half a day.

There are two 24-hour quarantine check points, one at Border Village going west and the other just outside Ceduna going east, and they are pretty strict about what you can take across. I watched a convoy of vehicles stopped at the border, carrying their horses and bales of feed. They had all the feed which wasn't still in sealed bags removed and burnt. All fresh fruit, veggies, open packets of nuts, seeds, plants, etc, are taken. All I had left at Ceduna was a banana, which I ate before crossing. I enjoyed the spoils of the quarantine checks as people would pull over and give me their extra food which the quarantine officers would have incinerated. However, I have developed an intolerance for raw apples from eating too many of them. I can't eat them anymore, and it is sad because they were great, travelled well and were a refreshing juicy snack.

You meet all sorts travelling across the Nullarbor. The friendliest people gift food and water, there were even a few who passed and came back an hour later with cold drinks for me. Someone gave me $300 cash! There were also the ones who wanted to save my soul. Very early one morning, one of them screeched her car and caravan to a dangerous stop in the middle of the road and ran back in a panic asking if I was okay. I quickly assured her I was fine and asked her to move her van off the road so nobody ran into her. After she did this, we chatted about what I was doing, walking for suicide prevention. I had sets of special mental health cards made by a supporter, to hand out as I walked. I gave her a set of them. She seemed very out of sorts, anxious, so I wanted to give her as much time as she needed, it was difficult to get anything sensible out of her; her plans were elusive and she didn't want to talk about her life. She circled back around to mental health. I was relieved as I didn't want her travelling in such a confused and stressed state of mind. It didn't take long for her to make it very clear she didn't believe in mental illness, that it was of the devil and only faith in Jesus can heal it. I knew this old trope from my younger years but held my tongue and heard her out as she tried to convert me.

Eventually, I tired of it and decided to turn the tables. I spent a year in Bible college as a teenager and hated it, but it taught me how to talk to fanatical Christians using their own language and quotes from their scriptures*. I quietly asked "If our god is everywhere, is he in all of our hearts? If he is in all of our hearts and minds, we are all of god. How then can the devil defile our minds?". This didn't go as well as I had hoped, even though I was angling towards an open dialogue about love, which had worked in the past. She yelled "Blasphemer!" spitting into my face and raising her hand up ready to slap me. Standing my ground and looking into her eyes, I came straight to the point, really hoping to avoid being hit, saying with as gentle a voice as I could "god is love". It worked, her hand went back down to her side, taking a few steps back as she said, "I will not listen to the devil anymore" and stormed off. She slammed her door shut and yelled out the window "Go to hell, you stupid bitch!" and threw her cards all over the highway. I collected the cards and gave them to a more grateful person later that day.

The eastern side of the Nullarbor is much like the west, almost identical in terrain except instead of walking into something like the Great Western Woodlands it was into farmland covered in flowering canola and ripening heads of wheat. Something-pollen or pesticides I thought-made me sick, and I nearly passed out a couple of times. This disturbed

* *Beware of false prophets, who come to you in sheep's clothing but inwardly are ravenous wolves.* Matthew 7:15 the Holy Bible. That's one of my favourites.

me: was it from genetically modified plants or chemicals? Whatever it was, my body was poisoned and I fought the effect it had in my lungs. Canola looks pretty but is dangerous for anyone sensitive to either pollen or pesticides. I asked about it in Ceduna, but nobody could give me clear answers, until a journalist confirmed it was probably the chemicals they spray. Remember this next time you want to wade into a farmer's canola field for a photo opportunity.

I'll add one final thing about the Nullarbor. If you walk or ride across for a fundraiser, don't be surprised if most of the roadhouse owners don't support you. Most of them have been out there for decades, most of their lives; for some it is a family business, handed down through generations. In that time they have seen hundreds of people walking, riding, running, roller skating, skateboarding, unicycling, you name it, trying to cross the Nullarbor. There are even 'regulars' who walk across every ten years or so, just because they can. To many of the roadhouse owners and staff, you're just another kook. Don't take it personally. Focus on your own journey and enjoy each step through this marvellous, rich landscape and the moments spent with the people you meet on the way.

CHAPTER 5

WHY?

There were other motivators for taking a very long walk around Australia, not just my psychologist's advice to go for a walk. If that was the sole reason for the trip, I would not have made it far before returning to the familiarity of wild places in the mountains.

In high school there was a brilliantly intuitive librarian who often recommended books for me to read. I was a keen reader and spent a lot of time in the library, it was a quiet space and safe from bullies. One of her recommendations was *Tracks* by Robyn Davidson, a book on the reading list for older students. *Tracks* is the story of Robyn's 2,700-kilometre trek with her camels and dog from the centre of the continent to the west coast, solo, in 1977. It has since become an award-winning film. I was only 12 years old when the librarian gave me *Tracks*. My young autistic mind didn't understand some of the mature themes, but I did understand Robyn Davidson—her connection with animals and nature, the drive to self-discover new places, bush foods, personal limits, the pain of abuse and frustration of not being believed. *Tracks* put a hot coal in my soul, a burning for being alone in wild places, for learning from the landscape, listening to plants and animals. As soon as I had accumulated enough outdoor survival skills I was out, free as an alpine dingo, on my own solo multi-day walks. It wasn't until I found this freedom that I began to see the fuller impact of Robyn's influence.

Starting out with short solo weekend walks at the age of 18, it didn't take long before I had the confidence to walk alone for more than a week and eventually that wasn't enough alone time. I read *Tracks* again as an adult and Robyn's journey resonated with my heart even more strongly, louder, longer. It was only a matter of time before the multi-month treks began calling.

In 2008, I decided to start doing long treks to help campaign for environmental conservation issues. I started with a 600-kilometre walk down the southeast coast of Australia raising funds for marine mammals, following the coastline through national parks, swimming across rivers and walking all the beaches from Tathra, New South Wales, to Bairnsdale, Victoria.

Each subsequent walk became harder and longer, the one for sharks in southwest Western Australia stopped at 450 kilometres because of death threats, stalking and glass bottles being thrown at me. In only a few years I walked over 5,000 kilometres for marine conservation and clean energy campaigns.

The strength of my stubborn nature came through in Western Australia, as well as the dangerous side of that trait. Trying to be strong and unfazed by the violent reaction against shark conservation I kept pushing that walk until I began receiving multiple death threats daily. It became too risky being out there alone without a support team or vehicle. The impact of that walk on my mental health started slowly but after getting back to the east coast it hit hard and fast. I went into hiding as the anxiety, depression and trauma took over. I kept getting death threats on social media, email and phone for over a year. The police in Western Australia, and the states I hid in, refused to help. Only one officer took a report over the phone, and nothing was followed up.

I had been back only a few months before I became suicidal again, thanks to a seemingly inescapable position between an abusive partner and campaign trauma. I called the NSW Health suicide number but after falling through the cracks of a bad system, and waiting months for them to never call back, I wanted to quit life and attempted to take my life three times, ending up in hospital. It was time to quit trying to quit; obviously it wasn't my time, there was unfinished business. To be honest, when I decided to live, to seek help, it was the death threats and an abusive partner who helped engage survival mode. They wanted me to die, I refused to give them that satisfaction.

Bronnie was not my first therapist. It had taken almost a year going through a counsellor, army psychologist and visiting psychiatrist to find someone I could trust, only one hour away from where I was hiding at the time. I used that turbulent time between therapists as best I knew how, in libraries.

My survival had become the new campaign, and I poured all my energy into researching mental illnesses, my symptoms, treatments, management and prevention. I read scores of medical journals and papers, completed tests, downloaded all the resources from mental health non-profit organisations and travelled down many rabbit holes of information, and tried many complementary and alternative therapies. I spent a lot of time distinguishing between reliable sources and misinformation.

Before the campaign fatigue and abuse began, I already knew I was on the autism spectrum, but it was a surprise how often it came up in studies. Anxiety, depression and PTSD are common with autism. People on the spectrum are more likely to go through greater hardships, traumatic events, learning difficulties and identity dysphoria in their childhood. The dangers were even greater before autism spectrum disorders (ASD) were generally understood by parents, doctors and teachers. It wasn't until the end of the last century that female and non-binary child behavioural specialists and educators began assessing autism more comprehensively, adding their own critical perspectives. It was an even longer time before such specialists were taken seriously and allowed to contribute to studies, education and non-profit awareness campaigning. There was a lot of bias against females and misinformation from non-autistic parents and quacks. There still is. It is frustrating that something so prevalent in society today is still worsened by so much unnecessary stress through wait lists, under-resourced and inadequate health support, unsupportive education systems and greater confusion through increasing online misinformation. The causes of co-occurring mental illnesses have shifted but symptoms are still experienced by many of us.

The further I explored down the rabbit holes of information on depression, anxiety and PTSD, the more I was shocked by the state of mental health and its treatment in Australia, as it was then in 2010-11. It was in a very bad state, especially regionally and in remote areas where services sometimes simply didn't exist or where only one visiting practitioner came through for a day every few months. The Liberal government had also started cutting funding to mental health non-profit groups. The Aboriginal youth suicide rate was at its worst and the highest for any youth group in the world. Suicide hotlines didn't have enough funding or volunteers to keep the lines open for the increased calls for help. Police training could not keep up with the increasing number of mental illness call outs, and the police service sometimes caused trauma, injury, wrongful incarceration and even death in situations it was ill-equipped to deal with.*

Climate anxiety was just beginning to be taken seriously. Defence veterans and families still didn't have access to adequate compensation or the support they needed. Mental health therapy sessions on doctor care plans were reduced from ten to six per year, while the cost to see a professional therapist was unaffordable to many. It is estimated that one in four people in Australia had a mental illness. One in ten of those had tried to take their own life or had suicidal ideations. It was a mess.

The self-help campaign began to take the form of something far bigger than myself, it became a campaign to

* Some police forces are now talking about dropping all responsibility around mental health call outs: I suspect they have caused so much trauma and have been reported so often they are creating a loophole. I have experienced police brutality myself, including extensive bruising, aggravated shoulder and spine dislocations and wrist sprains, caused while having an autism meltdown in quarantine.

help the nation. The Happy Walk was my name for this big continental circumambulation. Emboldened by therapy, recovery and hope, I wanted to walk myself to happiness and help others along the way. I thought to myself, if I can help just one other person on my own path to recovery then it will be worth it. How hard could it be?*

There were other motivating factors. Why hadn't a female walked alone around Australia without any support crew? When I was planning my walk, only two males had completed solo circumnavigations without support vehicles: Colin Ricketts in 2005-06 and Andrew Cadigan in 2011-12. Two more had already embarked on their laps when I started mine, Scott Loxley (2013-15) and Mike Pauly (2012-16). I had heard of only one female who had walked the whole way around, including lutruwita, with support crews, Deborah De Williams in 2003-04. Two males had walked around mainland Australia before this. I consider walking around or across lutruwita an important part of the claim to have walked around Australia. Too often it is left out, but it is only an extra 300 kilometres across or 1,300 kilometres around, following roads and tracks. For me, if it didn't include lutruwita and Canberra, was it really a walk around Australia? I can also get a bit antsy about being challenged on my claim. I did not include the distances where I needed assistance and I really did walk 'solo', alone with no company, for all except five kilometres.

Somewhere in the planning and excitement of it all, I failed to realise that what I was about to do would, if I

* That's rhetorical!

succeeded, become a first. From the time I met Deborah, near Merimbula during her walk, I always thought of her as the first female to walk around Australia solo, despite having a support crew all the way. I knew males had walked and were walking solo without support. I hadn't yet connected this to mean I would be the first female to walk without support. I did it differently, for a different reason. The record was never my goal, instead I was proving it could be done without support, by a female. The record was only pointed out to me by a news crew on the way out of Boorloo, on the third leg. Even then I was careful to do my research and make sure I wasn't treading on anyone's toes, taking their accomplishment and making it my own. Regardless of being non-binary, I was born into a female body, therefore it was a female accomplishment, for women and non-binary people.

The reason I can get defensive of my achievement is the number of times people tried diminishing my effort compared to men's. There was a rage in my belly driving me to walk around Australia. I knew I could prove it to myself, and I was very proud of each leg I successfully completed. Women want to see other females doing great feats of adventure. It motivates women to go out and set their own goals, stretch the horizon and stop listening to the people who say it can't be done by a woman. This drove me to do it better. It took longer, but I walked the furthest distance of any recorded circumambulation around Australia, with or without support crews.

I also needed to prove it to all the businesses and philanthropists I wrote to who had expressed no interest in supporting or sponsoring my walk around Australia for suicide prevention. I took those hundreds of rejections and channelled them into the drive I needed to show them it could be done. I was, and still am, bitter about the lack of support from the majority and the bad etiquette I often experienced; it was a negative motivator but a strong one, a reminder that I could do it with or without them.

Also, one last reason 'why' was my personal ambition to complete one big thing in my life. Leading up to the walk, I had had twenty years of instability and insecurity with work, homelessness and domestic abuse. My mental health was at an all-time low and I was unable to complete many things I started; there were a lot of failures and lessons learnt the hard way. This walk needed to break that pattern. I was not going to allow myself to fail. I had a drive for personal success, completion, competence and self-worth.

CHAPTER 6

THE WATCHER

One day, on a section of quiet highway between Boorloo and Tarparrie, I decided to push on further through Blackwood and Milyeannup National Parks. It would make it a 37-kilometre day and require walking into the night—my longest day until that point (there were much longer days to come)—but would mean I could camp at a rest area near an intersection. Most rest areas have at least a few people camping in their motorhomes, caravans or roof top tents, and always someone to have a chat with. Rest areas are good for company and safety in numbers when travelling through unfamiliar places.

The three-month rainy season had just begun in the southwest of Western Australia, but in the evening it was dry, so I walked under the stars. As the long day caught up, exhaustion began to hit so I ran intervals for the last nine kilometres, walking uphill and running down the other side, jogging the flats. Getting there quicker meant climbing into the sleeping bag sooner.

On the map the road curves around not far from the rest area, but when I came round the bend at 9pm I couldn't see any lights from campers or hear chatter or smell smoke from campfires. I knew I was in the right place, the reflective road signs for the rest area and intersection were bright in my headlamp light. It felt strange that it was so quiet, but it was too late to find somewhere else to sleep.

With ears tuned to pick up any human sound, I trotted the last kilometre. Still no sign of other campers, but plenty of the usual wallabies, possums, frogs and crickets. Turning into the rest area I slowly walked past empty parking bays, picnic tables, an information board, a pit toilet. After parking the barrow, I looked further into the bush, following 4WD tracks until they stopped at rocks or a wall of scrubby bush, in case someone was there. I even looked for fresh tyre and foot tracks made since the last band of rain. If I decided to camp, I didn't want any surprises during the night, like someone wandering through to the toilet.

It was a moonless night, and the stars were shining brightly through the tall trees. Still not 100 percent sure of the rainy season patterns, I decided to set up camp under the stars and trees, close to a shelter in case it did get wet. There was no mobile phone signal, so I sent a satellite check-in message to my parents with the location of my camp. I was too tired after such a big day to pitch the tent, it was quicker and easier to just lay out a ground sheet, blow up my sleeping mat, puff out my sleeping bag, secure the barrow at the foot of the mat, climb into the warm snuggly bag and drift off with the next wave of exhaustion. I had a basic safety system in place at night: under one side of the clothes stuff sack that I used as a pillow I had a pocketknife, on the other side was my emergency beacon, and above the pillow was my headlamp and a book. Maintaining a little order helps counter the midnight disorientation of sleeping somewhere new every night.

I fell asleep quickly, with the night sounds of the Australian bush as a lo-fi lullaby.

When you spend a lot of time trekking alone in the bush you learn all the natural sounds: screeching wildlife, clicking insects, chirping amphibians, the movement of reptiles through dry grass, all the different owl calls, sonar pings and flapping wings of bats, howling dingos, the rhythms of each animal running, hopping, scurrying and sliding. To the untrained ear it can sound like a cacophony of noise and some of those screeches bring up imagery of either a creature from the pits of hell or what it's torturing. One thing about the Australian bush is how safe it is for humans (so long as you don't roll over onto a snake lying alongside you for warmth in the freezing cold desert).

I'm a heavy sleeper and a bit of a snorer, so I rely on my brain to keep one eye open, so to speak. Our brains are amazing; I don't think we utilise even a small portion of our neurological potential. I can trust mine to wake me if something isn't normal: a sound, smell or shift in the air which doesn't fit the pattern or forecast. So I slept soundly, completely oblivious to the world outside my dreams.

SOMEONE IS WATCHING YOU! My brain's tripwire screamed an alarm.

My consciousness struggled to rise out of a deep sleep. I couldn't open my eyes and was fumbling around for the sleeping bag zip, trying to remember which side the beacon was on and beginning to panic with indecision about what to reach for first, the beacon or headlamp. In those few frantic seconds, I was thinking of how soon the watching stranger would attack. Did I have time? Could I escape? Would I be able to talk to them? Would I need to fight? Were they drunk? Why hadn't I heard their car?

I managed to free my arms from the sleeping bag and open my eyes. As my pupils expanded to take in the darkness, I looked down to the foot of my sleeping bag and up over the barrow. The breath caught in my throat, and I missed a heartbeat as my eyes met theirs, staring unblinking directly into mine.

A whirlwind of thoughts rushed through my head in those precarious moments. The people who asked, "Aren't you scared?" The ones who boldly claimed, "You'll be attacked" or "You'll be killed". The accusations of naivety, ignorance and stupidity came to mind. Was I over-confident, was it about to be my undoing, and so soon?

So, it was with a great sigh of relief and a quiet chuckle that I smiled into the eyes of a large masked owl perched on the handle of the barrow. The knife, headlamp and beacon stayed under the stuff sack as I watched it watching me in the light of the stars filtering through the tall trees.

It took a few minutes to will my heart rate down, then sleep rushed in fast. The last thing I remember that night was the soft silky rustle and down draft of wind from the masked owl's wings as it flew low over my face to catch its prey.

CHAPTER 7

AREN'T YOU SCARED?

No.

Well, okay, sometimes.

There were a few situations that were frightening.

Considering the distance and time it took to walk around Australia, feeling nervous only a handful of times is testament to how safe this country really is.

"Aren't you scared?" was and still is the most common question I'm asked when out on solo expeditions. Until people started asking this, I hadn't really thought about it, I hadn't had any reason to.

Typically, my roadside response was polite, succinct and light-hearted. "It is safer out here than in town", "Nobody is out here with intentions to do others harm", "Most people think I'm a bloke when driving past at 110 km/h", "Even the crazies think I'm next level crazy and leave me alone" or "The truckies have my back".

In longer, more serious conversations we would discuss the perceived dangers which don't exist and the perpetuation of fear through misunderstanding and films such as *Wolf Creek*. I had to learn what others fear in order to understand their fears for my own safety and reassure them. Yes, I had watched that film after hitchhiking around Australia in the '90s and heard all the stories which inspired the film, while hitchhiking.

As I walked across the bottom of Australia on the second leg of the continental circumambulation it became evident this was not a conversation I could brush off. Almost everyone asked the same question. Sometimes this was a reflection of their own fears, often it was simply because I was a female walking alone through remote landscapes. Fear is a thing which can erode our confidence, steal our joy, stop us from fully experiencing life, *if* we don't understand where it is coming from and have the courage to face it.

Let's address my own female/non-binary view first. I was raised fearless. Also, I have always struggled with my identity as a female. As a toddler I was stronger than the boys and often engaged in punch ups; into puberty I competed ruthlessly with the males in physical sports, such as street cricket, football, short and long-distance running, and cycling. If I didn't win a race in the top of the male field, I would get bitterly angry with myself.

In bodybuilding and boxing, I tried matching males of a similar size and took great joy in being stronger and faster. I envied the androgynous, the eunuchs and the sexless angels I read of in stories. Most of my employment has been in male-dominated fields of work. I have never fit society's traditional role of 'girl', 'lady' or 'woman'. I never felt comfortable as female. In recent years, as the discussions around gender fluidity and sexuality have become more public, I now identify as non-binary, neither female nor male, born in a female body. I don't want facial hair or external genitalia; I don't want menstruation or breasts either. I want strength, equality, independence and recognition based on achievements and character. That's not asking too much, is it? Isn't this what we all want?

This psyche has meant learning to put myself in the position of women to understand their fears and the more disturbing exercise of understanding why men also fear for women's safety. It puts me in a unique position to see both sides from the outside. I'm not going to get political (gender should not be politicised), but I am a feminist and will always err on the side of equality and safety.

Women are strong. To live in a world where they are treated as a weaker sex, paid less, expected to work more and whose academic, creative and physical accomplishments go uncelebrated, they need to be stronger emotionally, psychologically, spiritually and intellectually. This is the society we live in now: it hasn't always been this way and hopefully, we can break free again from gender discrimination in the near future. Don't ask me how, but it will involve everyone choosing to overthrow institutionalised thought through empathy, logic and compassion, a worldwide evolution of belief and values, starting with us. Somewhere back in history, in the dark ages of witch-hunting, religions violently took control of women's freedoms and harmony with the natural world. Women were forced into submissive roles, and it has been an endless cycle trying to gain back equality.

Men know this, which is why I had to understand both sides of the question, "Aren't you scared?"

The funniest encounter was a long day walking between Penong and Ceduna. It was a warm 28°C, but it was a breezy day and I aimed to walk 50 kilometres. More traffic was on the road around the Eyre Peninsula farmlands and people were heading to their favourite weekend camps. As I walked, I waved to people passing. I couldn't always see through the sun glaring off the windscreens, but I could usually see their friendly wave back.

An old 4WD with four gruff-looking bearded men inside, with fishing poles tied from the bull bar over the roof, loaded with ice boxes and swags, passed. They had their windows down and hooted a "Hey!" out the window as they drove by. A moment later they turned around and came back, pulling up off the side of the road and piled out to ask what I was doing. This was not an unusual occurrence. What was different about this encounter were their reactions on realising I wasn't a bloke. They were stunned.

"You're a woman!" they exclaimed, not believing their eyes.

"We thought you were a bloke. What on earth are you doing out here?"

After explaining my expedition, they expressed their full support but had more questions. "What does your husband think of you doing this?"

I tapped the lid of my barrow and asked the box what it thought, giving the men a cheeky smile. To their credit they understood immediately, laughed and apologised for their assumptions. We chatted for a while about life on the road, camping, the people I met, and the beauty of the landscape.

Eventually, one of them of course asked, "Aren't you scared?"

We had built up a fast rapport, so I felt safe challenging them and asked in return, "What should I be scared of?"

"Us, men, strangers," they replied.

I pushed them harder, "Why should I be scared of you?"

One of them looked at the ground, scuffing the dirt for answers, two looked at each other and the scruffiest of the men looked at me very seriously and said, "You've got us there, you shouldn't be scared of us, I just thought because you are a woman, you'd be more vulnerable to attack, but out here everyone looks out for each other."

"If I was a man, would you have asked me the same question?" I asked.

"No," he answered, as they all nodded, giving them thought about what they had assumed.

We shook hands, they gave me a beer and an orange, climbed into their 4WD and continued on to their fishing spot for the weekend. I have wondered how many times they mentioned this encounter to other men and discussed women's safety and how our fears are shaped by assumptions.

I do know what fear is. I have an unhealthy fear of wild boar, which I am always trying to overcome with each wild boar encounter. It is actually a phobia because no matter how much I learn about them and see them in the wild I am still scared witless of them. The fear itself isn't irrational, but my response is. They are a large, strong, dangerous feral pest, territorial, violently protective of their young. They can tear you apart with razor sharp tusks and throw an adult human body in the air. I have an uncanny ability to find them on every adventure and it unnerves me every time. My reaction varies little: I freeze, then I start shaking as my breathing gets fast and shallow; I get tunnel vision and cry, classic signs of anxiety, before logic and self-preservation returns.

I reckon that's a phobia because the same thing happens at the dentist. My confidence builds when they run away, boars and dentists both.

To face my fears, I learn as much as I can about what it is I fear. I have feared boars since I was a teenager when they made me very sick after polluting the water where I lived in Kosciuszko National Park. While working on farms, I asked hunters about their behaviours in different seasons and what to do if I cross paths with them*.

Despite putting the fear of Odin in me, most of their advice wasn't helpful because I didn't have a ute to jump on the back of or a gun or a big knife. But learning about their behaviour has helped me realise when I'm in a dangerous situation and need to take measures to avoid confrontations. To this day, I have never been charged by a boar, and I put that down to being aware of how they will react to my presence.

My advice to others is stay away from them. If you see one or fresh tracks, retreat and find another way around. Be especially cautious of sows with piglets, as they are the most volatile and will charge if you present a threat to them. As with most wildlife, never get between a mother and her babies. They usually travel and forage in family groups, droves or sounders, so if you see one there are probably more. The largest is the male and their behaviour is unpredictable at any time, but more so in rutting season. They will protect the family drove, usually from behind. Young males, who

* Every animal has its place and boars don't belong in Australia: hunting is the only solution to this growing feral problem which is causing far too much destruction to endangered habitats in our wild places.

often form a drove with other young males, will follow a leader. Usually, they will run away from you. If you give them a berth of a couple of hundred metres they will warily watch and take guard positions. Sometimes they will charge, so make sure there is something between you and them to hide or run around or climb up.

Currently, I am trying to diffuse this fear by aligning myself with Gullinbursti Viking berserkers, Gullinbursti being an old Norse god of war, a boar with bristles that glowed in the dark. When I'm not on my meds I display certain berserker traits so being an ally to the Gullinbursti tribe might help in a roundabout psychological sense. But I'm not a doctor.

Fear, as a general rule, is a safety mechanism. Without it we would do a lot more stupid things like play with snakes and pat bears. Mostly it is a learned reaction from parents, teachers, media and personal experiences.* To understand your fear and not let it restrict your life, the fear itself needs to be understood and sometimes this involves facing it.

In autumn 1998, as I prepared for my second solo crossing of the Australian Alps Walking Track (AAWT), a helpful local advised me of a certain "wild man" living in the Victorian Alps, let's call him Mr Patches (name changed). He was described as dangerous, a hunter, stalker and unfriendly. I wouldn't even know he was there until it was too late. At the time I was more concerned about packs of feral dogs on the track than people, so it was more of a side note on my list of things to check on the way.

* There are nuances like respecting the law/fearing authority.

I completely forgot about Mr Patches until one day, as I stopped to make an early camp somewhere east of Mt Buller, I saw fresh boot tracks at a freshwater spring. I hadn't seen anyone else on the track for four days, or any other fresh human tracks. It was then I remembered Mr Patches. All my senses suddenly snapped from "Ah, fresh water, what a relief" to high alert, quiet and calm breathing, pupils dilated, every hair follicle (bristles) standing up to feel any change in motion, still, crouched position hiding in the bush, peripheral senses tuned into every sound, smell and movement. I looked over towards my pack, dumped on the grass, leaning against a tree, and saw someone walk out of the bush just beyond it. Plain as day, not hiding, and looking over his shoulder, straight at me.

I realised it was too late to do anything but stand up, with my water bottle visible, and say "Hi". I needed to turn a potential fear into a learning experience. As I walked back to my pack, he walked over to meet me, put his hand out and gave me a good firm handshake. "Are you the notorious Mr Patches?" I asked and he laughed in response, neither admitting nor denying.

He was rough as guts, a tobacco-stained beard, mouth hidden by a bushy moustache, his clothes dirty and patched, a big knife strapped to his canvas pack and his trousers held up with rope. Mr Patches didn't ask what I was doing out here alone or if I was scared. He was used to watching people trek through on their own, many of them never even knowing they were being watched. He also knew how safe it is in the Australian bush for the experienced adventurer. We chatted about his self-sustained life in the bush and how he followed old Aboriginal paths and hunted feral animals. Mr

Patches told me about other places to find water along the track and where I might encounter feral dogs or a family of dingos. We compared notes and camping styles, I gave him a muesli bar and he invited me back to his camp for rabbit stew. I declined, but camped not too far away and could smell the smoke from his campfire that night.

I could have worked up an irrational fear about Mr Patches for the previous 500 kilometres of walking, and probably would have if I wasn't focused on feral dogs, but it turned out he was a decent human, living a happy and solitary life in the mountains. He gave me no cause for fear. People still talk about Mr Patches with a sense of fear and caution. He doesn't squash these rumours; in truth it helps him maintain his peace and solitude.

Some of our fear is unfounded, we often take on the fears of others, nurtured or instilled by those we meet throughout life or in our travels. This is why it is so important to understand where it comes from and how real the threat is, if any. You may have heard the adage "Question everything" or "You don't know what you don't know". These should come with a warning: awareness can't be reversed. Once you challenge your ignorance you begin to see the world around you differently and wonder how much more you have taken for granted or assumed. It is a stage in life we all go through to varying degrees, it is why we change our values or lifestyles, adopt new beliefs or discard previously cherished ones. It is also how we face our fears and overcome them.

Ask yourself about your fear. What do I fear? Where does this fear come from? Do I have a reason to fear this? What exactly is this thing I fear? Is it stopping me from following my dreams? Is it holding me back? How much am I altering my life to avoid confronting this fear? Is it impacting my quality of life? Is this fear rational? Is it my fear or someone else's fear? How can I face and overcome this fear safely?

You can also reframe how you use the word fear, replacing it with concern, caution, wariness: a healthy respect of something you don't know enough about yet, crocodiles for example.

While planning the walk around Australia I made a list of all the potential dangers I might face on the way. Top of the list were heat, dehydration, infected blisters, fire, flood, cyclone, packs of feral dogs, boar and ... crocs. I knew almost nothing about saltwater crocodiles and my path would take me through a lot of croc country in northern Australia. In 1993 I swam with freshwater crocodiles in the Northern Territory and learnt about their behaviours. When I say swam with, I mean I tagged along with locals—the freshies had the bottom three quarters of the swimming hole and we had the waterfall, watching each other at a distance which didn't bother them or us.

Salties are a different species all together, and you should never swim with them or swim anywhere they just might possibly have reached in the last wet season— that is, up to 500 kilometres inland from the ocean anywhere roughly above the Tropic of Capricorn, between Rockhampton on the east coast and Exmouth on the west coast, unless a local confirms it is 100 percent safe, and even then you need to be careful.

It is healthy to have a little fear for the saltwater crocodile, and to learn as much as you can about it in order to prevent doing something which will endanger your life. The saltie is a formidable creature, a stealth hunter which eats wild boar, cows, dogs, anything or anyone meaty who strays too close to the water's edge for too long in its territory. A magnificent creature which hasn't needed to evolve much for 170 million years. The saltie you see today looks much the same as its ancestors that ate dinosaurs. They grow up to 6 metres long, can live up to 70 years, can weigh a tonne and are individually identified by their scute armour pattern. The saltie is also a much maligned and misunderstood creature. Like sharks, they are deadly, but we choose to go into their wild territory, so the onus is wholly on us to take measures to stay safe. If a human is attacked the fault falls on them for not adhering to warnings and safety advice, whether they are collecting water from a creek in croc country, fall while fishing beside a waterhole with a resident saltie, or swimming a reef off the North Queensland coast.

It is a tragedy when a human is taken, and can shake up a community, but people who live in croc country know the crocodile was only doing what comes naturally. Killing the crocs for fear they will do it again does not fix anything, in fact it makes it more dangerous as a younger one will come in and assert itself in its new territory. I'm not an expert but I have a good understanding of salties because whenever I looked at the list of potential dangers it was only the crocodile (and boar) which made my chest tighten with anxiety.

From learning about salties, the next step was to learn as much as possible about safety in croc country. It is actually pretty simple when travelling in the dry/cold season. In the wet season the saltie travels further inland, but in the dry season they usually retreat towards the coast, large rivers and estuaries. They don't like walking over rocks or up hills and tall embankments but can still get to a speed of 20 km/h when they want to. They are more of an opportunistic feeder; when something meaty comes down to the water they either grab it immediately or watch and wait for it to return to the same place. Good examples are wild boar drinking at a billabong, a fisherman's dog hanging around the edge of a river, or campers washing dishes in the creek. They don't specifically prey on humans, they just don't differentiate us from other mammals.

So, with this knowledge, I have a set of rules for camping and walking through croc country.

- Observe and follow all warning signs.
- Talk to locals as you approach croc country in northern Australia to find out if saltwater crocs have been sighted and where they have been sighted. Saltwater crocodiles have been spotted as far south as K'gari on the east coast and Kalbarri on the west, and climate change will only extend their range.
- Talk to locals about safe places to camp and swim, but never take it for granted that it is safe that season, as it changes each year.
- Camp on high ground at least 100 metres from the high tide line or water's edge. Crocs don't like walking on dry land and are bad climbers.
- Never go down to the water's edge to clean fish, prepare food or wash dishes.
- Don't leave food or scraps at your campsite and don't camp near other people's food scraps.

- Keep your dog away from the water.
- Don't harass crocodiles.
- If you can smell a rotting carcass nearby, move on, it could be a croc's food cache.
- Stay away from croc slide tracks, they might be hanging around.
- If you are not sure, it is better to assume there could be a croc rather than take the risk.

There would be no need for croc culling if we all avoided the dangers. In some cultures, crocodiles are gods. On saying all that, one night I did have a close encounter with a big saltie and didn't realise it until the next morning—which I'm glad about because I would not have slept a wink if I knew what was really happening.

That day I had walked 50 kilometres from the quiet little town of St Lawrence in Queensland to the Tooloombah tributary of the River Styx where I could camp next to the service station and get a shower. On the way out of St Lawrence I walked through a koala colony and stopped to watch some of them, filmed one jumping from tree to tree and recorded their mating growl, a low rumbling drumming cough sound. Neither the film or recording worked out very well on the phone from a distance, but I remember the moment my senses picked up the tell-tale smell of a koala's eucalyptus scats, and I began to see them in the trees along the road for about five kilometres. There must have been a dozen of them, some were sleeping with their fluffy butts wedged into tree forks and heads bowed down onto their chests, others were grazing on gum leaves or climbing up another tree, and the one who was jumping was spooked by me walking so close underneath. Every moment with wildlife is a delight, especially the unexpected ones.

It had been a long day and my body ached, so I found a flat patch of grass near some eucalyptus trees and fell asleep quickly. I had a strange dream of exploring a dry creek bed for emeralds, dinosaurs and endangered wildlife with conservationists Bob Brown and Phil Zylstra, my geography teacher Mr Simms, writer Tim Winton and a couple of faceless science friends. We were on our way back to basecamp and checking one last creek bed, rock hopping down until the banks were lower and we could climb out. We occasionally stopped to turn over rocks and sift through silt, identify scats and tracks, and take photos. Then Bob Brown stood on a rock, to hop over a pool of mud, but the rock moved and turned into a big saltwater crocodile. Bob leapt so fast, and we all managed to scale a three-metre embankment with the help of some tree roots as handholds and steps and pulling each other up to safety. Once we were all safe, we stood watching the amazing prehistoric beast emerge from the mud; it growled, rumbled and drummed its mating call and the mud vibrated around it in a symmetry of dancing crests.

I woke from the dream but could still hear the rumbling sound from the dream. Remembering the koalas mating call from earlier, I relaxed and went back to sleep.

In the morning, after packing up camp, I had a look around for the koalas, I couldn't see any, there were no scratch markings on the trees from koalas climbing and I couldn't smell them or find their droppings. Interesting. That morning the walk began with a narrow creek crossing, the Tooloombah Creek. It was a bridge crossing with the creek far below. I liked these crossings, and if the traffic was quiet, I stopped to take photos of the lush green scenery. On this particular morning I had to wait for a truck to cross before the road was clear and stopping above the creek, I looked down the bank to the water. I think you can guess what I saw. A huge old saltie slipping into the water from the flattened grass on the edge. So the dream was true, the sound of the crocodile had filtered into my subconsciousness. It was probably supposed to wake me in alarm, but the sounds of koalas and crocodiles mating are similar to the untrained ear. Despite the high, steep embankment protecting me at night, that encounter was too close for comfort, and I am now more responsive to subliminal warnings.

How about people? It is easy enough in the age of information to learn about other animals, but humans are all so different and not always predictable. I'll share something very few people knew while I walked around Australia. When my mental health was so bad, I tried taking my life, I was scared of people. I had even, for no logical reason, lost trust in my family. It was simply part of the illness: when they get severe enough, depression, anxiety and post-traumatic stress disorder can impair rational thinking. My therapist helped me get over that. Did I mention how good she was?

I can understand the fear of strangers in the city, especially at night when walking alone. Women, men and trans people have been attacked, raped and killed walking home alone. This is a serious problem and something to be cautious about. I don't even walk through dark places in cities alone at night, unless that city has a sterling reputation for safety, like Singapore for example. I have had my own terrifying experiences in cities; Darwin for instance, where I was raped by a white man while I walked home from a friend's place, New Years night in 1997. Darwin still has a long way to go to gain my trust even during daylight hours. I do not call being cautious in cities a fear, it is being sensible. If I found out a friend was walking through a dark, unlit city park at night to get home from work, I would also ask if they ever felt scared.*

In preparing myself psychologically for this walk I needed to learn to trust humans and trust my instinct for trouble. Being completely alone, without support crews travelling with me at any time, I needed to be able to ask strangers for help if something went wrong. I was also aware many people would be stopping on the side of the road to ask what I was doing or just have a chat with another traveller. I had some experience of the attention this would attract from my previous long-distance walks. The difference in preparing for this was coming straight from two years of therapy back out into the world. It felt like taking a leap into space. Exciting but daunting. An opportunity to see how much the intense work with therapists had paid off, a test of how my strength of mind and will had recovered. Was I ready?

Once you get out of the dense population of a city, people treat you differently. Suspicion, caution and avoidance drop, replaced by helpfulness, friendliness and genuine curiosity. One day, walking into the town of Scamander in lutruwita, a woman out walking her dog came up and invited me to stay

* Obviously, the problem is not the person walking home through the park. It is the system that has failed society by allowing a criminal to be nurtured without respect and responsibility. This kind of crime is never the fault of the victim.

at her place for the night. I politely said no thanks as I hoped to walk a little further before dark. As I walked through town, two more offers of places to stay were made. I was overwhelmed by the hospitality proffered by Tasmanians.

But it wasn't only Tasmanians who showed their kindness and support, this was repeated throughout Australia. I began the big walk unsure of what would happen and the reception of people along the way. This was quickly allayed, and an assuredness of safety was built. As word spread of what I was doing, supporters would follow my slow progress and make sure I was looked after with somewhere to stay, meals, fundraisers and speaking events while in their towns. I have so many memories of the people who reached out and helped along the way. They were my support crew; with the community support I received scattered around the continent, there was rarely any need for more.

Travelling up the west coast I had a bad scare which turned into something overwhelmingly wonderful. One particular roadhouse used to be owned by an older couple who had let it go a bit (well, perhaps more than a bit). I didn't know this until I arrived and saw how filthy it was. As with many places on the way, I had phoned ahead and asked if I could get a new pair of shoes sent to their address to pick up on the way through. They had no problem with this. As was my habit I also explained what I was doing and asked if they could support me with a place to stay. They said it would be no problem. I admit I didn't clarify a donated place to stay.

On arrival I went to the counter inside and introduced myself to the young backpacker working the cash register. He had no idea who I was, so I asked if one of the owners was around. While he went out the back, I peeked behind the counter looking for my post parcel. It was there. As the backpacker returned, an old man disappeared out the back door and, mysteriously, the owner was not in. I explained they had said they would help my walk for suicide prevention with accommodation, and this offer also disappeared; I could camp or pay $100 for a tiny room where the door didn't even fully open before hitting the bed (which filled the entire cubicle), with shared camp amenities. I wandered over to the amenities to find the filthiest showers and toilets I had ever seen. Biting into my budget I booked an ensuite room but quickly discovered it was also dirty; rat poison was sprinkled on the floor under the bed and the toilet had not been cleaned since the previous occupant, who clearly had a bowel problem. I was eventually offered a clean room at an exorbitant cost.

Getting my shoes was an ordeal. I had to argue with the backpacker for my post parcel. I pointed to the parcel behind the counter, showed him my ID and pleaded before he handed it over. I had to tell him what was inside and open it to show him I was speaking the truth. He apologised about the fuss, explaining the managers had instructed him to not give it to me. I never found out why the owners didn't want me to have my shoes.

The next day, after a morning of admin work, I decided to brave the filthy amenities and stay another night camping. I was tired and didn't have much energy for walking. I asked after the owners again, and again they were not available. I asked the young backpacker if he could ask the owners if they would donate a night camping, for the cause. Suddenly, an angry voice with a strong Australian nasal drawl yelled out of the kitchen, "She can pay, just like everyone else!"

I stepped into the kitchen and asked if the owner of the voice, a squat, gruff woman with thick glasses, wearing a stained shapeless dress, was the roadhouse owner. I put on the charm and was very friendly, joking about how elusive they were. She forced a smile as the kitchen staff watched amused. I explained what I was doing, how far I had walked, thanked her for allowing me to send my shoes to her roadhouse, and dropped a mention into the conversation about my interviews with ABC regional radio, Nine News TV and the Pilbara Motorcycle Sisters support in Karratha. Not only did she become less gruff, she also decided I could camp for free that night.

As I went to the camping ground it dawned on me that they would likely mention to others how generous they were supporting my walk. I didn't feel generous enough to give them that, so I wrote a scathing post on my social media before heading up the highway, away from that awful place. I camped in the bush 15 kilometres north instead.

Unfortunately, that night someone in Port Hedland following my page tagged the owners in that post. On the highways in Western Australia there is usually some mobile phone range, it is finely tuned and falls out within ten metres leaving the bitumen, but as I kept walking the next morning my phone rang. Answering it, I was hit with an earful of abuse from the husband, blaming people like me for not being able to get customers, for not being able to insure his place, for getting only the worst backpackers to work there. When he said he was getting his shotgun and coming up the highway to "sort me out" I told him I was hanging up to call the police. I did so immediately and went through to a call centre and was told to stay put until the Port Hedland police called me back.

There was no way I was staying standing beside the road as the crazy roadhouse owner with a gun drove 30 kilometres up the road to shoot me. When I hid behind some scrub, I had no phone range. For thirty long minutes, I expected every car I heard to be him passing north or coming back south in search of me. When I couldn't hear any cars, I ran out to the highway to check the phone.

I checked my social media and updated all the events as they happened. Friends sent me screenshots of TripAdvisor and Google reviews, truckies commented that they don't ever stop there because of how horrible the owners are, backpackers relayed horror stories of being abused by the owners for asking for water.

A call came in while I checked replies. Hoping it was the police, I answered quickly. It was his wife calling to abuse me, repeating exactly what her husband had said, demanding I take down the post. Another call was coming in, so I hung up on her. This time it was the police.

I had to repeatedly explain the situation, while standing beside the highway waiting to be shot. It was an insane and terrifying situation to be in. After the police understood what was happening, the officer on the phone told me it was an empty threat; he was in Port Hedland that day and in the station that morning to see a parole officer. The owners apparently regularly threatened the lives of anyone who wrote negative reviews. The husband had his own mental health challenges.

"Would you like to press charges?" the officer asked.

At least I could relax now I wasn't going to be shot. I asked why he was allowed to continue doing this, why had he not been stopped already, was it really an empty threat, and what if one day it isn't?

The officer could only reply that they knew of him, what he did and would file my report to add to the others. There was nothing else to do. I decided not to press charges because no one else had been successful. It would be a waste of my time. My social media post and its commentary was enough to warn people about never stopping there. I would follow it up with a blog post when I reached Broome.

By the time all this had played out it was mid-afternoon. I desperately needed to sit down and stop shaking. The adrenaline rushing through my system every time I heard an engine had exhausted me and I was far from reassured by the police. I didn't relax for another 100 kilometres, a few days further up the road. How can a person like that, with a fat police record of abuse, be allowed to continue doing that to people?

Now let me tell you about something wonderful which came out of the awful situation.

By this stage of the walk, about 8,000 kilometres in, I had a good organic following on social media. I had met many truckies along the way and had the support of the Pilbara Motorbike Sisters. When they began seeing the roadhouse posts, they were on it. I began receiving messages offering help, some were even offering to "sort him out" for me. I was offered all kinds of protective equipment from all corners of my support network: guns, dogs, tasers, OC spray, baseball bats, bush knives. Bike clubs from both the Pilbara and

Broome rode out hundreds of kilometres to check on me. I had a two-way radio and truckies checked in regularly, many just happened to stop to do a tyre check where I would walk past them and have a chat. Some of them bought me cold drinks, fruit salads, sandwiches and muffins when they filled up their fuel and would pull over their huge heavy trucks to hand off the much-appreciated gifts.

The truckies and bikers had set up their own support networks, checking in on me and sharing my location and news with others travelling my way. I was flabbergasted by their caring compassion. Until then I thought they were all a good bunch of rough, tough people but this gave me so much valuable insight into human nature and how we instinctively look out for each other. These awesome people made me feel safer on this, one of the most remote sections of the walk than I had felt anywhere else, or would feel anywhere else.

I didn't carry any weapons and accepted none. I was once in the police force, a lifetime ago, and one thing I remember was the risk of drawing a weapon, having it taken from you and used against you. That was one reason. When I worked as a pub bouncer, also another lifetime ago, I learnt I could talk down almost any face-to-face aggression which arose, which mostly involved listening to the antagonist's problems, which rarely have anything to do with you. That was another reason. I also felt that preparing for trouble only invited trouble. If I carried a baseball bat expecting to need it for self-defence, I was very likely to run into a situation requiring it; you attract what you give attention to. That was the main reason.

Over the decades, since a teenager, I have dabbled in martial arts, not disciplined in any one sport but picking up many useful defence techniques from ninjutsu, jiu jitsu, taekwondo, judo, karate and boxing, as well as intervening in a few bar brawls. You could call my style street fighting. I'm not proud of it but it is good for self-confidence, and I do not look like a person who knows how to fight dirty, so I also have the element of surprise (evil laugh). Plus, the unique autistic ability to snap into superhuman strength and feel no pain. In another world, another time, I would have made the perfect berserker, but to stay safe walking around Australia I needed to know how to communicate and stay calm in all situations, maintain a friendly and benevolent yet strong persona and stay away from troublemakers.

You are right in thinking I had many advantages over others who embark on such an adventure, but it still does not excuse the fact that literally thousands of people asked, "Aren't you scared?"

Think on this: males who walk around or across Australia are not asked this even half as much as females. What happened to me could happen to anybody, regardless of their gender; worse has happened to males and most of the time people passing at 100 kilometres an hour assumed I was male anyway.

It was never far from my mind how lucky I was to be prepared physically, mentally and with years of skills collected for just such an endeavour. I am always in awe of people who set out with a purity of passion and purpose but with no experience. We have all started somewhere, we all learn the lessons required for success, we have all had to face uniquely personal fears in order to achieve our dreams.

It is the unexpected, unplanned for events which catch us

out, the things we could not have prevented or anticipated. When you think about it, do we really have any control of what happens around us? Realistically, we only have control over how we react and respond. For this we can prepare, train, equip, go over potential scenarios in risk assessments, research, be mentored by someone who has succeeded, learn from others' failures, read books, have conversations, hope for the best but prepare for every possibility. Preparation, knowledge and experience sets you up for success and reduces the chances of bad things, scary things happening. I might be making it sound simple but when you break it down into steps, when you don't rush into it, it is an easy process.

Have you ever camped in the bush alone? Your first time can feel scary, hoping you have everything you need to stay safe, listening to all the new night noises, animals, wind, storms, noticing new moon shadows and smells. You wake, or just get up if you didn't sleep, and you survived your first night out alone. That wasn't so bad, it was exciting and you have opened up a new level of freedom. After a few nights your brain begins to adjust to all the new sensations, recognise the sounds of nocturnal animals; each night is more enjoyable and fear-free. This can be applied to many new experiences in life: jump in, have a go, get experience, learn, enjoy it and become more ambitious. Maybe turn an overnighter into a full week of trekking, then start looking at some of the epic end-to-end multi-week and multi-month treks.

This subject of fear is, I believe, at root a large part of why, even today, far fewer women than men attempt the extraordinary. The (almost always male-created) glass ceiling effect and perceived (or imposed) gender roles are of course, critical hurdles but I think women have been treated by virtually all societies as the 'weaker' sex for so long that the assumption is as ingrained in women as it is in men–that women have simply *more* to fear. It is almost incomprehensible for many women, particularly in more repressive cultures, to think of stepping out of their comfort zone and conditioned roles and imagine pursuing anything remotely like a continental crossing, particularly without a role model. When women are constantly questioned about their safety, they of course start to question it themselves. A friend once told me something very disturbing: as children, girls are told to "be careful" about six times more often than boys. No wonder women have a different perception of fear. If women believe they have much more than men to fear, then their psychological 'barriers to entry' are simply all the greater. Until someone is shown something is possible, that the associated fears are mostly illusory, they are more likely to think of all the reasons why it is not possible, those reasons likely perceived as fears. When women are shown what they can do, their vision widens, dreams grow and the impossible becomes a new goal.

It was shocking to hear some of the things men said would happen to me. According to my nay-sayers (all men incidentally) I was going to be attacked, everything was going to be stolen, I was going to be kidnapped, raped, murdered. I was also going to die of animal attack: snakes, crocodiles, dingos, stampedes of wild animals, boars, wasps, scorpions, centipedes–they were all out to get me. And if they didn't finish me off, I would get lost, die of dehydration, heat stroke, bushfire, dust storms or freeze to death.

Men automatically called me stupid, ignorant or naive, and asked if I had ever been to Australia. Some even accused me of not walking, insisted that I had a support vehicle hidden somewhere and that 'we' stopped to take photos on the way. Seriously! They did not, as far as I am aware, say these things to the men who had walked and were walking around Australia. Sometimes I dreaded what would come out of their mouths when they stopped on the road beside me. I wondered if they were the type of person who would attack, rape or kill a woman? How would they feel being in my place and told of their own demise by a stranger on the road? It made me very angry. And this might partly be why women are often afraid of men and what they are capable of doing to them. It's not helpful nor conducive to a healthy society when women are continuously told to expect the worst and men are brought up to believe it will happen.

Fixing this shameful flaw in our nation will require all of us to change our attitudes, behaviour, thought patterns, education, nurturing, legal system, policies and prejudices. We need a concerted message in young families, schools, workplaces, government, courts, social media and news media to be better humans. Have I missed anything?

The question "Aren't you scared?" really means: "We live in a society which breeds fear, how have you escaped from it?"

I haven't escaped what causes fear. I have learnt what causes fear, both the hard way and through studying it, I understand why, where it is coming from and how to face it. Still, I only really react badly to my fear of wild boars. All other things which could have given cause for concern were okay because I had prepared, researched and was confident in my skills and experience.

Are you bored yet? Does the theme of fear feel repetitive? I was tired of hearing about it, over and over. If I wrote the solutions to fear a thousand times, would they sink in? Prepare, research, get the necessary training and experience to increase your chances of success and joy in the journey. And, above all, trust in yourself.

CHAPTER 8

WONDERFUL PEOPLE

"You must meet a lot of interesting people."

People were the highlight of the walk: their kindness and generosity, forging new friendships and sharing stories.

At the Balladonia Roadhouse, the first roadhouse on the Eyre Highway, 180 kilometres east of Norseman, I met Lluis and Kylie, a dynamic garage punk duo, the *Thee Cha Cha Chas*, who were travelling across the country. I had just arrived at the Roadhouse and was walking out with something cold to drink, probably a can of Solo. I was trying to avoid human contact because I stank and was covered in dirt, sweat and sunscreen. When a couple pulled up in their van for fuel, I thought I recognised the guy as he walked into the roadhouse, so I smiled and nodded. Horror upon horrors, Lluis stopped, said hi and we shook hands as he asked what I was doing.

I had booked a budget donga to stay in for a couple of nights, a single bedroom in a portable with a fridge. After settling in I walked over to the amenity block for a shower. The van was parked in the camping ground on the other side and as I walked across, the woman made a beeline for me. I was so embarrassed, I truly stank; surely she could smell me from there? Kylie didn't care, inviting me over for dinner.

I cleaned up and wandered over with some nuts and fruit to share, wishing I had a bottle of wine instead. We had a campfire, Kylie cooked a delicious veggie pasta, Lluis played guitar and we shared stories all night while the dingos howled. They produced a bottle of wine! It was a wonderful night with beautiful people. I didn't know Lluis before, but I know I was meant to meet them. We caught up again in Perth the next year and the map in this book was drawn by Lluis.

Do you ever get that strange intuitive feeling when meeting new people, that feeling of already knowing them? I had that feeling often. I can't explain it. The next day, relaxing at Balladonia, I chatted with one of the roadhouse staff about intuition, connections and coincidences. You know, those light conversations you have with strangers. Everything I have learnt about it contradicts the science I believe, but I can't help thinking about how much we don't really understand: life, fate, the before and after, premonitions, deja vu, and all that woo woo. What if there are such things as past lives and inherited memory? What if we don't really have any control of our lives and are at the mercy of the Fates? If I can believe in Aboriginal spirits, then why not these concepts too? At least I can play with the ideas in my head. Chatting in the warm sun on the front veranda of Balladonia Roadhouse, reminded me to keep an open mind.

Curiosity is a main strength of humanity, alongside diversity, wonder, kindness, a sense of community, values and a zest for life. Inside each of us is a desire to discover the world around us, a wanderlust, and this desire unites us, especially when we're out on the road following our hearts.

It delighted me to meet so many people travelling around and across the continent, exploring. The grey nomads (the "adventure before dementia", spending-the-kids'-inheritance crowd) were everywhere, in almost every free camping area. They would often pull over for a chat, make sure I was okay for water and, if they weren't in a rush to get a good spot at the next free camp, we would talk more in depth about life. I had a guilty pleasure, used only occasionally I promise! When reaching a free camp, I timed my entry just before dinner, walking in as the sun set, pushing the barrow with the lights flashing. Heads would turn. "Who is that?" "Where did they come from?" "That's the walker we saw earlier. What is their story?"

Sure enough, I would be greeted with invitations to join them for dinner, a beer or wine, fruit cake, cheese platters. A feed was guaranteed. As well as conversations about depression and suicide, friends and loved ones lost, those who sought help and recovered. Many of these were personal stories of survival.

It wasn't only the feed, it was the company, listening to their life stories, the places they had travelled, hearing their pride as they spoke of their children and grandchildren. The grey nomads were a source of a wealth of wisdom for me, each of them sharing a library of fascinating stories and experiences. Every few weeks I would sit down and soak it all in, thinking one day soon I will be an old grey-hair myself, inviting other travellers to the campfire and exchanging stories over dinner and wine.

People from all walks of life are travelling around Australia. Some have sold up and bought fancy motorhomes, others leave their adult children at home looking after the garden and animals to tow their new home in a caravan. There are also many young families, home schooling their children and allowing them life experiences they will carry for the rest of their lives. Perhaps those children will then take their own future families on the road. The families were often excited to see a walker on the road—for them it was like meeting a teacher, for me it was a spontaneous roadside classroom. They usually asked lots of questions, inspected the barrow and its contents, and we would chat about mental health, wellbeing and their family support network.

Backpackers from all over the world passed by and stopped. They were here on holidays or working visas, many were seeing as much of Australia as possible—full of energy, enthusiastic about their next destination, sad to be leaving too soon. They saw more of Australia than many Australians will ever see.

The backpacker crowd help keep this country going. They take up jobs that are often hard to fill—employment in roadhouses, harvest picking, cleaning, remote cafés. I have been lucky to have worked alongside many backpackers on the harvest trails, and they were some of the most humble, hardworking people I met. It would always upset me to hear them accused of "taking our jobs". They don't. They take the challenging jobs, out in the elements, in remote places, strenuous back breaking jobs, cleaning dirty toilets, being abused by racist customers. They work hard and then they travel hard. Many buy campervans, rooftop 4WDs, old shit boxes they can sleep in the back of, spending all their money here, traversing the country, so they get the most out of their visas and Australian experiences before going home. I have been a backpacker, many times, outside of Australia, and those were some of the most eye opening and enriching life experiences. Take that gap year, even as a much older adult you won't regret it.

On my walk, I would often run into the same people multiple times. I first met Naomi and her travelling companion, a kitten called Boss, at a pop-up party on Murchison River. It was pouring with rain, but we all squeezed in under the shelter, played music and had a wholesome good time. A few months later, while walking somewhere between Mardoowarra/Fitzroy River and Halls Creek I was thinking about that night, and suddenly Naomi drove past in her unmistakable old bus. Ten kilometres up the road, at a free camp, she was there. We spent the afternoon together and I added my signature to those of many others on the back wall, people she had met on the way. She had also picked up another passenger, an orphaned kangaroo joey whose mother had been hit by a car. The next day, as I sat in the shade beside the road, someone pulled over with a big bag of fresh food and snacks from Halls Creek, sent by Naomi! A couple of years later, as I walked through Meanjin, we caught up again. Friends met on the road are special, they are part of the story, some become more than a fleeting meeting.

And then there are that special niche of travellers and remote workers who always carry bottles of chilled and frozen water, just for the cyclists, runners and walkers they pass on the road. I had to postpone the section from Katherine,

Northern Territory, to Queensland for two weeks. I had tried to start too early when it was still too hot. In fact, the police came out to take me into hospital after the heat knocked me over, at 11 am. By the time the daily average dropped to 33°C I was ready to go. It was still hot, but I was more careful this time. I met a road work crew two days out and one of the guys handed me a couple of bottles of frozen water and another bottle of electrolytes. He had heard news of the false start and wanted to help in his own way. On that same stretch of Stuart Highway, further south, a young woman in her ute pulled up ahead of me, rummaged through the back of her cabin and met me with two bottles of chilled water. In Western Australia, a few days south of Geraldton, I found a parcel sitting beside the road, in my path, of grapes, juice and fruit cake, all still cold and covered in condensation. In the north, just past Kununurra, the Grey Nomad I had breakfast with that morning pulled over, about a kilometre ahead. By the time I caught up he had made us a cup of coffee and opened a pack of biscuits to share. There are so many more stories like this, of people generously helping out each other.

We are a tribe. I was part of two tribes, the travellers and those supporting suicide prevention. We made up a community of people watching out for each other's safety, helping when and how it was needed, and being there for each other, for company and support. Even on my worst days, I knew help was never far away.

Then there was the biggest group of amazing people, those travelling vicariously around Australia with me and supporting the suicide prevention campaign. At that time, I had all the popular socials—Instagram, Facebook, Twitter (now X) —with a following of about 8,000 people at its peak. Most days when I had phone range, I tried posting an update and came to rely on all the encouraging comments and messages. On the days of complete exhaustion, it was my online social support network who provided the empathy and compassion needed to get through. They made donations to the non-profit fundraiser I walked three years for, and later when I set up a fundraiser to cover my costs of the final part of the walk, they were there to support me again, help me continue carrying my message around Australia.

As I wrote this chapter, while I was staying at Cape York, one of the backpackers working there asked me, "What is your honest opinion about Australians, as a whole?"

I think, as a whole, we are a pretty good bunch.

CHAPTER 9

THE FLY PLAGUE

Between the two cyclones was the most horrendous two weeks of walking.

Flies have their place in nature as composters of dead animals, breaking down organic matter, and are great little pollinators. They can also be revolting and extremely annoying.

The day before my 43rd birthday I stood in the bush screaming, covered from head to toe in a blanket of little black flies, thousands of them. I was shaking with rage and defeat. The blighters had succeeded in driving me over the edge of sanity. I was unable to think coherently, completely broken. I had to ring my brother and his wife and ask them to help me escape. I was lucky; my parents were visiting Steve and Sil, so they teamed up and came up with a plan. They called the next roadhouse, 100 kilometres away, and arranged for the owner to drive down in his big 4WD to collect me and the barrow. I spent the next three days resting, reading, eating, luxuriating in their donated donga accommodation. The roadhouse cooks made a special dinner to celebrate my birthday and I watched a huge lace monitor lizard, the longest and fattest I have ever seen, steal a kid's meat pie.

Two weeks after Cyclone Olwyn the flies had arrived. It was not too bad at first, a few buzzing around my head during the day. But they were only the forerunners. Within a couple of days, they came in plague proportions: hundreds, then thousands.

I was prepared for this. I put the fly net over my hat, tucking it into the shirt collar, tucked my trouser legs into my socks and wore long-sleeved button-down shirts. I sprayed tropical strength deet insect repellent all over; it worked for about twenty minutes. Flies would still find a way under my clothing, getting trapped inside then crawling and buzzing on my skin. There were always a few under the fly net, getting under my sunglasses, in my ears, up my nose and in my mouth. I swallowed a lot of flies.

Eating was impossible. I stopped eating during the day—if I tried, my food was shared with hundreds of flies—and I ate them too. Instead, I would just sit morosely in the shade trying to rest with an incessant loud buzz all around my head, crawling on my hands and covering the book pages I tried reading.

Drinking water was difficult at first. I would carefully manoeuvre the mouth of the bottle under the fly net, trying not to let any into the bottle. A score of them would swarm under the net and onto my face. When the bottle was finally to my mouth they would swarm over my lips. One day, after a few days doing this, I forgot I had the fly net on and drank straight through it. I nearly puked thinking of all the fly shit on the net, but started drinking that way anyway, it was easier.

The fly shit! Hel's Bells! It was on everything: a coating

of black fly dirt on every exposed surface of my skin, clothes and barrow. There were no laundries out there to clean my clothes. Each morning I had to put on the same filthy gear as the previous two days, changing to a clean set only when the trousers stood up on their own and tried running away. Each night, it took ten baby wipes to get all the fly dirt off my face, neck and hands. I tried cleaning the barrow, but it ineffectively smeared into fly shit mud.

This was the only time, the whole way around Australia, I wished I had a support vehicle. All I wanted for the full two weeks was somewhere to escape, guzzle water, rest and sleep in peace. An air-conditioned car, free from flies, a quiet place to breath, relax and eat without sharing.

As the plague worsened, the flies woke earlier, so I had to wake earlier to eat breakfast, dress and break camp before they swarmed. At its worst I was up 90 minutes before sunrise to beat them at their game. Nights were worse (could it get any worse?) They clung to me and the barrow until two hours after sunset before finally going wherever it is flies go at night to sleep. I would be walking until after 9pm before I could safely set up camp, eat lunch and dinner and sleep in silence. If I tried camping any earlier there would be a massacre inside the tent as I swotted a hundred and more of the little shits who came in on my back.

It felt bad killing them. I try to live a life that does no harm to other animals. But these weeks were an exception. Mind you, I only felt bad for a few days, until I switched to survival mode; it was me or them.

Nobody stopped to talk and when they did it was very brief. I would be given looks of alarm and sympathy. Roadhouses were great! I could share my flies with other people, have a shower, wash clothes and clean the barrow. Roadhouses were a refuge of cool air, where I felt myself completely relax, all the tension would slowly leave my body until I was nearly sliding off the seat. But it never lasted. My money would run out and I'd need to keep going, back into the nightmare.

Each time I walked past roadkill I would swap some of my little friends. The worst thought was of their dirty little carcass paws walking all over me. The mouths that were just before sucking on rotten meat were now sucking on my sweat.

After ten days covering myself in deet spray it began to impact my health. I felt poisoned, my body was not functioning properly or recovering overnight. Prior to the fly plague I used a great brand of repellent, an Australian company called Nature's Botanical, made with rosemary and cedarwood. A miner I had met on the Nullarbor introduced me to this—the above ground crew used it at work. He had a spare tub in his glove box and gave it to me. It smelt nice and worked really well, but nothing could match a fly plague, not even Nature's Botanical. I had to stop using the deet, for my health, and smeared the natural stuff thickly on the front of the fly net regularly through the day. It worked for about half an hour.

They were so thick on the fly net I had trouble seeing through them. If I swiped a hand across my face, the flies would jump out of its path only to immediately return, like they were on elastic bands. There was nothing I could do.

The day before my birthday, I was covered in shit and the flies were not letting up. There was a slight headwind, so the fly net was stuck to my face with the flies' little legs and suckers probing every crevice, eyes, nose, ears, mouth. I felt something wet on my mouth. Reaching up under the net I wiped my lips and saw maggot eggs on my fingertips. It was the final straw that broke my sanity. I dropped the barrow, yelled and ran like a wild beast into the bush.

A few days later, after my much-appreciated rescue, they were gone.

The fly plague has had a long-term effect on my mental health. Even a few flies near my face triggers anxiety: I get twitchy, my chest gets tight as my breathing shallows, my heart speeds up and if I don't catch the signs early, I have panic attacks.

CHAPTER 10

THE WEST

On the third leg, walking up the west coast from Boorloo to Garramilla, I started from my friend Deb's home in Mullaloo. We both share a passion for marine conservation, and I learnt a lot from her about the destruction of valuable marine habitats as the city expands along the coastline and marinas are built where there was once vibrant coastal diversity, known habitats of endangered species. These new estates and marinas are built because people once enjoyed the beauty of the area; only, in the process of development that same beauty has been largely destroyed. I walked past developments for two days before I could see what the coast looked like before the demand for house and land packages and berths for luxury yachts was met by a government with little care for the environment. Western Australia has the worst extinction record of all states of Australia and as a nation we are the worst in the world. It was good to head north and put all that behind me.

On the way to Lancelin I re-read Tim Winton's novel Dirt Music: many locals believe, with mixed feelings, that it is a story about their town, with detailed depictions of traumatic events still real and raw for them. I loved the book, both times, and saw Lancelin through both his eyes and the locals. One of the women living there took me under her wing for a couple of days, introducing me to the elders, men and women who had lived there for their entire lives and knew Tim personally. They are proud of him, despite knowing the book is about them. It is a friendly town, popular with travellers for its dune slides, and has amazing conditions for windsurfing. One evening I walked down to the beach, bought some hot chips and watched the windsurfers, silhouetted against the setting sun, racing across the waves and leaping into the air.

The rest of Western Australia was captivating. The colours of the different vegetation, rock formations, wildflowers everywhere (even though it wasn't the season), the blues and greens of the ocean, red and gold earth and wildlife, especially the nocturnal animals. I saw my first western fat tailed gecko in Nambung National Park after taking a walk through the Pinnacles at sunset. The Pinnacles is a geological oddity and tourist attraction: hundreds of tall limestone pillars standing in the yellow desert dunes. These were formed from shells and marine life breaking down and blown inland, into the limestone sand dunes, depositing in swales or caught in plant roots. As the dunes continued to travel west the pillars were left behind like sentinels to aeons past. (This is one theory, the precise way the pillars were formed is still debated.) I arrived too late to take a guided tour but followed the self-guided walking track as the yellows, orange and purples of the sky set the sand and pillars on fire with colour.

One of my favourite camping spots was at the Wedge Island lookout. I was trying to push out a big day and walked into the evening, through gently undulating dunes covered in stunted banksias, grevilleas and xanthorrhoea. There were euros, emus and echidnas out foraging across the hills. I wanted to get to Wedge Island but coming up over the last hill I stopped at the lookout and watched as the sun dropped below the horizon. It was a clear night with zero light pollution; the Milky Way was so bright it cast shadows, and meteorites blazed through the sky all night. I woke early to watch the soft greens, yellows and blues of the sunrise to the east before eating my turmeric porridge and making my way back down to the sea.

It is a harsh environment beyond the coastal and mountain catchments, where farmers and communities rely on the wet season and storms for water. In the wet season it floods and in the dry season it bakes under the relentless scorching sun. Flood plains crack into red cakes, curled around the edges, stretching to the horizon, the only fodder for animals being salt bush, spinifex and acacia. When it rains out of season the soil is so hydrophobic the water spreads out across the plains and over the roads before it begins to soak in. In the banks of the dry creek beds, swallows build nests, intricate hollow towers and bowls of spiralled mud, painstakingly collected and moulded into shape. After the rain, burrowing frogs wriggle to the surface to feed. Every native animal has evolved and adapted to these conditions.

My favourite is the thorny devil lizard, an alien looking little creature, dappled in reds, browns, white and tan to camouflage against sandy and stony ground and under the shade of acacias. Its entire body is covered in a thorny armour, its feet, tail, nose and back have millimetre to inch-high 'thorns' as a defence mechanism against aerial predators. They walk painfully slow, in jerky movements like a cryptic robot, making them vulnerable to being squashed under wheels when they cross the road. I rescued one which had frozen in the middle of the road when a truck rushed past it, carrying it to the other side, in its direction of travel. I placed it under a small acacia bush in the shade and took some happy snaps until it was obviously losing patience with me. I turned to the road, just for a moment, and when I looked back it was scampering at high speed, running on its toes with its belly clear off the ground. It was gone in a flash.

I considered taking the Gibb River Road through the Kimberley but while in Derby, watching the sunset from the jetty, I caught up with some grey nomads who offered to accompany me on the dirt track. They left the day before I did but came back down the track and met me at the intersection, just as I reached it, warning me the traffic was very heavy, so dusty drivers would not be able to see me beside the road, and confirmed what I had heard from cyclists: the 4WD tourist buses were dangerous, too fast and threw rocks up, cutting cyclists faces and breaking windscreens. Seeing as most of the seasonal traffic was on the Gibb River Road, I took the much quieter highway to Kununurra; it was like my own big, sealed footpath with the occasional car and truck. I could walk for an hour without another vehicle passing on the highway.

While walking through the Kimberley, a bunch of young Miriuwung Gajerrong rangers pulled up for an impromptu chat before they began their work in the Ord River Ranges and Purnululu. That day they were out weeding, picking up rubbish and planning a traditional burn. They were a great bunch of young people, one of them gave me a NAIDOC wrist band, "Respect Culture", which I still carry in my pack and on my bike everywhere. As I walked through their country, the old stories, spirits, dreamtime were alive in the gorges, valleys, wide riverbeds, promontories, pinnacles and bluffs, carved by ancient rivers, floods and wind.

Walking through East and West Kimberley there were days when a turn in the road would take me to another planet—the view enclosed by a pass, tall forests or steep mountain ranges would open up into sweeping lowlands and new environments. On one side it would be hot and stifling, in the lee of the wind, and on the other cool, dry with a welcome breeze and big sky.

Growing up on Worimi Country, Awaba/Lake Macquarie, Mulubinba/Newcastle and Port Stephens, I loved being near, in and on the water. Many days were spent at the beach. I still remember the first time I body surfed, and the first time a wave dumped me: Novocastrian rites of passage. In Rubibi/Broome I had mental health problems and needed to rest for ten days, I remembered the previous times in Rubibi and how healing a swim in Cable Beach felt. One of those visits was shore leave from a ship, recovering from a hairline fracture in my hip. Each day I would catch the bus to the beach, hobble down to the 'clothing optional' side and spend an hour in weightlessness, floating on the gentle waves. There were always a lot of people, so I was never worried about crocodiles.

This time I did the same, sought healing in the water. Each afternoon, after the sun had lost its burn, I walked to the clothing optional beach and enjoyed a cooling, calming swim. This time was a bit different; on the last afternoon in Rubibi I stayed in the water longer, chatting to some of the other swimmers. I wanted to leave the water before sunset to be croc and shark safe, I began walking up the beach and looked up to where my towel was, above the high-water mark, and a long train of camels were walking past. On the back of each camel were tourists, most people modestly kept their eyes forward, but a few kids and mothers gawped as I rushed to get my towel around me. I really hope they were warned first! They were there to watch the sunset; they didn't pay to see the moon. You go to Roebuck Bay for that.

CHAPTER 11

THE WATER BUFFALO'S BED

It began to get unseasonably warm as I walked through the Top End between Kununurra, Western Australia, and Timber Creek, Northern Territory. It was going to be an early hot season. To take advantage of the cool nights, I had started waking at 5am, resting a few hours in the afternoon, walking into the dark and stopping around 10pm. This added to the challenge of finding an ideal camp spot at the end of each day. Having no idea what my surroundings were in the dark, some mornings I would wake up to strange and delightful surprises.

Since starting multi-day walking in 1989, I have developed a checklist for campsite safety and comfort which works just about anywhere. This list is a little longer for safety beside roads.

Do not camp on vehicle tracks, animal pads, ant nests, spider web funnels or holes someone might live inside. You don't know when someone might use that track for hunting or wildlife tracking. They won't be expecting you and might not see your tent, so don't risk it being the night you camp on the track. Same goes for tracks other animals use—animal pads indicate high use areas and they might be nocturnal. Some of our wildlife can get up to very fast speeds and can't stop before careening into you. Ants, funnel web spiders and snakes do not make great bed mates.

Do not camp under overhanging eucalyptus branches. They can kill. Eucalyptus trees can randomly drop large branches, day or night, sometimes in drought, or after too much rain or in the heat or when heavy with snow or in the wind. Don't trust them. That's why they have nicknames like the widow maker and murder tree.

Do not camp in dry riverbeds, creeks or drainage depressions if it is rainy season or rain is forecast, for obvious reasons. Adding to that, don't camp close beside a dammed river in case they release water. I was caught out by that once, and once only.

Pick a flattish spot and clear away stones and sticks so the tent or ground sheet won't get damaged, and you don't feel them poking your back and hips through the night. Pick a campsite which does not require clearing of living plants, leave no trace.

I like to add choosing somewhere delicate plants and vulnerable animals will not be disturbed or damaged by the tent or my feet.

Traversing or going around a continent will involve travelling on roads, depending on how much access you get to private and traditional land and how hard you want to make it. I walked mostly on roads: main roads, back roads, 4WD tracks, beach roads; and most nights I wasn't anywhere near a rest area or town. I needed to choose a campsite out of sight of the traffic, so headlights, high beams and engines didn't wake me and curious travellers didn't stop to ask questions while I rested. After dark, all I needed to do was find a reasonably clear patch of ground behind a rock, some low bushy trees, tall grass or mound of earth. Preferably not near a cattle pad and definitely well uphill from saltwater crocodiles. Some natural screening was useful in the morning when I needed to use the toilet hole I had dug the night before.

One night, somewhere between Kununurra and Timber Creek, my careful approach failed me. The day had been glorious and I was entering a new landscape with new vegetation, animals, plants and colours. I saw glimpses of a big, beautiful river winding its way between ancient red outcrops of carved rock and pockets of palms and pandanus. A couple travelling by stopped and gave me an orange, muesli bar and water. The sunset was magic.

As the evening cooled, my headlamp began picking up the reflections of animal eyes in the dark, both wildlife and free-ranging cattle. The stars were bright and, sensibly, there were no vehicles on the road. All was still and quiet, my rhythmic footsteps gently crunching the road surface added to the spell cast by a purple sunset and star shadows. I could have been the only human on Earth.

After 45 kilometres of walking and pushing an 80-kilogram barrow my feet were beginning to hurt so it was time to find somewhere to pitch the tiny single-person tent. The cattle property on either side of the road had fences, which limited me unless I could find the end of their land. Lucky, on a bend in the road the fence kept going straight, leaving a large patch of vegetated, flat and dusty ground covered in cow pats, spinifex grass and a big thorny acacia tree.

Pushing the barrow off the road I took a closer look at the acacia tree. It was a three- to four-metre-thick mass of tangled limbs, spread across the ground with a circumference of about 10 metres, it might have been a stand of trees. Behind the bush, under a couple of straggly hanging branches I found a clear patch of soft dusty ground.

Perfect! There were some hoof prints in the dust, the free-ranging cattle must sleep there for shade during the day. I was overjoyed to find such a great little hide.

Within 15 minutes I had the tent up, sleeping gear down and sent a satellite check-in message to Mum and Dad. I read by the headlamp briefly before falling asleep.

I was barely asleep when I heard the snorting of a cow, probably another brahmin or longhorn. I had seen many of them grazing beside the roads in Western Australia. I quickly drifted off to sleep again until I heard the stamping of a hoof. Okay, it wasn't happy having a stranger in its paddock, if I kept my light off and stayed quiet then it would probably go away or tolerate my presence. I went back to sleep. I had done this before, nothing to worry about. A moment later I heard the stamping of hooves and loud aggressive snorting right beside the flimsy little tent.

What could I do? It was on the door side of the tent so there was no running away and no way was I going to confront a cranky longhorn or brahman bull. I froze, stopped breathing and hoped my pounding heartbeat wasn't making the tent shake. Please, please, go away. Are animals telepathic? With one last snort in my ear and kicking dust on the tent it left and lay down not far away, so it could keep an eye on the strange tent and barrow—things which did not belong there.

I can understand its perspective, but it took a long time to fall asleep again.

In the morning I peeked very cautiously out the door before getting up. There were fresh hoof prints at the very edge of the tent, but nothing was damaged and most importantly, I couldn't see any cows or bulls. Although, there was one surprise, a clue to whom I had spent the night with, a message, like a letter on a pillow. The biggest, most humongous wet cow pat I had ever seen.

Turns out I had a one-night stand on the bed of a wild water buffalo, and was very lucky to survive.

CHAPTER 12

EYE OF THE CYCLONE

There was something irregular in the scrub, about ten metres off the road. Parking the barrow, I walked in and had a look. It was a warning sign for cyclone season, torn from its posts and thrown away by the cyclone that had just passed through.

The thing about walking is that you don't get to decide the weather. To some degree I was able to plan each leg of the walk to avoid the worst of the heat but just about everything else just happened, a reminder of how exposed I was every day.

The first cyclone warning came in when I reached Billabong Roadhouse, five days out of Northampton on the west coast. That morning one of the wildest storm cells passed over me. You know the ones, where you wonder if it is going to be your last day on Earth: everything goes dark, the air is thick with electricity, lightning strikes everywhere, so close you see it hit the trees and ground around you. I was pushing a steel and alloy barrow, and the only places I could hide were being hit. At one point I just walked away from the barrow and squatted in the dirt until I could count a few seconds between the strikes and thunder.

Once the storm cell passed over it left a colourful landscape in its wake, all the bark and leaves were washed of dust, vibrant reds, yellows, browns and greys of rocks and foliage stood out against the dark red wet earth and brilliant blue clear sky. The bruised and battered plants and leaf litter filled the air thick with fragrances. One species of tree smelled like choc chip biscuits, another smelt of peppermint, and a small bush steaming in the sun was like fruitcake. It made me hungry. The herbs released their own sweet smells. I walked through invisible clouds, inside nature's aromatherapy spa.

The air was still heavy, I could feel the pressure increasing inside my head. It was a new feeling; the heat, humidity, stillness, thickness and sunlight were all strange, unlike anything I had felt or seen before. The weather was fine most of the way between the storm and the roadhouse, but a big monsoon shower came in just before I reached the pub. I was running to beat it there, but it caught me only a few hundred metres before I could dash under the shelter of the veranda, and it soaked me to the bone once more. More lightning; the power flickered out and came back on with the generator out back. I bought a cold drink and watched the stormburst with the locals until it passed. Water poured off the roof, a flash flood covered the road; within a minute of it passing the flooding had soaked into the ground.

There was a TV in the pub, and I saw a weather warning for the Gascoyne region with the familiar cyclone symbol out at sea off the coast. My mind slowly ticked; it likes to slow down when it receives incomprehensible new information, putting together the strange and unfamiliar feeling in the air and what I was watching on the news. Still not quite comprehending the situation, I walked next door to the service station to book into the donga accommodation and dry my clothes.

The manager had been hearing reports of some crazy person walking up the highway for days, and he was excited and relieved to see me. Excited because he had a printout of the Bureau of Meteorology weather report and cyclone warning to show me, relieved because he knew I would not be caught out in it. The cyclone was named Olwyn.

The next morning, I helped the roadhouse secure everything in shipping containers and rooms. We put anything which needed to stay dry up high on bunk beds and shelves. I parked my barrow in one of the shipping containers and made up a dry sack of emergency overnight gear. After all the lifting was finished, I hitched a ride with a truckie back to my hosts in Northampton, who were expecting me to retreat there.

Olwyn was expected to make land early the next morning, hitting Northampton between 5 and 6am. When I arrived, on the eve of Olwyn, I went directly to the supermarket to get some water, dried food and, most importantly, red wine to share with my hosts. The supermarket was busy as everyone else was doing the same, buying emergency supplies. We secured everything in the yard and put away anything which might cause damage around the house. Once we were ready, we had a delicious dinner, drank the wine and retired. I made sure everything was fully charged and had my cameras ready to record.

The next morning, waking up to some wind, getting up as the sun rose, I asked what happened to Olwyn. I slept through it! How unfair. My first cyclone and I missed it. I felt cheated. We tidied up the yard, checked everything was okay, and listened to the news on the radio before I hitched back to Billabong.

In Billabong it was carnage. The worst of Olwyn hit Carnarvon and Coral Bay at category 3, badly damaging the resort, then tracked inland to Billabong, hitting at category 2, before going down the coast to Northampton where it was only a category 1, finally dissipating to a low-pressure system before Geraldton.

It was easier to get away from the cyclone than it was to return. News quickly spread of the damage, tourists were asked to avoid travelling there until repairs had been made, many places had to close down for a couple of weeks to rebuild. The only traffic on the highway was either locals or contractors heading up to help.

By the time I reached Billabong, they had fixed everything they could, without the help of contractors. I picked up a shovel, tagging along with work teams, throwing trees on the back of the trailer, doing what I could for a few hours. That night I retrieved the barrow from the shipping container, then slept the sleep of the dead on a dry top bunk in a room which had escaped demolition.

Hitting the road the next day, I noticed how light my head felt. Not a light-headedness associated with illness or substances, but a clear head with no strange atmospheric pressure. This was when I realised I could sense barometric pressure change and, reflecting back on the many storms I had walked through, it was something I had been experiencing for a long time, but had not tuned into it until then. This was a pretty cool trick and would come in handy, once I learnt how to use it.

Exactly one month after the first, there was a second cyclone. This one was called Quang. It landed further north, late in the season and was not as strong as Olwyn. After Olwyn I made my way to Hamelin Pool Caravan Park to see the prehistoric stromatolites growing in the bay. These are sometimes called 'living fossils', and are an example of an ecosystem found in only a very few locations on Earth as they require very specific and rare conditions to survive. They are a clear sign of microbial life, and fossilised versions have been dated, astonishingly, to more than 3 billion years old (interestingly, the oldest that have been found are from the Pilbara, only a few hundred kilometres away). Finally seeing them was a milestone in my 'See Them Before They Disappear' nature list. There are only three places in the world where stromatolites still live, and only two of those are accessible to the public. I spent a few days there, watching the tides come in and out, studying their forms and symbiotic tidal life. Hamelin Pool is regularly hit by cyclones, but the caravan park was built on the leeward side of some large dunes, to protect it from predominant weather patterns. While here I quizzed the owners about cyclones and how they survive living in Cyclone Alley. The wealth of cyclone survival information they shared became invaluable.

Three days past Nanutarra Roadhouse, a mining vehicle pulled up on the road, a guy wound down his window and yelled through the wind, "A cyclone is coming!"

"When?" I shouted back.

"Tonight!" he replied. And drove off.

It had been blowing a gale force crosswind all day and I was already feeling exhausted. The news, although a surprise, was oddly welcome. I could stop early, just as soon as I could find the safest place to camp. It was a sparse landscape, not many trees or hills, no roadhouses or farm stations nearby; the closest emergency shelters were in Onslow, 140 kilometres back or 130 kilometres further north in Karratha. I was in Quang's path.

Using what I had learnt at Hamelin Pool, I walked until I found the perfect place to bunker down for the night. There was a hill, about 40 metres high. On the windward side it rose gently but on the leeward side it fell away steeply. At the foot of the leeward side was a stand of young two- to three-metre-high acacia and mallee trees, spindly, springy and not likely to break. Even better. There was an unlocked gate in the fence bordering the road, giving me access to the hill and trees. Thank you very much. Reaching the hill, I was instantly out of the worst of the wind and found a space just big enough for the barrow and tent in the middle of the trees. After making camp and eating dinner, I checked my water and anchored everything down, ready for a rough night.

The wind built all afternoon and through the night to a crescendo of noise, sometimes roaring, other times screaming. Gusts of wind forced their way down the side of the hill, flattening the trees against the tent, but the hill and trees protected me from the worst of it. The tent barely buffeted.

At 2am, when I thought the storm could not get any louder, it suddenly stopped and everything went quiet. There was still wind, but still deafened from the earlier roar I could barely hear it. The little trees were swaying, like waves on the ocean, but they were not slapping the tent anymore. I climbed out of my Mont Moondance to check the barrow was still there and look at the sky.

Quickly, walking a short distance from the trees, I lifted my eyes to the sky and saw stars, shining brightly above. It was the eye of the storm.

Clouds began scudding across the stars and I rushed back to the tent. The next three hours were far more violent than the first, as the other side of the cyclone came in from the opposite direction. It was not as loud though, and soon after it passed over me it weakened from a category 1 cyclone to a tropical low.

At sunrise, a strange light filtered through the air as I rose to survey the damage. I had survived. The tent and barrow were unharmed. But the trees were nearly shredded. It was the strangest feeling to have survived camping through the eye of a cyclone. Seeing one was never on my bucket list, but the memory of seeing those stars, even now, gives me goosebumps.

CHAPTER 13

HOW MUCH WATER DID YOU DRINK?

Our body is more than 70 percent water, the surface of our planet is more than 70 percent water. Water keeps us alive and makes the planet thrive.

Early on, the question of water consumption mostly came from other bushwalkers, people who knew the weight of water, having had to carry litres of it in their packs, on their backs. As the walk went further into remote Australia, other travellers knew I was pushing days of water in the barrow.

Bushwalking across the mountains I normally drink three to four litres of water a day, five if it's hot. I can refill at creeks, rivers, springs, melt snow or collect rain every day, sourcing water is not a problem most of the year, up there.

When backpacking around lutruwita, clean water was available almost every day. On hot days, a lutruwita 28°C feels like 38°C—summer heat is more intense being close to the ozone hole, but being an island, it is also surprisingly humid. I could chug through six litres, even walking shorter distances on those days. I carried water storage for ten litres—that's ten kilograms—when I didn't know if I could refill overnight. In the mountains I caught big fat snowflakes in my mouth...does that count for water collection?

On the east coast, when I switched from the barrow to the pack, I knew I could get water every day and carried only five litres of bladders and bottles for storage. I often needed to clean it, some of the water was from dodgy creeks, puddles and bores.

For years I carried a LifeStraw when my little treks took me to places where the water could be contaminated by feral animals. Trekking overseas I carried iodine tablets to dissolve in the water, but it tasted strange. In the mountains I often boil my water: a rolling boil is all you need to get the water to a temperature that kills the parasites and bacteria. Of course, the higher the altitude, the lower the boiling temperature so you need to boil it longer. There are many brands of filters for water filtration and cleaning, but when I did an outback survival course I learnt about Condy's crystals (potassium permanganate). It is part of my first aid kit for washing wounds and for the last nine years I have been using it to clean my water. A few small crystals in a litre of water, wait thirty minutes and it's safe to drink. Don't use too much. If your water looks like pink cordial, you have overdone it. It is important to clean any water if you are not sure it is safe to drink. There is nothing worse than getting a stomach bug out in the middle of the bush or desert, especially if there are no trees to run behind.

Water hygiene is also essential. If you are in a water catchment area, channel country, or near creeks, rivers or dams, other people are going to use the water. Collect your washing water and clean cooking utensils, pots and pans at least 100 metres from the water so the soil can filter out the contaminants, oils and food scraps. If you're taking a natural bath, don't use soap of any kind in the water—even the "ecofriendly" stuff is a chemical cocktail for native fish and plants.

What about the native bush soap tree? Nope. When you rub the leaves into a lather it kills fish, so it is better to use a potato bucket when making a soap leaf lather. Swimming is also restricted in sensitive alpine lakes where the build-up of sweat, sunscreen, oil residue from our bodies and detergents in our clothes harms endangered fish and plants growing around the shore. Toilet waste, in many places, needs to be carried out in a bag or tube when you leave; it is a good habit anywhere you trek as the popularity of hiking increases. If you dig a hole it needs to be at least 15 centimetres deep and 200 metres from the water, so torrential rain won't wash it out and animals can't dig it up. Using water hygiene keeps it safe for others to use, and parks won't need to restrict our access to beautiful places because we've abused the privilege.

Accurately judging how much water you need depends on how much you drink normally: most of us drink around two litres a day. Add terrain: once you start sweating up hills and down steep declines you need more, depending on your fitness. Add the temperature forecast: over 20°C and you will use a little bit more, about three litres, and your need for water incrementally increases as it gets hotter. I use five litres a day walking through the mountains in 28°C. It isn't safe to be walking in anything over 33°C unless you have a support crew travelling with you or you have gradually, over weeks and months, increased your endurance.

I tried to avoid anything over 35°C. Walking beside the

road was much hotter than on a bush walking track. One day, just south of Katherine in May, walking into winter, I measured the ambient, road and radiant heats. Ambient was 33°C, the road was 65°C, and the radiant heat was wavering between 45 and 55°C. I was walking in that radiant zone. The water in the bottles hanging in woven bags on the outside of the barrow was hot enough to make a cuppa. Inside the barrow I could insulate it with clothing, but it was still warm. The only cool water I drank was first thing in the morning or the gifts of chilled water from travellers passing by. On those days I drank about eight litres a day.

There were some days unexpectedly over 35°C; they were the days even the locals commented on as being hot, usually as I walked into town, asking me, "Are you crazy? Are you not right in the head? What are you doing walking in this heat?"

A few times I was caught out in really unseasonable heat, up to 40°C. Once it was a Bureau of Meteorology error, forecasting a much lower temperature. The other occasions happened while walking long stretches between towns. All I could do to get out of the heat was sit in the shade, hoping for a breeze and reading books for the hottest part of the day; walking six hours before noon and another four hours into the night after the air began cooling.

When I was in Broome, I met one of the local young men, Brett, who drove a regular run between Darwin and Perth in his truck. It was July, I was about halfway between Fitzroy Crossing and Halls Creek when a surprise heatwave hit. I had 45 litres of water in the barrow, seven litres a day in moderate terrain walking 50 kilometres a day. The water was for drinking only, no washing. Even my teeth were cleaned with a dry toothbrush. I had to carefully ration my water out over 289 kilometres as there were no stations, mines or roadhouses near the road for a refill. As the temperature crept up, I had to drink more, just a little, aware of how close I'd be to running out if I used too much.

Almost exactly halfway, after making camp I checked my phone for messages. Brett had sent one from Halls Creek asking if I needed anything from the shop and offering to drop it off on his way through to Broome. I immediately replied to request five litres of water but had missed him by an hour. We messaged back and forth when he was in phone range. He could drop off three litres of his own water.

It was dark and my tent was hidden from the road, so I pulled out the two-way radio, put on the bright headlamp, sent a text saying I'd flash him (forgot to clarify headlamp which gave him a chuckle) when I saw his headlights, and turned the radio on ready. A few minutes later I heard his truck and soon after saw the high beams come over the horizon. It was a cold night, about 5°C—a 30-degree difference from the day. I sat in the warmth of his truck cabin to thaw out as we had a chat. He gave me some snacks and crackers along with his three-litre cordial bottle full of water. Best unplanned rendezvous ever, and I now had enough water, if it didn't get any hotter.

Two nights later I saw a shed and windmill, attached to a bore and cattle trough. It was late and time to stop and camp. Squeezing the barrow through a gap in the fence, I made my way over to the windmill. The water trough was full, and some Brahmin cows were drinking in the dark. There was a flat smooth patch of ground behind the shed for the tent. I stripped off all my stinking clothes, took the 500ml cooking pot over to the trough and, dipping the pot into the slimy water, I had a wonderful soapy shower. The cows were watching but I didn't care. The next morning I made sure I had ten litres of water, topped up and cleaned from the slimy trough. It was only another 45 kilometres to town and I smashed it out, chugged my last litre of water at the 5-kilometre road sign and arrived before 2pm.

That night, staying at The Kimberley in a lovely air-conditioned donated hotel room, I watched as all the dirt I didn't see the night before made mud on the shower floor. I stayed under the water so long I went pruney. That was the only time I miscalculated my water; from that point on I always carried a reserve.

Electrolytes are a must when walking in hot conditions. You can't replace them with a normal diet when sweating profusely all day, unless sucking on a salt rock is normal for you. I put electrolytes in every fourth litre of water and had another 250ml before sleeping to help muscle recovery. For the walk I was supported by Shotz, an Australian sports nutrition company, with donated and discounted tubes of tabs. They tasted good too, even disguised the taste of some of the nasty bore water I had to drink. When I started the walk I used powdered coconut water, but when the water was warm it was disgusting, as bad as bore water. My throat would constrict and gag. Shotz was one of the most important parts of my nutrition. When you sweat you lose essential minerals, magnesium, potassium, sodium and calcium. Hydrating excessively with only water, without replacing these, can result in a heart attack.

Then there was frozen water. When you wake up and want to make coffee, but nothing comes out of your bottle, it can feel like the end of the world. There is nothing like starting the day with a hot brew, without it the day doesn't feel right. Camping on the snow I expected this to happen and would sleep with a water bottle inside the sleeping bag. Walking through the outback and the Nullarbor, I knew it was going to drop to below zero but forgot that water would freeze. I woke up at 5am: frost covering everything, gloved but aching and numb fingers pulling out the tent pegs, and frozen water. I had to go without water, breakfast and coffee until it began thawing three hours later. I only had to do that once to remember to sleep with my water every night after.

I am immensely grateful to all the wonderful people who stopped and offered me water, soft drinks and electrolytes. Anything that came out of an air-conditioned car was such a welcome relief from the heat. I would stand there and roll the can or bottle over my face and neck, luxuriating in the cold condensation dripping off it, before drinking. The feel of it cooling me from the inside was ecstasy.

CHAPTER 14

FIRES AND FLOODS

Australia is a continent of surprises, some of these can present logistical challenges and unplanned diversions to the long-distance traveller. I faced not only cyclones and massive electrical storms; the west coast also gave me floods and fires.

Not long before cyclone Olwyn hit, I had been staying with my wonderful Geraldton hosts, the Wellies. Sue Wellington had a special interest in what I was doing as she was planning a big a continental traverse of her own, and a couple of years later she successfully walked across Australia, raising awareness for dementia. I stopped here for five nights; time to heal, rest and be a tourist. On the last night a monsoon storm hit at about 1am, flooding most of Geraldton, including Sue's kitchen, and opening up a sink hole in the backyard under the far corner of the house, where the boghouse used to be. I waded outside through knee deep water to check the barrow, safely locked onto a post. Fully expecting it to have taken on water, it was a surprise to see it floating. I went back inside and started bailing out the kitchen with Sue and Dave. The storm passed, we mopped the last of the water out and went back to bed. Everything else could wait until daylight.

Walking out of Geraldton I was shocked by the power of the monsoon downpour. Gutters were still flooded, SES and emergency crews were putting tarps over roofs, roads were closed, paths had been displaced and bitumen eroded under washouts. More rain came in as I walked up into the hills, feeling safer on high ground.

A week later I stopped beside the Murchison River for a night. The river had two crossings, the old lower ford, still functional, and the new high bridge beside it. On the south side was a rest area with picnic tables and a dozen caravans and motorhomes parked along the riverbank. A couple were fishing, on their camp chairs on the dry ford, when I arrived but there was an approaching storm which forced them back to their caravan before they caught anything. The river water was murky and running swiftly, there was no way to see the depth or any obstructions under the surface, so my planned dip was abandoned. The storm hit hard and fast, forcing me to camp under the picnic shelter and set up the tarp as a weather break so I could pitch the tent without getting too wet from the horizontal rain. In the gloomy dusk I could see the water rising and covering the ford, a couple of the more sensible campers packed up and left. I was on higher ground and hoped to be okay; if the water reached the shelter I could move the tent onto a table, I had nowhere else to go. The weather was perfect in the morning, but the river had risen over a metre flooding the ford and lapping at the steps of the remaining caravans.

On a few other occasions, after heavy or prolonged rain,

I had to wade along stretches of flooded road, pushing the barrow like a small dory floating on the water, while watching snakes swim across in search of dry ground, hoping they didn't climb on the barrow, or me.*

It feels like I walked through or camped near many floods, but there were only a handful of them. I just happened to be strategically placed by the Sisters of Fate to experience each of them. I started making it a habit to find places to camp on high ground. Sometimes this meant foregoing rest areas and the company of other travellers to stay safe when a storm began brewing in the region. The storm doesn't need to hit where you are for you to be flooded down river.

Up north in Western Australia and across the Top End of the Northern Territory, I experienced the complete opposite, walking past fires from traditional burns. These were managed by the Aboriginal communities and rangers in the right seasons to prevent catastrophic fires later, promote regeneration and conserve wildlife. They were fast moving, cooler grass fires, usually lit in the evening and allowed to run through the night, with a crew keeping watch.

Walking through the traditional burns of northern Australia, inching their way through the cool damp evening grass in a uniform low flame, was relaxing to watch. The flames were surprisingly peaceful, lazily crackling away, casting a golden light into the trees above. All I needed were some marshmallows. However, I made one silly mistake. A

---

* I named my barrow Dory, not for the small boat but after the *Finding Nemo* movie. Before leaving on the first leg with the barrow my family wrote messages inside the lid. Sil, my sister-in-law wrote "Just keep swimming, swimming, swimming."

burn had just finished where I had planned to stop for the night. Rangers were packing up and leaving, they advised I didn't camp there yet, but wait an hour. There was no smoke or flame, so I rashly assumed the ground had cooled and rolled the barrow off the road onto the freshly cleared ground, looking for a good place to put the tent. I paused for a moment, just long enough to feel the heat through the soles of my shoes. Quickly, I ran the barrow back to the road, checked for melted rubber and waited while licking the wounds of my injured ego.

CHAPTER 15

WHAT DID YOU EAT?

Fuelling myself on this expedition was very different to most of my previous walks. I needed to choose food with a lot of slow-release calorie energy and high nutrients, which I wouldn't get bored with too quickly. I was not out there to lose weight, but that was going to happen whether I liked it or not. For this reason, I bulked on weight, about 20 kilograms for each leg of the walk, and always lost it. On the 4,000-kilometre Boorloo to Garramilla section I was underweight when I finished, despite eating double breakfasts and mountains of hot potato chips in roadhouses. Admittedly, I enjoyed the bulking process. As well as eating lots of healthy food, I indulged in chocolate and potato as much as I wanted without any guilt.

Lutruwita was a short section with regular shops, so I ate a lot of fresh fruit, salads, toasties and cake. There were many roadside fruit and vegetable stalls and farm gate shops, not to mention ice creameries, fudge and truffle shops. Okay, so maybe I didn't lose all the weight I put on for that leg! I carried a small camp stove for coffee, porridge and soups, all simple and fast foods which didn't require too much energy or imagination. I made double serves of porridge in the morning to give longer lasting energy, and in the evenings, camping away from towns and friends, I made a double serve of soup to replace lost energy overnight.

All the way around Australia, I was on a mission to find the best veggie burger. The winner was in Eucla, but there were many close contenders. In some places I had to order a hamburger-with-the-lot without the meat. Vegetarian and vegan were alien concepts in the heart of carnivore country. I have been vegetarian most of my adult life. When I was 17, I told Mum I didn't want to eat any more meat. It was not for any altruistic reason, I just didn't like the taste and texture and my digestive system struggles with all meats, fish, birds and mammals. The only times in my life I've craved meat were when I was depleted in iron and protein from excess exercise in extreme heat without adequate meal options, like when I worked on ships. I was prepared this time and only craved eggs when I ran out of cashew nuts.

I had previously dabbled in veganism. I was a navigation officer with Sea Shepherd, and they have the most amazing vegan cooks. It was the healthiest I have eaten on a ship (in fact ever) and the meals were wonderful. I wanted to go vegan for the walk, but trekking meal options were terrible, snacks were limited, and I had no way to refrigerate food.

In the year between lutruwita and walking across the bottom from Boorloo, there was a sudden increase of online stores selling nuts, seeds, dried fruit, powdered fruits, spices, powdered soy milk, fruit leather and all kinds of healthy goodies I could carry in the barrow without them spoiling. Before Tasty Bites left Australia, I dehydrated weeks of their vegan Indian meals and vacuum-sealed them ready to cook. Another new company started up in lutruwita, Strive Food, specialising in vegan and vegetarian trekking meals, including pasta, risotto and dahl. These gave me a great variety of healthy, high-energy meals. It was never boring. I was vegan for seven years after that, I'm now a lapsed vegan vegetarian, but mostly vegan.

The more remote the walk became, the harder it was to get fresh food. Some small towns and roadhouses didn't have any for sale, unless it was cooked in a meal. When I could get fresh supplies I chose what would take the longest to ripen: capsicums, citrus, carrots, plastic-wrapped cucumbers, hard tomatoes, beetroot, three different colours of bananas (two green, two light green and two yellow), rock hard avocados (safely wrapped in the sleeping bag, they always ended up ripening too fast anyway), flat bread, hummus, dairy-free cream cheese, peanut butter, nutritional yeast sprinkles and tamarind sauce. I had big clip-top food storage boxes in the barrow for the fresh food and filled them as often as possible, eating everything quickly before it had a chance to rot. Sometimes I was not quick enough and had to feed the ants. Across the Nullarbor I arranged with IGA to put in a weekly order which came out of Norseman with the roadhouse orders, right up to the South Australian border. After that it was dried and powdered rations, with lots of a brand-new vegan energy bar, Blue Dinosaur. This brand had only two flavours when they began, ginger nut and cacao, but I ate them until they came out of my ears. It was a delight (and a relief) when they expanded into more flavours!

Breakfast varied. I couldn't eat porridge *every* day, but it was my usual go-to. Another new company, Lovin Earth, made a variety of buckwheat cereals; chocolate was my favourite. Mostly, I ate a porridge mix I prepared with hemp seeds, cranberries, goji berries, golden berries, linseed, cacao, turmeric, cinnamon, powdered acai, pumpkin seeds, raw cashews, coconut milk powder and rolled oats. It tasted fine, but it was made with nutrition and fibre in mind, over flavour and texture. When the bananas began ripening too quickly they were added to the mix. This breakfast would sustain me for about four hours before it was time for lunch.

When fresh food was in the barrow, I used it in wraps with hummus dip. Without fresh food I ate dried fruit, nuts and seed crackers. Lunch was always a bit boring, not memorable for the food. It was more of a forced break for my body. I'd sit in the shade under the trees and read books, update social media if there was phone range, wander around the bush taking photos of native bees and flowers, talking to birds or stalking reptiles. Some days it was more of a logistical stop to dry out the tent, sew up holes in clothes and put out the solar charger. If I had stopped a few times to talk to people throughout the morning, lunch was shorter and more hidden in the bush for alone time.

Snacks were my favourites. Obviously, I couldn't carry chocolate (I tried, it melted), so I had sugar cane syrup sweetened cacao nibs: my small expensive luxury food. Muesli and energy bars and nuts were my go-to, but my favourite gourmet treat was banana dipped in peanut butter with pieces of sesame snaps stuck in it. Yeah, I'm a sweet tooth. Sometimes, on the longest days, I ate as I walked, skipping the breaks, grazing all day from pockets stuffed with bars, nuts, seeds and dried fruit.

I had a few quick and satisfying meals for the nights when I was too tired to put much effort into it. For instance, I would boil a cup of water with some dehydrated peas, corn, carrot and shitake mushrooms. That's ready in three minutes. Then turn off the flame, add powdered potato and make veggie mashed potato. Garnish with a few saffron stigmas, pink rock salt and smoked paprika, and *Voila*!

Here's another favourite: cook up some basmati rice, put in a little extra water and add a sachet of vegetable soup. When this is cooked through, turn off the flame, stir in a teaspoon of vegemite and garnish with foraged leafy greens you collected waiting for the rice to cook. Seaweed flakes also taste good with this.

If you want to get fancy, try powdered coconut milk, garam masala, freeze dried vegetables and rice. Garnish with dried chickpeas, broad beans, chilli flakes or wasabi peas. This cooks fast and tastes amazing.

A nice quick hot snack is a miso soup sachet and seaweed flakes in a cup: add boiling water and garnish with dried shallots.

Roadhouse food is (and some people would be surprised by this), mostly very good. Some roadhouses have amazing dinner menus, and the cooks were often happy to make something vego especially for me. There was one roadhouse (which closed down in the pandemic unfortunately) that heard I was coming up the road and made a beautiful mountain of fresh crisp salad, decorated with garnishes, ready as soon as I arrived. That was wonderful.

Usually, if I was at a roadhouse, I had a double serve of hot potato chips or wedges to carb up for lunch and a vego truckies breakfast before leaving. A truckies breakfast is everything: eggs, bacon, baked beans, spaghetti, toast, sausage, mushroom, tomato, hash browns, and maybe some spinach if it was a fancy roadhouse. The cook would make me the same size without the animal stuff, and sometimes I went for seconds. Many roadhouses also have healthy truckie options: fruit, salad and Mexican bowls, big sandwiches and wraps full of salad; those days I bought everything and ate until my sides split.

I don't normally use vitamin and mineral supplements, but I don't normally exercise for eight to twelve hours a day. Before I started, and during the walk, I saw nutritionists to make sure I had a balanced diet. We guessed a triathlete's diet would come close to meeting my nutritional needs. Walking around Australia is not a common thing for a nutritionist to be asked to plan, and my expedition was made more difficult by not having a support vehicle for cooking and refrigeration, and a limited space to carry supplies. We added supplements as insurance in case my natural reserves depleted faster than anticipated. I'm glad we did. I had multivitamins with extra vitamin Bs, omegas and iron, magnesium powder, as well as spirulina for protein, iron and potassium.

After about 3,000 kilometres along the west coast, I knew for certain my body was running low on some important nutrients. If you have ever smelt spirulina, you know it smells like a swamp. One day I reached a stage where I opened the bottle of spirulina tablets and took a long sniff, my brain was convincing me it smelled great. I knew immediately I needed to double my supplements and tripled the spirulina from six daily tablets to a handful. Within a week it went back to smelling like a swamp and I could cut back to normal.

I carried books on edible weeds and bush foods, foraging and trying new plants as I went. Around the southwest, through farmland, I focused on learning the edible weeds from *The Weed Forager's Handbook – A guide to edible and medicinal weeds in Australia* by Adam Grubb and Annie Raser-Rowland. Most days I could find fresh greens to supplement my rations with plants I recognised and grew up with. I was surprised by how many of them I had tried experimentally as a kid. Native bush food took a lot more care: learning the toxic and hallucinogenic ones not to touch, what parts were edible, how to prepare them and in which season they could be harvested. I never touched fungi, that's far too risky.

Not having an Aboriginal guide to show me all this, I used the twenty-hour five steps of safe testing for anything I was unsure of:

1. Rub it on your wrist, wait four hours for a reaction
2. Rub it on the outside of your lip, wait four hours for a reaction
3. Rub it inside your lip, wait four hours for a reaction
4. Rub it on the side of your tongue, wait four hours for a reaction
5. Try a very small amount of it, wait four hours for a reaction

If you have any reaction at any of these stages, stop: it isn't edible. Wash your hands and knife and remember what that plant looks like so you don't mistake it for something else. If you have no reaction then it is safe. If you're using this in an emergency situation, don't worry, starvation is usually the last thing people die of and you'll probably be rescued before you reach step five.

CHAPTER 16

EARTH MOVING

In the middle of the Gascoyne region, on the west coast, I saw a green burning flash fall through the sky and moments later a muffled boom and the ground shook. It wasn't until the next day, seeing a local interest article on ABC about meteorites, I realised I saw, heard and felt one fall so close I could have found it and made headlines for reasons other than just walking around Australia.* I think my brain registered what I saw at the time, but I recall my surprise at being so close to mining explosives. That was what my brain said the noise and tremor was, even though I was far from the mines, walking through cattle country. I have watched many meteorites burning through the Earth's atmosphere. Most burn up before hitting the ground. They come in many colours, depending on their mineral content, and can be spectacular events at night, but to be seen during the day they need to be a decent size, fist to football size. This one would have been larger than your average to have sent out a noticeable shockwave. I have made a mental note

* And probably enough money to cover the cost of the walk.

to never dismiss this again, drop everything and go find it. The crossover between our planet catapulting through space and space debris entering our safety zone is not rare but uncommon enough to want a piece of the action.

I was often filthy at the weather gods for headwinds, rains, heatwaves and blizzards, but dust storms, well that was like throwing sand in my face.* Dust storms look destructive, apocalyptic, but they aren't, they only looked like they were about to swallow me into an abyss. The build-up, watching them form and roll towards me was real-time Hollywood action and adventure suspense: huge, angry, red storm clouds, sucking sand and dust into themselves, getting taller, darker and faster as they moved closer.

When the gale force wind suddenly changed direction, feeding the storm, I knew I had only enough time to cover my face and stand side on to it before it slammed me from the other direction. The sky went dark and all visibility was lost as I was engulfed by a moving wall of earth.

In the worst of these, I fully expected the barrow to be lifted and lost, as I squatted behind it. I was lashed and scratched by sand, pebbles and plant debris as the wind tugged and tore at my clothes and hair; I felt like a rock being polished. The storm front didn't last long but I trailed dust as I walked for an hour afterwards. I was covered from head to toe in sand and dust and whatever else it had picked up across the desert. The finest particles had filtered through my clothes, filling every skin pore, and my hair was standing on end from static energy and dry dust clinging to each strand.

---

* Not sorry.

Not a speck of rain fell during these storms.

The first time I experienced a dust storm was years earlier, working on a ship anchored in Roebuck Bay off Broome. I watched what I thought was a huge fire building and swirling around like a tornado on Roebuck Plains. The 'smoke' was spreading out over the bay towards us, but I couldn't smell it; it was unnerving and put me on edge. As the cloud kept growing and getting closer, I let out more anchor chain to hold us. Suddenly we were in it, getting tossed and bucked on the choppy water. It passed very quickly, losing a lot of its power over the water, whipping around us, and twirling us around the anchor, leaving us with the inconvenient job of washing all the red dust off the ship, which we had just washed two days earlier. It helped prepare me for the dust storms I would encounter during the walk: that is, I was ready to get very dirty.

For the third dust storm I was better informed and better prepared. As I saw it forming into a long bank of cloud, and felt it begin sucking the air into itself, I zipped my rain jacket up to my ears, tugged on my rain pants, pulled a balaclava on over my sunglasses, pulled the sides of my wide-brimmed sun hat down tight with the drawstring, and tucked pant legs into socks, so ensuring that almost no skin was exposed to the blasting I was about to receive. I had to stop and huddle on the leeward side of the barrow. If I tried walking the wind tried pulling my legs out from under me. As soon as it was past, I carefully removed the rain clothes and gave them a good shake; they had kept out most of the sand but had also proved to be great wind protection. Under the hat and balaclava, I still had a little bit of dirt, but this time it wasn't getting into my eyes, gritting between my teeth and cementing onto layers of sunscreen.*

There was one other earth-shaking event I remember clearly. This was on the east coast, just south of Bowen. At this point in the walk my body and mind were beginning to deteriorate, hip pain was taking its toll on my health, but I was stubbornly pushing on. Only 15 kilometres out of town a couple of backpackers invited me to stop at their camp, shared with about twenty alternative-minded travellers. It was a hot day, so I pulled up around lunch and introduced myself; everyone was so welcoming. We all pitched in food, helped cook and clean, and people sang and played instruments around the fire late into the night. We were our own tribe. The next morning, the camp stayed silent, except for birds and distant traffic; it was snug and warm inside the tent so I decided to take a rest day and sleep in. With nothing to do but rest my tired body I lay there reading, snacking and napping, it was a 'go slow' day.

Mid-morning, as I drifted into sleep, the ground under me rolled like a wave, bucking my body up and down, it felt like my thin mat was on water, not earth, but it wasn't soft as I tried clinging to the floor of the tent. For a few seconds I lay there in shock, then the adrenalin kicked in, pushing me to rush out of the tent and check on the other campers and anyone inside the rickety old kitchen shed. As I climbed out

* Although, in the appropriate storm situation, layers of zinc sunscreen can help protect against wind burn. I've seen people deep in the Papuan jungles coating themselves with pig fat for the same reason. If you don't like sunscreen or pig fat, you could just cover up with the right clothing. It is cleaner and more comfortable.

of the tent, everyone else was emerging from their rooftop campers, vans, tents and the shed. We all looked at each other. We were all safe, but we were all shaken, excited, relieved, pumped. Someone turned on the radio and tuned to the local ABC station: yes, as we suspected, we had experienced an earthquake and we were only two kilometres from the epicentre. There was no phone range in the camp; that night everyone exchanged contacts and social media handles so the next day, as soon as I was back in range, I posted the "We're okay" update, tagging everyone. Their families and friends replied with gratitude to hear that we were all safe.

CHAPTER 17

HOW DO YOU CAMP?

Camping gives you a lot of freedom when travelling. With the right set up you can visit many more places of beauty and find more opportunities to connect intimately with nature. When camping, remember to relax, sit back and allow the senses to tune into the sounds and smells of the great outdoors. Feel the breeze on your skin and watch the light play with trees, observe the path of the sun in the shadows and the warmth of the hills, and let the water cool your feet. At night, after the magic of each sunset, notice the darkness come to life with nocturnal activity; gaze up at the stars, their colours shimmering, and watch meteorites blazing across the Milky Way; look between the stars and let your imagination fill the emptiness. The best adventures are camping adventures.*

Having already had a few decades of camping and trekking experience I was at an advantage in choosing set ups. I even tried out some small luxuries I had seen reviews for in

* Children don't always appreciate camping holidays when they are young, but many grow up to love them and take their friends and their own young families camping. Immersion in nature is an important part of early education and a great way to instil into young minds the value of conservation and protecting our wild places.

adventure magazines, such as a pillow and a down sleeping mat. Totally unnecessary if you're trying to keep weight down but lovely if weight doesn't matter. It was a good way to field test a lot of gear and upgrade accordingly.

On one of my Australian Alps solo traverses, I used a lightweight tarpaulin and alpine sleeping bag. It was a good choice for autumn and a fun challenge trying out all the ways I could imagine setting up a tarp, from the A-frame tie ups to the tarp tortilla roll and the good ol' lean-to tied down over a big log. It was with this confidence I was able to do most of lutruwita with the same set up.

Once I had the barrow, I could buy a light one-person tent. A good quality small tent is perfect for solo adventures. It is all you need: enough space for sleeping and stashing your pack at your feet or in the vestibule. Mine didn't take up much room in the barrow and it wasn't a problem distributing gear around the poles. My first little tent weighed 2.1kg. I can't remember the brand, but it wasn't very good in the rainy season in southwest Western Australia. Mont Adventure Equipment, an Australian company, came onboard as a supporter, offering an industry discount. All their gear was top quality, and I could use it knowing I could sleep warm and dry. My first Mont Moondance tent lasted over 10,000 kilometres, through temperatures between minus 5°C and 38°C, one flood and a cyclone, before delaminating in the monsoon season in the Northern Territory. That is a pretty good test of durability, and they replaced it with a new and improved Moondance model. At the time I bought my first Moondance it was a unique design: mesh inner for air flow and watching the stars, sealed floor to protect against high rainfall events, very quick and easy to put up and pack down (five minutes), plenty of head room when sitting and pockets for storing essentials like book, headlamp, snacks, toilet tissues, emergency beacon, phone and power bank.

The only disadvantage of the mesh inner is in cold weather (admitting snow when you want the full silnylon wall option of the Moondance) and in dust storms, of which I had a few blowing in at over 90 km/h: the dust blew up under the fly, sifting in over everything. If the rain quickly follows the dust you get mud. Even the deep floor walls were not high enough to prevent that happening in a desert storm. Tell you what though, I could get the tent up in a record time of four minutes when those storms hit; and it stood up solid through the worst of them.

The only other problem with sleeping every night in a tent for months is the toll it can take on your hips. I had a good inflatable sleeping mat but about four months into any section my hips began aching while sleeping. This meant shifting a lot through the night. I found a little relief when I could dig a shallow hollow into sandy ground under my hips and shoulders or when camping on thick, soft grass, but these ground surfaces were relatively rare. Learning to sleep on all sides helps prevent sore hips.

Condensation is a common problem with all tents. Most tents will collect water on the inside surface at night because it is warmer than the outside and of course you exhale moisture. If it is cold enough it freezes and can be shaken out, if not it needs to be wiped off or dried out during a rest break. It is uncomfortable when you forget to dry it and need to pitch a wet tent at the end of the day. The Moondance is designed to reduce condensation in most environments, and there are enough venting options to get good air flow through in fair weather. This is important if you plan to set off for extended treks, or when base camping in extreme cold—too much condensation can result in wet sleeping bags which can be dangerous. Your tent is part of your safety net.

I used the Mont Moondance tent until switching back to an ultralight set up on the east coast where food and water were available every couple of days. This time I added a Tier Gear hammock and tarpaulin to the kit. Tier Gear is a small cottage industry business, family run from their home in lutruwita, and they were one of my first sponsors with donated gear.*

The lightweight silnylon hammock and tarp set up was so good I've used it for almost every expedition since. I'm on to the third hammock now. The first was getting threadbare from nightly use for years. The second Tier Gear hammock succumbed to damage after a neighbour's campfire lost control in high winds and burnt tiny spark holes into it. It is always a sad day when I need to say goodbye to a hammock. The third is only a recent acquisition and is even better than the others.

The hammock has a sewn-in fly mesh and a four-pocket pouch on the ridge line, making it a very comfortable place to hang out on rest days. With the hammock I don't need to carry a stool or chair; it is usually an easy task to find two trees, shade and a relaxing view. One small thing I do before setting up is to ask the trees if it is okay and reassure them that I won't do any damage. I have broken part of a tree only

* A good business 'sponsor' offers significant donations, financial assistance and/or social media love.

once and it made me feel like a criminal. I'm usually much more careful and even place soft paperbark under the tree slings to spread the pressure around the trunk or branch.

Hammocking is a very old style of sleeping and resting during the heat of the day. The name's origins go back to South American First Nations, but it was first adopted onto ships independently by the English to save space in sleeping quarters. I imagine there are many other records dug up by researchers of hammocks being used throughout history instead of, or as well as, traditional beds and mats.

The most common question I'm asked about hammock camping is back comfort. Most people find sleeping in a hammock very comfortable. It is a different comfort to your bed at home, with a banana sway and a limit to the positions you can lie in, but after a few nights you get used to it and find ways to curl over. Personally, I end up in a foetal position, happily snoring away like a hibernating bear, kicking out a leg or arm if it gets too warm. Honestly, in three season weather, it is much better than on the ground in a tent. You do not need to get down on your hands and knees to go to bed or sit down to read and write. When the ambient temperature drops below 15°C you will need insulation against the cold underneath you. For cool summer nights I use a cheap $5 silver car windshield foam sun visor or the emergency bivvy. For cooler seasons and on the snow, I use a hammock under-quilt. If the hammock is long and wide, you can stretch out a bit. The only disadvantage to a long three-metre hammock is finding trees, poles or rocks wide enough apart for the slings, but it's not that hard if you give yourself enough time to find a spot before sunset. I have been caught out only a few times, usually in caravan parks.

Like all sleeping systems for trekking, if you want to try hammock camping I recommend borrowing a good quality one first, don't try a mediocre brand or style and decide it isn't for you because you had a lousy night. Always set yourself up for comfort and safety for an enjoyable experience.

Wherever and however I camp, I practise 'leave no trace'. This is the habit of treading lightly on the earth, leaving a place exactly as you found it, or even better if you pick up rubbish and repair damage made by other campers. I like the feeling of packing up camp and looking back to see only a soft indentation in the grass where I had been sleeping. It makes me feel like I have a gentle connection to the places I visit.

Body waste can compromise how well we do this and in some sensitive environments, such as alpine regions and water catchments, you are required to carry out your toilet waste in a bag or tube. I use compostable starch bags or doggie bags and put them inside my used zip-lock camp food pouches, which in turn go into a garbage dry sack. Others carry out using compost bags inside a homemade wide conduit pipe with screw top caps (you put your poop bags into the poop tube, don't try pooping straight into it!). In most places you can dig a 15- to 30-centimetre hole, back fill it when finished and place large rocks on top of the hole so other animals don't dig it up. Rarely, but occasionally, the ground is too hard to dig so I choose a very discrete and hidden place to safely burn the paper waste and build a rock cairn over the rest. That is only a last resort, and never inside a national park.

Toilet tissues are one of the things people seem to struggle most to dispose of well. There are several alternatives I have tried. The stand-up pee funnel, a small silicon funnel women can put into their undies and pee standing, you still need to pat dry and wash the funnel. Or a small natural fibre cloth can be used to pat dry, this can be disinfected by the sun when hung to dry on your pack. These days I just use tissues and put the used ones into a zip lock bag for disposal later. My sisters, please stop leaving used tissues in the bush, nobody is going to pick them up for you.

As a general rule, I don't light fires, except a very small fuel fire for cooking, which leaves no mark. Fire scorches the earth: I particularly avoid fires in alpine areas, even on snow, as it can take generations to recover. Smoke alarms wildlife and causes them unnecessary stress. Removing deadwood off the ground and cutting down branches takes away the homes of many animals, including small reptiles, amphibians and insects, as well as fungi. Too many bushfires are caused by campfires which get out of control in wind gusts or which have not been fully extinguished. I was a volunteer fire fighter for many years, and know the risk is too high most nights to even consider one. If you do light a fire, clear the ground for two metres around the fire, then keep it small and contained. When you pack up camp make sure the coals are cold as winds can create sparks and restart warm coals which can then cause catastrophic fires. Fires are lovely but deadly serious and always leave a mark. Think carefully before you make one.

Pocket rubbish, including the little bits and pieces such as tissues, hairbands and snack wrappers, the things you have stuck in your pocket and forgotten about which sometimes fall out onto the track when you pull your hand out of your pocket. It is unintentional but someone coming along behind you has to pick it up. I suspect I've dropped a few things this way too. These days my packs have front pouches, either on the shoulder straps or waist band, where I stuff those little things so they can't go astray.

My last big no-no is digging trenches for rain run-off. DON'T! You don't need to. Pack prepared for rain, use a footprint (a groundsheet made to the shape of the tent floor) under your tent for extra protection, camp on a slight slope and avoid hollows for natural run-off; move the tent if the ground becomes saturated, don't go if the forecast is bad. I've walked through wild places above the tree line where the alpine grasses and herbs have been dug up for drainage around someone's camp. It made me cry knowing it will take many years to recover from that damage. I tried my best to replant the delicate grasses but when I went back the next year only half had survived. I see this repeated in many places around Australia. It is an old-fashioned out-of-date practice taught in the army and scouts decades ago but should be replaced by smarter and more environmentally considerate practices. Our camping gear has technically advanced a long way from canvas tents, our practices can too.

Enough lecturing for this chapter. I can get quite worked up about this, so let's move on to more specific tips for camping while walking across a continent. To put it simply, you can camp almost anywhere, with a few exceptions.

"Where do you camp at night?" was one of the most common questions people would ask when we met along the road or track.

"Wherever I get to at the end of the day," is the answer.

I would hear stories of international cyclists and walkers camping right beside the road, but I tried to get some privacy by camping further back in the trees or behind cairns of rock. After sunset, when there was no more traffic (apart from a few trucks), it was quiet. I would lie under the stars listening to the wildlife and enjoy being alone and safe, out of sight of anyone who might pass through the night. Nobody knew I was there, except those I had sent my position by satellite.

A traverse or circumnavigation of Australia, depending on which route you take, is mostly through regional and remote landscapes. If you choose a more challenging direct crossing, for example, Cape York to Cape Leeuwin, 99 percent of your route will be remote. If you walk between Melbourne and Cape York, you will be in a new town almost every day until you reach Queensland and then it gets progressively more regional until remote Cape York. When passing through populated areas it is safest to stay with friends, supporters, in backpacker hostels and holiday parks. If you feel confident enough, you can try sleeping rough in town, but you will be woken by random strangers or the police. Once beyond the towns, camping is as easy as looking for a good spot to stop while you have daylight to set up.

One of the exceptions to this is on Aboriginal traditional land where you need to ask for a permit or get permission from the owners. When I walked across the bottom of Australia, from west to east, I needed to pass through Mirning and Wirungu land on the Nullarbor and Head of Bight to Yalata. Just east of the Nullarbor Roadhouse was a small sign with a phone number for the Traditional Landowners. I stopped and called them.

I spoke to a female ranger, explaining how I was walking around Australia alone for suicide prevention awareness and requested permission to camp as I passed through their country. She asked a few questions and explained that their land is used for men's and women's business, so I could not camp further than 50 metres from the road. It took only three days and two nights crossing to Yalata and each night I was able to pick a camp 50 metres from the road. On the way I visited Head of Bight to see the right whale calving nursery and learn more about the Mirning and Wirungu nations. Years before I had watched Julian Lennon's documentary, *Whale Dreamers*, about the Aboriginal connection to this land, and it helped my understanding of their culture and country by visiting and being on country.

Make sure you are allowed to camp on traditional land by contacting the traditional owners, talking to the rangers or applying for a permit. Otherwise, make other plans.

There were evenings when the sun was about to set and I had not yet found a place to camp, as the cattle fences along the highway went on and on and on for days. On those nights I looked for gates where I could camp just inside the property. Many were locked and I had to keep going. Sometimes I had to resort to camping behind long grass. The main thing I was wary of were the cattle ranging along the highway, as they often walked along the fence line, so my camp needed to be clear of their tracks. As with anywhere else, it was important to leave no trace of my camp.

Rest areas varied from filthy human waste strewn dumps to tidy places full of friendly travellers and clean drop toilets. As a rule, I avoided the rest areas because of the rubbish and excrement. When I wanted company or to hear a yarn, I made my way to the official free overnight camps full of motorhomes, caravans, campervans and converted backpacker 4WDs.

The worst camp ever was one where a truckie pulled up while I was eating dinner and took a dump on the road in front of me. The best camps were places I could wander a few hundred metres off the track, and silently watch the sunset and spot wildlife in the trees and tracks in the dust.

CHAPTER 18

AN ATTEMPTED MURDER

It was a horrible day as I walked along the Barkly Highway near the Northern Territory/Queensland border. A cloudless day but cold, with a relentless 70 km/h headwind blowing in from the east as I slowly made my way to Camooweal. The terrain was gentle, slightly undulating and wide sweeping bends in the highway broke up the monotony of long straits. Beside the road was a 1.5-metre-wide sealed shoulder and red marbly gravel falling away to either side into a tough landscape of patchy mallee scrub, stunted acacia, spinifex and saltbush. I had three layers of clothes on, including my big yellow rain jacket to block the wind; over my head I had a beanie, balaclava and hood with my headphones blaring a podcast to try cutting out the painfully incessant roar of wind over my ears. I don't normally cover my ears; I like to hear the traffic coming up from behind. It was an uncomfortable and energy-sucking day.

I stopped at a roadside ruin to find shade for a rest and to eat out of the wind, and I ended up having a snooze—but it was scorching hot out of the wind. The wind and sun dehydrated me quickly and very soon I had finished off my daily water ration and had started drinking the next day's supply; I had six days of water in the barrow, seven litres per day for 250 kilometres of walking. There were buildings in the distance, old mud brick or mud-stained huts, a strange place to be but maybe they had water. I pulled out my spare water bottles and began walking towards them on a dry disused track with one set of barefoot prints tracking in the opposite direction. About halfway there I suddenly had a really bad feeling about the huts. Listening to my instinct, I turned back and continued walking along the highway. If I ran out of water before Camooweal I could ask other travellers to help out at the rest areas. From that point on I felt uneasy and on edge. It could have been the wind stirring me up or a sixth sense, but I kept walking, adjusting my anticipated 50 kilometres to 40.

At about 2pm it was getting warm, so I took off the bright yellow jacket and wore a silver heat reflective thermal shirt over a T-shirt with brightly coloured leggings and yellow thongs (flip flops). The highway is not a fashion runway, but I was highly visible. I found more energy after guzzling a litre of electrolytes and was able to quicken my pace. There was to be a hot rod/drag race in Katherine or Darwin the next weekend so many of the vehicles passing were car trailers and trucks heading to the event, mixed in with travellers towing big vans and cattle road trains—trucks pulling two or three trailers of hot and dehydrated cows to the Mt Isa train terminal for export overseas.

In all states of Australia and most places around the world, where there is no footpath or shared track for pedestrians we must walk on the opposite side of the road to the flow of traffic, facing oncoming traffic. Here in Australia this meant I walked on the right-hand side of the road most of the way. Wide sealed shoulders made it safer: I could see the vehicles approaching me and if they were not going to give me a safe passing distance, I could move off the side of the shoulder. I also had a side mirror which I used to see if the approaching vehicle could pass wide, and it let me anticipate moving off the shoulder sooner if another vehicle was coming up from behind. I usually had a few kilometres from seeing the oncoming traffic to when they passed by; plenty of time. On long quiet highways like the Barkly, I didn't need to use the mirror much and just concentrated on what was ahead. I always tried to be as considerate as possible to traffic on the road, understanding from experience there are a few drivers out there who get angry about sharing the road.

By mid-afternoon I had somehow managed to find that sweet meditative walking state, a steady pace and peace of mind, with a reluctant acceptance of the wind conditions (after hours of swearing at all the weather gods). I had given up on listening to podcasts, the wind was too loud to hear the talking, so I played some relaxing classical music of which I picked up a few bars here and there.

I had just come out of one of those wide sweeping bends with the road stretching ahead to the horizon, and began thinking about what to eat for dinner, maybe some fruits and nuts, more electrolytes. I still had an avocado carefully buried in the cool centre of the barrow, it would be nice on crackers with a sprinkle of pink rock salt and seasoned seeds. I began thinking of stopping even earlier.

And then I had that awful sinking feeling in the pit of my

gut that something was wrong, urgently and terribly wrong. All my senses blared their alarms. Nothing was in front of me, nothing was running or sliding out of the scrub at me, I glanced in my side mirror and to my horror it was filled with the front of a huge black truck on the wrong side of the road heading straight for me, from behind.

I let my reflexes and instinct take over and jack-knifed the barrow off the shoulder and ran, following it down into the gravel ditch. As I looked back at the road, the truck and all its three fully-loaded cattle trailers sped over the exact spot I had just been walking. I caught a glimpse of the driver in the cabin and he looked directly into my eyes with a maniacal grin.

His intention was clear, he wanted to kill me. He was not asleep or on the phone and there was no way he could move his truck and trailers back to the other side of the road to miss me without rolling over. This wasn't just a scare, it was an attempted murder.

I had become accustomed to idiots thinking it was funny to drive straight at me and run me off the road, and people side-swiping me from behind while overtaking abreast of me, usually on a long straight empty road. But this incident really shook me and before I thought about getting the rego number he was too far away. Instead, I pulled out my two-way radio and gave him an earful. I was shaking with fear and fury and wanted everyone listening in to hear what had happened. The only information I had was the colour of his cab, black, his load (three trailers of cattle), the logo of the company he drove for, a longhorn cattle image, and a rough description of his face. I made radio contact with anyone who travelled past for the next half an hour, asking them to look out for him and report him if they caught up.

Initially, I didn't know what to do, I was still shaking for another 40 minutes and every vehicle passing from behind made me jump and cry. I began wondering what would happen if he came back to finish off the job he started. It was necessary to get off the Barkly Highway and hide.

Luckily, I don't often freeze in these situations; being a fighter I automatically override my fear and take action. The first life-preserving action in this circumstance was finding somewhere far from the highway to camp and sweep over my barrow tracks.

On a bare patch of soft dry red earth, scattered with round gibber stones, between small lithe acacias and spinifex grass, I sat beside the barrow and tried to find enough calm to think clearly. I could ration my water for two weeks and collect some on trees, from tent condensation and dew. Food rations would also last a few weeks and I knew from experience I could fast without food for a month without any problems. There was also the fact Mum would come looking for me if I didn't check in at Camooweal within a week. I was prepared to stay put for as long as it took to find my confidence again.

Once the tent was up, I lay inside, controlling my breathing and heartbeat, bringing them both down to their resting rates. Instead of meditating I thought about the walk, why I was out there, questioning if I needed to continue and if it was time to stop. Was stopping failure? What were my options? One thing I knew for certain, I needed to get off that highway.

That night I finished reading the *Tibetan Book of the*

Dead. I used that leg of walk to expand my understanding of world religions and always had a few books in the barrow. Sleep was not to come that night, so I began re-reading His Holiness The Dalai Lama's book, *The Art of Happiness*, and kept reading all night until I finished as dawn began lighting up the horizon. He reminded me of the purpose of this walk, the role I had played in the lives of others for more than 12,000 kilometres. He gave me the courage to keep going.

There is so much to process in his book, but the message I needed at that time was about purpose and compassion. My purpose was/is to be compassionate, reduce suffering and increase happiness in this world. In the darkness of the early morning, I remembered the many people I had spoken with beside the road, in roadhouses, on the radio, in newspaper interviews, emails, messages on social media, phone calls and public speaking. I thought of the times I stood beside the road with someone as they shared their story, as we cried and hugged together, easing their pain, of the phone call from a friend who was about to take their life and thought to call me instead. I'm crying now, writing these precious memories. I had to keep going, there was still work to do.

For a couple of days I relaxed, feeling safe hidden in that sparse beautiful landscape, the bowing branches of wattles feeling protective, mesmerising, hypnotic as they swayed in the wind. I sang pieces of songs to the birds and wrote bad haiku.

Finally, I nutted out a way to safety. Removing all the reflective strips from the barrow, I packed up at dusk then used the cover of darkness to walk to a rest area about 10 kilometres up the road. Each time I heard a vehicle approaching I dashed into the bush. The rest area was empty when I arrived, apart from one drunk, a sick man coughing in his swag. He didn't even notice me quietly walking past so I kept walking another five kilometres and hid in the wattles again. The next morning, early, I used the last of my water to wash and put on my last clean set of clothes before walking back to the rest area, weaving between the trees, well away from the road. At the rest area I settled down at a picnic table and began writing notes to send with grey nomads to the police outpost at Avon Downs, asking them to come and help me. Having a big barrow made it impossible to get a lift so I chose for them to come to me. By now you are probably wondering why I had not used my emergency beacon, and on reflection it was probably a good enough reason, but I prefer to reserve it for a life and death injury or illness where there is no physical way to extract myself. This was serious and I needed help, but I was okay, I just needed a lift and to make a report to the police.

Travellers began arriving by 9am and my notes began going out. By 11am, Robyn arrived in her police paddy wagon. The first thing she asked after establishing that I was the walker was, "How many notes did you send out?" She had received them all.

Thank you so much to all the people who delivered them, especially for understanding how serious the predicament was, some of whom compassionately consoled me while crying uncontrollably. I was finally able to feel safe. We jostled the barrow into the back of the police wagon, tying the door shut with rope, with the handles poking out, and went directly to the station.

Robyn and I chatted about policing on the Barkly Highway.

It is known by many as the "heartbreak highway" or "suicide highway". All kinds of things happened out there: cattle rustling, UFOs, drug running, but the most common callouts were for solo vehicle accidents ('male, deceased'). I made my report but couldn't give them enough information to make an arrest, unless someone else reported hearing him talk about it. They would keep an ear out and let me know if anything developed. We went into Camooweal, this time with the barrow comfortably tied down in the back of her ute and found a lift for me into Mt Isa. In Mt Isa, ABC radio and the local newspaper interviewed me about the attempted murder. They helped get the word out and asked the community to report anything they heard.

During the few hours looking around Camooweal I updated everyone on social media, called my parents and had my last cleansing cry. One of my friends, Simon from Tier Gear Tasmania, messaged and asked if I would like to do a house sit for his sister and her rescue cats in Mt Isa for 10 days. It was just what I needed. Another friend in Townsville, Belle Sinclair who I had met a couple of years earlier in southwest Western Australia as she rode around the world on her postie bike, called and offered to then drive out and collect me for a break at her place. That was an 1,800 kilometre round trip, for which I very gratefully covered the cost of her petrol and accommodation. My support network are superheroes.

Now I had another event to add to my already long list of causes for post-traumatic stress disorder (PTSD).

Thankfully, this time I had somewhere safe with friends in Townsville to process things. I could sleep as much as I wanted, walk along the river, sit by the ocean and eat gelato. The PTSD affected me physically as well as mentally, and all the little niggling pains became exaggerated. The worst was a twisting pelvis from walking along the right-hand camber of the road for thousands of kilometres. There was a yoga studio near Belle's and I went there every other day. The owner gave me private sessions to work on the twist, strengthening my back, hips and pelvis. It helped a lot, in a holistic way, to work on myself, body, mind and spirit. It was a time for self-care.

A few weeks in Townsville and I was ready to keep going. Instead of returning to the Barkly Highway, I calculated how many kilometres I had missed and measured that distance up the coast from Rockhampton. I jumped on a bus and left for Cairns. It was still difficult to walk beside any road as every passing truck spooked me, but the feeling eased off and I was finally able to get far enough south to use quiet detours, tracks and farm roads.

I have heard nothing from the police since, but I had a long chat with Ben Ferris Gump, a long-distance runner who was running the East Savannah Way heading west as I walked parallel on the Barkly Highway east. He had the exact same thing happen to him, same truck, within days of it happening to me. I spoke to some cyclists touring across the continent who had been physically pushed off the Barkly Highway by a cattle road train. We were not the only ones.

Years later a documentary was made to try finding the driver who had wreaked much more havoc than that year of incidents. I still hope he is found and dished out some form of justice.

CHAPTER 19

MY POOR MUM

Dad requested this chapter be short so he can read it while sitting on the toilet. Apparently, it is frustrating when chapters are too long, and frustrating for Mum if she's waiting to use the bathroom.

You might have a mixed impression of my parents from reading about how they raised me in a fundamentalist conservative Christian cult. Understand that they didn't know better and thought it was the right thing to do. They didn't know it was a cult until it was time for us to leave and they treated us, the whole family, like pariahs. When I visit Mum and Dad it is a taboo subject and if I dare broach it, I usually begin unconsciously raising my voice.

Dad struggles with society's acceptance of LGBTIQ and gender fluidity, but still loves his eldest child (and grandchild) who identify this way. Considering he believes the Bible is law, this is a demonstration of the strength of his love.

Mum, like all mothers, has a prerogative to worry about us kids. My mum has a habit of going directly to the worst-case scenario when there is a small problem. My youngest sibling, Steve, being the most grounded of us, doesn't stress her out, but they had a couple of rocky years when he became a dad at 18. Linda, three years younger than me, is finally stretching her wings and discovering the joys of unshackled adventure. Even though Mum has had 50 years worrying about me, she still has plenty of worry left for Linda when she posts videos climbing cliffs.

Walking one day along the Victoria Highway, Northern Territory, west of Katherine, I made camp in a place where there was no phone range, so I sent a satellite check-in message with my location to Mum and Dad. My device made all the right noises for message sent and received, so I went to sleep. The next day, about 30 kilometres out of Katherine, I saw a police vehicle go past and wondered what they were responding to. Then another, and a State Emergency vehicle, then another police vehicle.

I thought it must have been a car accident, until the last police vehicle turned around and came back, wound down the window and asked, "Are you Terra?"

"Yes," I replied cautiously.

"Call your mum."

Shit! Has someone died? What's happened? As I picked up my pace the police and SES drove past again, returning to town. About 15 kilometres out of Katherine, on top of one of the undulating hills, I picked up a bar of phone range and called. The check-in message hadn't gone through. Mum had panicked and called the police, bless her. We had a quick chat. Later that day, in town where I could recharge the phone, we talked for longer.

That happened sometimes, satellite messages not going through. Back then the only SOS communication device providers for recreationalists were from the northern hemisphere and southern hemisphere satellite arrays were not as easy to connect to, simply because there were not as many up above. My check-in registered as sent and about 20 minutes later it came through as received but it ended up getting lost on its way back down. This is why I also carried an AMSA registered EPIRB/PLB for emergencies, which goes directly to an Australian rescue coordination centre, the Australian Maritime Safety Authority, that uses its own southern hemisphere satellite receivers and activates a rapid land or sea search and rescue response. The satellite communication device providers have improved since then and the sky over the southern hemisphere has plenty of receivers. Still, they cannot be relied upon 100 percent of the time and it's best to carry a nationally registered emergency beacon for real emergencies.

After Mum activated my search and rescue, I began weaning her off the nightly check-ins and eventually stopped. Missing a check-in was an anxiety trigger she didn't need and it was easier for both Dad and Mum to know I posted every few days on social media or sent text messages through other travellers if I couldn't.

Mum and Dad know they can't stop me from doing whatever it is I set my heart on. Instead, they try to support me so I can do it successfully; that is, without dying. One way they often help is with little loans when I run out of money: BMD, the Bank of Mum and Dad, is interest free. Because I live below the poverty line, this is vital support, like throwing me a life ring in a storm. I always pay them back, otherwise that support would run out. I'm not proud of needing this kind of help, in fact, it shames me. I'm like an embarrassed dog with its tail between its legs when I need to make that phone call and only use it as a last resort, when every other way of finding emergency funds fails. I don't take their generosity for granted. There was a time, in my younger years, when it must have seemed to them as though I only called when I needed help. I could almost hear dad's inward groan when he answered the phone. These days, on the rare occasion I need their help, I pre-empt his disappointment with something self-deprecating. It's easier for both of us if he knows how difficult it is to ask. The walk has provided many lessons on the importance of being able to ask for help but poverty, anything to do with money, still shames me.

How I funded the walk was a common question, but I didn't like to talk about it. Mum and Dad gave each of us kids a gift when they sold a block of land. This funded half the walk. For another year I just survived, and in the final year I opened a personal fundraising account where supporters, friends and family donated $8,000 to help the message of suicide prevention continue down the east coast.

Dad's main role during the walk was to reassure Mum that I was okay, that I had the experience, was prepared and could flag down other travellers or use the two-way radio to get help. There were things I did not write about publicly but would have a private chat with Dad about them, letting him decide if he would share them with Mum.

I'm writing this from Cape York, and he has already asked me not to post anything else about crocodiles, for Mum's mental health.

Can you imagine how much of a toll that anxiety must

have on her nerves? I can't, not having had kids of my own. You would think I could change my lifestyle. I have tried but that takes a toll on *my* mental health. These days, when I head out on crazy expeditions and adventures, I carry a tracker. If I'm stationary for more than two days without sending a text message, Mum can alert emergency services. It is an expensive compromise, but it looks after our wellbeing. Thankfully, the only emergency rescues I have needed*, I have been able to activate from my mobile phone, talking to the paramedics and sending my location with a map pin.

The only time I really disappointed Dad was when I changed my name from the one he gave me. To be honest, I never felt comfortable with it and when I was heading back to southwest Western Australia, where the shark fishers had abused me and sent death threats a few years earlier, I decided it was safer to change it to Terra Lalirra, so they didn't remember who I was. Before I finished the walk, I legally changed it with NSW Registry of Births, Deaths and Marriages to Terra Roam. It had become my identity, roaming the earth. The people I met during the walk didn't know me by any other name than Terra and I felt comfortable with it. Dad is okay with it now. I think he was just annoyed about the extra legal paperwork I made for him.

I get a bit of perfectionism from Dad and drive from his

* Breaking my leg on the Gold Coast Hinterland Great Walk during this walk. Succumbed to hypothermia in a blizzard after reaching a locked building and calling the national park. Tripping on a rock in new boots, falling two metres onto my shoulder dislocating it, dislocating two ribs out of my spine and breaking them which required an emergency airlift.

mum, Ooma. His side of the family are high achievers and Ooma was not only a sports champion but also a pioneer female entrepreneur, writer and adventurer. She was my role model. Before I began the walk, I visited her in her care facility; she was blind and had dementia but remembered me. I leaned in close to her ear and asked her to hang around until I finished, so I could tell her lots of stories. The day after I finished, Mum, Dad and I went to see her, and I told her about the walk. Ooma shared some of her own adventure memories with me. A few months later, at the age of 99, she passed away. We all went down to spend her last few days together and we told her stories, sharing our favourite memories with her. Dad was with her right to the end.

> *"Memories, I always think, are like flowers; you have the very real experiences, they linger a while then fade, but the perfume of the flower or experience lingers on forever and can be recalled as very sweet and wonderful, to be stored and nurtured in the long book of memories."*
> *Jean Nossiter/Ooma (1991)*

Between legs of the walk, I would return to the east coast and stay with either Steve and his wife Sil, or Mum and Dad. It was the hardest part of the walk, stopping to rest and recover while waiting for the cool season. I needed to be with family who understood how much I was struggling and would help when it became too difficult to cope with. I felt like a burden sometimes, especially when unwell, but then they would remind me of their love and acceptance.

Mum doesn't like it when I say I'm homeless. I don't have

a home, house or apartment, no car, camper or caravan. I spend most of the year in a hammock or tent, transient, on foot, bicycle, bus and train. There is always a room available at Hotel Mum and Dad, or Bonny Hills Hilton. Being a vagabond can get exhausting on a tight budget, so it is always good to be able to land at my parents' and call them home for a while.

On my recent sojourn at their place, we timed it so I could be there for six weeks while Mum, who had had foot surgery, recovered in a wheelchair. Dad and I cared for her, shared the cooking, cleaning and gardening. Taking the pressure off him helped them both. I was able to mother my mother and make sure she was following the surgeon's instructions, resting with her foot up. She was so frustrated; Mum is not used to being still. One week after surgery, I caught her outside trying to trim the hedge. Is this what it's like having kids?

One day, as I walked between Crescent Head and Port Macquarie, I was catching up with a friend, Kerryann Hayes, who began the women's adventure magazine, Travel Play Live. She was camping near where I camped at Delicate Nobby. Before setting off for the day we sat down for a chat. As I was getting ready to leave, I heard a familiar engine. It was Dad! I threw the pack on and ran down to the beach, looking up. And there were Dad and Mum, flying over in their little CT ultralight plane waving out the windows. I stretched my arms out like wings and dipped them from side to side. Dad flew over again and dipped his wings from side to side. I cried from happiness. It was so good to see them. I had hoped they would do a fly-by while I walked their stretch of coast.

Mum and Dad are my biggest supporters! And I never

need to worry about being lost or injured in the middle of nowhere for more than two days while Mum is on watch.

What I loved most about my childhood was camping almost every school holiday. We were a middle-class family; Dad was a sales rep and Mum taught pottery at night school once a week. They supplemented their income by selling pottery and bartering honey, eggs and organic vegetables from our garden. This meant, if we scrimped and scraped, we could go camping for one or two weeks every few months. It was always in a national park where we could go bushwalking, wildlife spotting, learn to light fires, play with knives, swim in the surf and join the free park ranger's guided tours. We went to Siding Springs Space Observatory, historic Trial Bay Gaol in Arakoon, walked up Targungal/Mt Kosciuszko and visited the ancient Gondwana rainforests in Queensland.

We were lucky kids. Without these opportunities I would not have formed a deep connection with nature at such a young age, a connection I have valued ever since.

Dad, I hope that wasn't too long for you to sit on the loo.

CHAPTER 20

THE NORTH

Garramilla/Darwin has been a psychological hurdle. I first visited the city in 1993, after travelling by land and sea from Bangkok, Thailand. I was there with my ex-husband, but the city was full of men who wolf-whistled and yelled obscenities at women. I felt like a piece of meat. We hitched out of there quickly. The second time I took my sister up to Kakadu, Arnhem Land, Adelaide River and Litchfield National Park. We hired a car for a week and stayed in nice places, visiting rock art sites, billabongs, took a tour up East Alligator River, walked through the wetlands birdwatching, visited WWII sites and swam under waterfalls. Only our first night was in the city; there was no way I was going to expose my sister to the Top End male culture of the '90s. The third time I stayed there, it was on shore leave from a pearl farm. That was when I was raped at knife point and ended up getting an abortion. On the fourth visit, as I finished the west coast leg, I was so nervous one of my supporters flew up and shared my donated room at the Value Inn, escorting me everywhere, to interviews, Crocosaurus Cove, botanic gardens, until we flew out. My view of the city was still tinged with trauma and I was never able to relax.

When I returned to begin the leg to the east coast I stayed with Deb and Roger, from Slappas thongs. I felt much safer and explored the city and coastline. The culture of the city had changed over twenty years. Even though the rape was still in the front of my mind and triggered PTSD flashbacks, I was able to relax a little and appreciate the coastal beauty. I saw endangered Gouldian finches in the wild and loved the colours of the coastline: the purples, reds, white and golds of the rocky embankments falling to dark coffee rock platforms covered in foraging shore birds, green, yellow and brown seaweeds, pocked with rock pools spilling into turquoise, aqua and ultramarine water. Filling my head with this bright rainbow of nature forced out all my worries. I'm now looking forward to the next visit.

I was once told by a clairvoyant that I was going to be a spelunker. I had to go to the library to find out that meant a cave explorer. I was thrilled. I have a lifelong dream of living in a cave, not the spelunking kind though, just a nice deep sandstone cave with a spring of water and lots of animal friends. I do love caving and visit them at every opportunity: day caving, night caving (yeah, I know, what's the difference), beach caves, limestone caves, lava tubes, they are all equally fascinating and beautiful. When you have an imagination like mine, all the beach caves have hidden treasures and all the limestone caves are full of precious jewels and portals to other worlds. I'll happily walk an extra fifty kilometres to visit a cave.

Cutta Cutta means 'many stars' in the Jawoyn language and as you walk down into Cutta Cutta Caves, just south of Katherine, the crystallised limestone on the ceiling and floor sparkle like stars sleeping through the day. It isn't a cool cave, in fact, it is quite hot, being so high into the tropics. When you exit, the breeze outside, under the shade of the curly bark acacias, feels refreshingly cool. My tour was lucky enough to see ghost bats and an olive python curled up in a dark nook. Formations of stalagmites and stalactites, columns, veils, ripples and crystal pools were an astonishing surprise find in the hot Top End, and I didn't need to detour to see them.

Bitter Springs. Sounds interesting doesn't it? An oxymoron, spring and bitter. It is a sweet spot at Mataranka, on the way down Stuart Highway. It has been used for thousands of years as a water source by the traditional owners and a fertile place for food and textiles. The biggest and deepest pool in the springs is off limits to tourists; it is a women's place, a birthing place. Following the track, wandering along the stream, under and around palms, cycads, pandanus and melaleuca trees, I was in a real oasis in the middle of arid Australia, fed by the Great Artesian Basin. The water was a clear crystalline mineral blue green with reeds, algae and delicate ferns along the banks. The bed of the stream was white quartz sand. Some of these plant species have barely changed since Gondwana separated from Pangaea.

Slipping into the warm thermal water at the swimming platform, I hooked the pool noodle, borrowed from the holiday park, under my arms and slowly, gently floated down with the current. Below me were small fish and a turtle with green algae on its back, above the sun peeked through the palms. The creek wound its way down to another platform where I climbed out, walked up the track and went back in again, this time floating on my back. It was so relaxing I returned again, early the next morning while the warm water steamed in curling clouds around me.

On my way out, I met an elder who was also a stockman on the old cattle station most of his life. It was just the two us standing on the platform above the women's pool, he shared first-hand accounts of when the station manager and stockmen fought, his sad eyes watered up as he told me about rations, slavery, murder, rape, as though it happened just yesterday, still fresh, raw, painful and personal. The Karrigari people are the unceded owners of this land; farming colonists murdered them, they were at war and fought over rights to the water and hunting grounds. The next day I met him again, as he joined a bus load of traditional owners travelling from Garramilla and Katherine to protest coal seam gas at a meeting with the mining company and cattle station owners.

There was an inconvenient resupply hiccup in Northern Territory, very annoying and potentially disastrous. Renner Springs Desert Inn had agreed to hold a resupply box of food, sunscreen, electrolytes and baby wipes until I arrived. I posted it at the same time as the resupply box for Barkly Homestead. My rest day was spent chasing up the missing box. Australia Post records showed it as delivered so all I could do was lodge a report with the parcel number. It was lost. There was some food left over from the previous resupply; supplemented with roadhouse snacks I was able to ration these and walk 160 kilometres to Tennant Creek, where the supermarket had overpriced and limited options to fuel another 211 kilometres. On arrival at Barkly Homestead, the owners were happy to offload two resupply boxes, one of which was clearly addressed to Renner Springs. I didn't think I would need to ration for a while after that.

CHAPTER 21

HAVE YOU HAD TROUBLE WITH ANIMALS?

Slow travel allows us to see and hear everything around: all the birds, lizards, kangaroos, frogs and other animals. At night, quietly sitting under the stars, the nocturnal animals come out. Some of the more cautiously curious are so quiet their only evidence of visiting are footprints in the dust or a fresh scat.

The mornings start with bird calls, and each new location brings a new ensemble. Listening to the bird population change as I walked through new ecosystems and habitats added layers of appreciation for the changing landscapes. Some mornings I would lie in my warm sleeping bag trying to identify each of them or get up early to make breakfast and in the stillness of the pale dawn watch their silhouettes dart from tree to tree. What were they talking about so exuberantly so early in the day? Perhaps they were sharing their plans of where to find nectar and bugs or checking in to see if everyone slept well. Or maybe telling off their neighbour (me) for snoring.

As the sun warmed the earth, lizards, snakes and dragonflies came out to bask and play. This was also the best time to see kangaroos, wallabies and wallaroos before they escaped the heat of the day to rest under trees or rocky escarpments. Those who did not hide from the sun were vulnerable to predation from the sky as kites, hawks, falcons and eagles soared overhead and perched high in trees, watching and waiting.

The dusk was just as enthralling as dawn, listening to the layers of animal noises, hopping, scurrying, whistling, fade away to be replaced by nocturnal noises, and everywhere I went, they changed. The nights I had spare energy I would wander through the bush and grasslands looking for the owners of the noises: night jars, owls, tawny frogmouths, frogs, crickets, dingos, wombats, koalas, quolls, bandicoots, possums, gliders. In hot regions, wildlife is more active through the cool of the night.

One night in the Northern Territory, I woke up with something nudging my back from under the tent. I lay still hoping for clues to its identity, which I knew pretty quickly. It was a snake, a very big one and it slid in under the tent floor and lay along the length of my body. For warmth I assume, not for company. And it stayed there, neither of us moving until I fell back to sleep, making a conscious note not to roll over. It was probably a python; they're okay, slow, methodical, not very venomous, even slower in the cool of the night. Unfortunately, it was gone when I woke and packed up the tent. I had hoped to meet it. I love pythons!

Dingos are my favourites. Since childhood they have fascinated me. Some of the national parks Mum and Dad took us camping as children had dingos and the sound of their howls evoked a sense of kinship in my soul. I wanted to go run with the pack, into the night.

Most places I trek through, the dingos' curiosity gets the better of them and I spot them walking by for a stickybeak. They can't help themselves, it is who they are. Normally, they are cautious and try to stay out of sight, watching or following at a safe distance, exploring my camps at night or camouflaging perfectly with their environment in plain sight during the day. We are as curious of each other and every encounter makes my heart sing, even more so knowing they are allowing me to see them. They are brilliant stealth stalkers, the ninjas of the Australian bush.

Their iconic family howl at night is usually how I know I am passing through their territory. One would start the howling circle and each member of the family took turns, sometimes they would all end by howling together. These howls are used to both locate each other and communicate where they have found something of interest, a stranger or a meal. Humans are not on the dingo menu; we rarely need to worry about them, unless they are in a larger than normal pack and very hungry in a drought. I could sleep soundly knowing they were around and would visit during the night but leave me alone. I was licked on the face by one in central Australia while sleeping under the stars, but I woke up and shooed it away. It was letting the others know as I fell back to sleep.

Usually, I join in their howling: it's so funny when I hear the query in the next round of howls. Only once has a dingo growled at me. It was in Alice Springs as I walked to the

Larapinta Trail before sunrise. A family of dingos had just crossed the riverbed and the track in front of me, and they were making their way up the hill. I crossed behind their path, watching them agilely leap from rock to rock. But I jumped as another dingo appeared beside me on the path and growled. I had just crossed between the male and his family, and he was warning me to move on, quickly. He followed the rest of the pack up the red rocks to the top of the hill, and I watched them sit there facing the horizon as the sun rose over their golden faces. I felt like a voyeur, watching a secret ritual.

On the way across the Nullarbor/Eyre Highway, I heard a family begin their howl circle. I listened for a few rounds until I knew when each set finished, and then jumped in adding my own howl. We did this a few times until they stopped. The next night, 35 kilometres down the road, the sun went down and I read a book by headlamp until I began feeling my eyes close. Suddenly, I heard them, the same family, howling. I jumped in at the end of the first set. They went straight into the next set and, to my delight, they paused for me to join them. We did this for three nights, travelling over 100 kilometres together. A confirmation of kinship.

The dingo is my spirit animal. This is not cultural appropriation: I believe deep in my soul and mind there is a spiritual connection. On the third night of walking between Naarm and Newcastle it was raining, I unrolled my sleeping bag under an historic school shed, three timber walls, a corrugated iron roof and dirt floor covered in swallow poop. It was near a service station.

All night cars went past, slowing down to pull into the station. Occasionally their headlights would sweep across the shed and wake me. A car pulled up right beside the historic school ruin and I felt uneasy. Waking fully and rolling over to check I was safe, I saw a white dingo sitting at the foot of my sleeping bag, facing out. As my eyes studied it, wondering where it came from, it turned its head, its glowing amber eyes looked straight into mine. Instantly, I felt safe, in my head I heard a voice, "I'm watching after you, go back to sleep. I will always be here." I fell asleep. I know the dingo walks with me, protects me, keeps me company, always.

There is a difference between dingos and feral dogs. Dingos are a naturalised Australian canine which has likely been here at least 8000 years according to the latest DNA studies, and up to 20,000 years according to some researchers. The more scientists look at the dingo the more they are learning about its heritage and the purity of different breeds across the continent and islands, how it is genetically substantially different to today's domesticated dogs. I have personally met and made eye-to-eye contact with five different alpine dingos in the wild. Some were males alone, others were from family groups, one was black with a tan front, another was white with a black spot. Usually, they were golden and blond with thick coats and pups. The dingos I meet in the outback are sleek with tan and gold coats. Up on Cape York I have met both the black and tan dingos and on K'gari they were the pure iconic slim tan breed.

In places like K'gari, humans should not interact with dingos. They can become accustomed to us and expect, even demand, food and get aggressive if it is not forthcoming. These dingos are euthanized for public safety. There are signs everywhere telling us not to feed them, touch them or encourage them, but people still do so without fully understanding the consequences. During the two weeks I walked the length of K'gari, I didn't see a single dingo until the last day. He was walking along the beach at low tide. I stopped to take a photo and he just kept going, glancing up once, putting his snout back to the sand to continue hunting for pippies.

Walking increases the chance of seeing endangered species and I was lucky to have a few rare and wonderful sightings. For their protection I will not give locations, but I inform conservationists what I saw and where. I have a 'Before They're Gone' bucket list of vulnerable and threatened species in the wild, made in earnest as Australia's extinction rate rises. Personally, I'm not a fan of zoos with animals in enclosures. I love their conservation projects as arks for threatened species and species which are now extinct in the wild, but I walk around zoos feeling the sadness and loss of those who were captured in the wild and placed in confined compounds and pools for our entertainment.

Walking alone means I can stop anytime, anywhere, and wait quietly, without distraction. If I hear or see signs of a species on my list, I can camp for a few days, waiting to spot it. In this way I have been fortunate to see palm cockatoos, golden shouldered parrots, giant frilled-neck lizards, striped numbats, hammerhead sharks, mountain pygmy possums, greater gliders, platypuses, koalas, cassowaries, a nursery of southern right whales, yellow footed rock wallabies, and many more, big and small, furred, feathered, scaly and finned.

When I walked down the east coast of Queensland, I made it to Agnes Water just before the butterfly migration finished. Oh! What a sight! My favourites were the blue tiger butterflies, so big and bright. I stayed there for a rest day and walked to the lookout. On the way I passed a tall xanthorrhoea flower spear covered in blue tigers. I grabbed my phone and quickly turned on the camera and tried taking photos. I was literally vibrating with excitement. The butterflies could sense how tense I was and flew away in a burst of sapphire. The letdown was immense and I scolded myself all the way to the lookout. On the way back I kept reminding myself to stay calm if they had returned to the flowers. When I reached the same place, the flower spear was covered in butterflies again. I stopped, breathed, brought my heart rate down then slowly approached the magical kaleidoscope; they allowed me to get within two metres before fluttering away again.

I had my hand pooped on by a little penguin while sitting on a beach watching electrical storms at night over Bass Strait in lutruwita. It was so smelly! A scorpion chased me around a picnic table while I tried eating dinner in central New South Wales. I watched a rakali/water rat following a platypus down a creek, eating the scraps of the platy's snacks in the Victorian alps. Families of noisy pink cockatoos doing acrobatics on an old telegraph line in Western Australia, playing, squawking and flaring their magnificent pink and yellow crests. A pod of at least 50 humpback whales being escorted up the Kimberley coast by a pod of more than 200 dolphins. Wedge tailed eagles feasting on the hot carcasses of roadkill. Lyre birds and bower birds in their fancy nests. Birds of prey catching snakes. Huge male red kangaroos fighting in the outback, their muscles rippling as they leaned back on their tails and kicked each other's bellies. In the rainforests of southeast Queensland, a little antechinus climbing all over my pack, searching in every pocket for a morsel of food. On the shore of the Great Australian Bight a male emu bringing 11 stripy fluff-ball chicks down to the ocean to cool their legs off in the water. I even saw a fruit bat catch a fish on the Broadwater!

It wasn't just wildlife I saw out there. There were many feral animals, including boar, goats, deer, cats, foxes, rats and mice, starlings, cattle, horses, donkeys, camels, rabbits and dogs. I saw the damage these feral species cause in our wild ecosystems, bringing native species of plants and animals to extinction, and their destruction of Aboriginal places. It is frustrating to watch places deteriorate because the governments don't have the resources to eradicate them (and often when they do, activists want to save them). Just 200 years tenure doesn't mean an introduced species is naturalised and feral horses should not be protected for heritage. If these people really cared for animals and heritage, they would want to save the native species and sites of significance being destroyed by ferals. That's my two bob's worth.

Very early in my solo adventures, in my early 20s, I had listened to stories of packs of feral dogs in places I enjoyed escaping too. I had never seen them but had stumbled upon some of their dens while walking off track, and also had heard them. Dingos are not feral dogs and you can tell the difference especially when they howl, or bark. Dingos don't bark at all, they howl, yip or growl. Feral dogs usually don't make a sound when hunting but they can bark and when they growl they mean business. Dingos are our conservationists: we know for a fact they help keep feral dog numbers down.

They should be protected for the job they do. Feral dogs, unlike dingos, are unpredictable, especially as a pack, and can take down a human if they are hungry or bored. In order to feel safer while out on long treks I learnt as much as I could about them, what to do and not to do when encountering them. They never bothered me until 10,000 kilometres into the walk around Australia.

Somewhere near Wijilawarrim, pushing my barrow beside the road between the majestic escarpments, on a quiet day without much traffic, I came around a bend to see some animals in the distance. They were moving on a natural cairn of red boulders, on the other side of the road. At first I thought I was going to be lucky enough to see rock wallabies, but it was a strange place for them to be, beside the road. Staring at the rocks I realised they were not wallabies, but three dogs standing. A few hundred metres further and another rock cairn came into view. Two more dogs stood up. Were they camp dogs? If they were then they would be no problem, but there were no Aboriginal communities nearby, or dirt roads off the highway. Were they a feral pack? As I walked closer, I could see they were a motley group of mixed breeds, tough breeds, dogs bred to guard, fight and hunt pigs, ridgeback, rottweiler, bull, healer, but they were very healthy. Not camp dogs.

The first three dogs had stood up, now the other two dogs stood. I knew who the alpha was when four of them looked to the one who stood on the highest rock. He walked down off the rocks and the others followed. They were now on the ground, on the other side of the road, alert, unfriendly, waiting for me.

"Here we go," I thought as dread sank in.

All the things I had learnt about feral dogs came back immediately and the first was "Don't let them sense your fear". Easier said than done, I was scared the moment I realised what they were. My own hackles were up and the adrenalin had hit. Flooding my brain with thoughts was the only way I knew to cover up the fear. "Do I have it in me to get through this unscathed?" "Watch them carefully." "No, don't stare at them, but make sure they can see you are watching." "Maintain your steady speed, don't stop, don't run, don't turn your back on them." "Don't smile, they are not humans, baring your teeth is a threat." They were now baring their teeth at me.

Over and over, I kept this dialogue going through my head to cover the fear; my heart was in my throat, I knew my heart rate was too high. "Keep your eye on them, don't speed up, walk straight, keep all emotion out of your face, no mixed messages."

The alpha began walking towards the side of the road, his pack fell in behind. I was almost opposite them and could hear them growling and see their fur standing on end from neck to tail. No mixed messages there.

Now came the moment I had been dreading for the last kilometre. As I walked past them, I would have my back to them. I kept my eye on them, and they stayed on their side of the road. Eventually, I could no longer twist my neck enough, and had to turn around and push the barrow backwards. In that moment, only seconds, I took my eye off them. That was their cue. They ran at me.

Dropping the barrow, I fully swung around facing them.

The only defence I had left was to scare them and make them realise this was going to be a meal they had to work hard for. I made myself as big as I could, summoning all my energy and courage. I stomped my feet out on either side into a half squat, threw my arms up into the air, hands in fists, and I growled as low and loud and menacingly as I could.

It worked! Like a cartoon, the dogs skidded to a halt, dust clouding up under their feet and they hesitated. In that moment, I picked up rocks and began throwing them, hitting the alpha with two. I picked up handfuls of gravel and dirt, spraying it all over the pack. They turned and slunk back to their side of the road. It was over, I was safe. The fear was replaced with a relief so huge I couldn't contain it and I yelled a primal warrior scream.

That was too close, I thought I was going to die. I walked backwards, pushing the barrow behind me until I watched them climb back up onto their rocks. Turning to face forward once more I increased my speed and kept going for another few kilometres before finally stopping to get my heart rate down again. My whole body was still shaking from adrenaline, and it took a long time to settle down. It was days until I wasn't walking on high alert for dogs, and weeks until any dog didn't make me jump and pump adrenalin through my brain.

That was the only trouble I had with animals.

CHAPTER 22

THE POWER OF AUTISM

Autism is a spectrum of superpowers. Being able to interpret the world and ourselves differently to most people, we have abilities to respond and react in ways that are surprisingly original, uninhibited, potentially more efficient and innovative. Our strengths, being intense and unique, are our superpowers, what sets us apart from those whose brains are wired neurotypically. It does not make us more or less equal; we fit into communities and groups differently and create our own niches. There are advantages and challenges in having autistic superpowers.

In 1972, not much was known about neurodivergence, people whose brains are wired differently. Attention deficit disorder (ADD) was relatively new and any hyperactive kid with learning difficulties was usually diagnosed with this—in 1975 I was one of them. Over the next three decades more was understood about different types of neurodivergence, because ADD didn't fit us all. Attention-deficit/hyperactivity and Asperger's were soon added to the list of behavioural 'disorders' (there is a massive crossover between them). These two, along with obsessive-compulsive, dyslexia, synaesthesia, sensory processing, savant intelligence, gender dysphoria, Tourette's and various developmental disorders, are classed together in an overlapping spectrum called autism.

It should not be described as a disorder. We are trying to eliminate this term so that everyone, of all learning abilities, has an equal chance of finding their interests, strengths and niche in life, without discrimination. For some of us, our autism does mean we need some special help, but for most of us it is the way people treat us which handicaps us.

I love this mental picture of a 'spectrum': wavelengths of light dispersed into a rainbow, each colour overlapping and blending with those around it. Not every colour can be seen by the human eye. So it is with autism: some of us had to learn how to camouflage (some still do) so you couldn't see us, so we could be treated as 'normal'.

I believe my story will help other autistic people find their path and thrive. It is not easy to write this chapter. I feel tired writing it, and I am choosing my words carefully to reduce misunderstanding. However, describing it in writing is much easier than speaking about it and I welcome any and all questions where you need clarification. Some of this story will sound familiar to your own experiences, everyone can, at some point, feel the same as someone on the spectrum. It doesn't mean you are autistic but maybe you can empathise with how we feel all the time. I'm sorry if you also had a rough time growing up and at work. What I hope to emphasise in this chapter, and book, is the power of autism, enabling us to achieve great things and triumph through tribulation.

As a kid, to survive school, I had to learn how to mask, or mimic. The process of learning how to behave like neurotypical kids, to hide autistic traits and act as other kids and adults expect is exhausting. To be different meant getting bullied and ostracised; both of these I experienced until high school, where I could make a fresh start and be someone else. In later years, I wondered how much my dual personality impacted my mental health and whether it would have been worse if I didn't mask my true self.

The main reason girls were not diagnosed with autism was because they could mask so well. For decades the focus of diagnosis and therapy was primarily for boys, and not much was known about girls. It is now known to occur as much in females as males, and is even more prevalent in transgender and non-binary people who experience the added stress of gender dysphoria. There is a modern phenomenon of mothers being diagnosed when they take their children to be assessed. Autism, the spectrum, ADHD: it is all changing rapidly as science and therapists try to keep up with terminology and how we, as a community, want to be identified and acknowledged.

For example, there is always a discussion of whether you say "I am autistic" or "I have autism". One is stating it is part of who you intrinsically are, the other sounds like something you caught.* The term 'Asperger's' is losing ground: this high functioning diagnosis delayed and cut people off from accessing the right level of care, and was overused when what people really required was an individualised assessment, more specific diagnosis and a customised approach to their challenges and needs.

* You cannot catch autism from vaccinations!

I had learning disabilities, including a hearing impairment until about five years old—my hearing was still developing after I started school. It was an impossible task teaching me word sounds, like 'au', 'oa', 'oi', 'ei'; my brain couldn't process these until my teens. Even today, in my fifties, I still can't remember what nouns, verbs and adjectives are, making learning new languages difficult without living in them for months. As soon as anyone mentions nouns, I switch off. It is like a wall goes up and I blank out, trying to block the memories of frustrated teachers losing their cool. Funny thing is, English was one of my stronger subjects at school. I was given special tutorials during free periods to improve comprehension and critical analysis. Without those extra classes, taught voluntarily, I would have been lost in the school system and my life would have taken a very different trajectory. Some of my high school teachers were remarkably progressive for the 80s, when neurodivergence was more science fiction than another way of thinking. Thank you.

Dyscalculia (number dyslexia) meant I only just passed maths. It was an unknown part of the spectrum. I wanted to be an astronaut or astronomer, but maths was one of my biggest problems (pun intended). To even begin the academic path towards exploring the universe your maths and science needs to be very strong, and unfortunately physics and chemistry were beyond my mathematical abilities. I could not understand algebra, mixing numbers with letters was so confusing and made no sense; despite all the extracurricular work I never figured it out. I would write numbers back to front, and my 3s looked like capital Es. I wrote numbers in reverse order, 234 became 432, and I accidentally wrote numbers beginning on the right side of the paper instead of the left margin, very much like Arabic is written from right to left across the page. I worked so hard to pass, but my teachers had no idea. If I had known it was a thing back then I believe there would have been a couple of teachers who would have happily helped if I had asked. But I don't think I would have handled maths at the university level. Sometimes our passions have to be enthusiastic hobbies, rather than careers.

Every autistic person has a special interest they excel at. We are not all stereotypical savant mathematicians; we are artists, musicians, writers, adventurers, athletes, lab technicians, teachers, chefs, carers, doctors, actors. You name it, there is an autistic person thriving at doing what they love and being exceptionally good at it. Unfortunately, the developmental learning stage, i.e. school, is often detrimental to us finding our special skill set and being allowed to follow it.

For me, it was geography, and later biology. I was good at earth sciences in high school and university, even better at solo travel and outdoor pursuits. Learning in my teens how to navigate, read a map and compass, about meteorology, animal behaviour and survival skills, opened up a whole new world. I found something I excelled at, my niche. Nature had been my classroom since I was a kid, and in my teens it became a refuge. In these places I could be my true self; nature only judged the weaknesses in my survival skills.

Social skills, being in groups, having conversations, navigating social niceties and body language, these were my biggest weaknesses. It made every day a living, exhausting hell. Always paranoid, I often did or said the wrong thing, sometimes accidentally offending. I worked hard at fitting in, and to varying degrees it was a success, so long as friends and acquaintances didn't get enough time with me to see behind the mask. Three hours in a social gathering requires three days to recover. Three months in a relationship requires moving on to a new place and three or more years of independence.

If I get to three months in a workplace it's a miracle. Working the harvest trail was perfect in my younger years, when I had the energy to pick fruits and vegetables. It was back-breaking work, but I made enough money to eat and at the end of the season I could leave. Harvest work is full of misfits (apologies to all the pickers who are not misfits!). Many of those working with me chose this type of work for the same reason I did: we didn't fit in anywhere else, and the only requirement of us was to pick as fast as we could. If social interactions were expected, I could mask now and then, just enough to avoid 'being found out'. After half a century of life I can see these interactions with a broader perspective, the way people would change the way they spoke to me, alter their body language and avoid talking. After they worked out I was different, they felt uncomfortable, unsure of themselves around me, I seemed "mostly normal" but people began treating me as though I had an impairment. That was my cue to move on.

When Mum read a book by Rudy Simone, *Aspergirls*, in 2010, she said it was like reading a book written about me. For 38 years Mum had been searching for answers. She was unfairly made to feel like a bad mother when I was a kid, and as I clumsily travelled through adulthood her concern never wavered. In early childhood I was not diagnosed with anything, apart from ADD, but this was a good thing as it allowed me to grow without labels.* By 2010, females on the autism spectrum were beginning to be recognised and treated seriously, even if we were all diagnosed with Asperger's and therapists never looked deeper into the spectrum than that. It was something, better than nothing, a place to start on a new part of the journey of self-awareness. Not all were diagnosed correctly, some women on the spectrum were incorrectly told they had borderline personality disorder. A good therapist takes you through check lists and tests every possibility, rather than prematurely jumping to conclusions and passing your case to someone else.

Aspergirls was the beginning of a deep dive into Asperger's that continued with reading medical and psychology journals and papers, learning everything and trying to keep up with all the changes in terminology and new categories of the spectrum, which is always changing. The large differences between each edition of the *Diagnostic and Statistical Manual of Mental Disorders* (DSM, now in its fifth edition) illustrate just how much the comprehension of and approach to autism has changed over the last decade alone. For this reason, important as it is, this book can be used as only a guide. It is the responsibility of the individual, parent and therapist to be thorough in their self-diagnosis or clinical diagnosis. People don't necessarily need a clinical diagnosis (it is expensive and takes a stressfully long time), but it can help them access specialised care and education, then prepare for university and choose a healthy workplace.

* I guarantee I would have abused the labels and used them as excuses for bad behaviour.

A diagnosis and an understanding of autism both help someone on the spectrum develop a skill set, find a safe group of friends, pursue recreational activities which enrich their wellbeing and enforce healthy boundaries, reducing exposure to overwhelming situations. My advice to younger people exploring their autistic identity is to:

- Go step by step, take your time, travel through this at a comfortable pace. There is no need to rush into changing your life all at once: that's meltdown material.
- Start with one thing which will immediately improve your mental wellbeing, for example, noise-reducing earphones or ear plugs.
- Remove unnecessary stressful group activities and create a quiet safe space for decompressing your stress without anyone watching or listening to your sounds and stims.
- Explain your autism to close supportive friends and family so they can understand why you need to say, "Thanks, but I can't" as you learn your sensory, social and spatial boundaries.

One step at a time, just like walking around Australia: it might seem hard, overwhelming, even scary, but they'll get there.

What is a meltdown? And how do you recover from it? A meltdown is not a breakdown. A breakdown is mental stress built up over a long period of time. A meltdown happens quickly when we are overwhelmed by sensory overload and have no control or escape. A neurotypical mind learns to filter about 80 percent of our sensory input; it's how you stay sane. An autistic mind does not have the wiring to filter our senses.

We see, hear, smell, taste, feel everything with much more force, and some of us, especially females, have heightened empathic senses on top of that. It is physically painful when too much comes at us at once. Shopping centres and public transport are particularly challenging.

For example, when I'm not travelling by foot or bicycle, I prefer to catch long-distance trains and book two seats together. I have space, a view, and it is usually quiet under the hum of the rolling carriage. I feel safe. On one of my trips from Melbourne to Sydney the train was cancelled and replaced by coaches. I explained to the driver I was autistic and asked for a double seat near the front. The coach was quiet and only half full, it was manageable for my hyper-sensory processing. Two hours out of Melbourne, the replacement coach in front of us broke down and all the passengers boarded our coach. It was now full, loud and smelly. I had earbuds in, listening to relaxing music but the noise of people shouting for their conversation to be heard over everyone else's was too much. When I asked them to talk quieter, explaining that it was triggering my autism, they just stared at me before continuing on as before.

Since I was a kid, I have been stimming. This is an unconscious, autistic way of trying to physically release sensory and social stress. It could be finger flicking, jumping, hair chewing, leg bouncing. My stims are spinning, bashing and thrashing my head on something, bashing a fist into my thigh muscles, hand flicking, picking the skin around my nails, humming, leg bouncing and body rocking. On the bus I went through the harmless ones. They weren't helping, so I ended up bashing my head on the window until the pain of that was greater than the pain of the other onslaught of senses.

As soon as the bus pulled in to refuel, we were told to stay aboard. I jumped up and asked for my pack to be removed from storage below, telling the driver I had to hitchhike, and collapsed under some trees in the shade, rocking and crying uncontrollably. One of the rail staff, travelling home on the coach, came over for a chat, asking what was wrong, and explaining they would let me have ten minutes, they wouldn't be leaving without me and assured me the yelling would stop so I could continue to Sydney with them. It was humiliating and frightening, my first public adult meltdown with nowhere to hide and with no family or friends for support. I'm usually pretty good at being independent but the circumstance was completely out of my control. It took a week to recover, and I now have some very good noise cancelling earbuds.

That is an example of one of the many challenges faced by autistic people and how some of us react to being overwhelmed. It goes some way to explain why I gravitated to spending days, weeks and months alone in nature. The sounds of nature have never caused me stress, quite the opposite. I bathe in the sounds of the wind, rain, thunder, rivers, birds, dingos, grasshoppers, gliders. It soothes the senses, like visiting a relaxation spa, but the soundtrack is live.* It is my sanctuary.

How is autism a superpower? It's more than that. It is precisely because I experience the world as I do that I can take on 'impossible' adventures. Of course, I sometimes

* I welcome all donations to spas and retreats.

overreach and need to ask for help, and as I get older and more experienced, I make more responsible decisions. For example, I now consider whether a proposed adventure will put other lives in danger if I need to hit the SOS button? This is also why I firmly believe outdoor education should be part of every child's school curriculum. If nature is where we feel safe, we need to know how to use it safely.

As a free-range kid, exploring the bushlands around where I lived, both in Mt Hutton and Kosciuszko National Park, I was allowed the freedom to learn from nature, the green classroom. Not everyone can walk out the front door into the woods (not everyone should). However, I encourage all parents of autistic kids to discover calming natural spaces together at every opportunity, teaching each other how to interact with and navigate the natural world. They will thank you for it later.

My spectrum of autism includes Asperger's, synaesthesia, dyscalculia, gender dysphoria*, hyper sensory, attention-deficit/hyperactivity, high empathy, and some special ones like high pain and cold tolerance, sensing hot as cold and cold as hot, and extreme stubbornness. Some of these can get me into trouble but I've learnt how to use them.

I didn't know about the hot/cold sensory confusion until walking around lutruwita. I found a great cooling muscle liniment I rubbed on my feet at the end of each day, it also dried out my blisters overnight. It was so good I posted about it on a bushwalking forum. One of my friends tried it out and she called me to say it was not cold but burning hot and

* Until I learnt about non-binary gender fluidity in 2018.

hurt like hell when put on her blisters. I asked a few others to try it out and they could only feel the heat. My brain had interpreted the sensation as cold and delightfully soothing. I don't make liniment recommendations anymore.

The nerve messages associated with pain are usually sent to my brain as a mere discomfort. I'm still learning to interpret them as warnings and pay attention, instead of ignoring them and causing more injury. Often, I need to see the injury to know something is wrong. Blisters, for example. I could walk with 17 blisters on my feet and at the end of the day, simply rub some alcohol or liniment into them, taping them up the next day to keep walking. I couldn't see them, only feel the pain and stickiness when they began bleeding. If my brain was wired 'normally', then when my knee started to struggle to take weight near Karratha, I would have felt the warning signs and have been able to take appropriate action, but I didn't. I only began feeling a sharp pain once it gave way, too late to do anything about it. Having a high pain tolerance allows me to push harder, find my body's real limitations, without thoughts holding me back. It is dangerous but, despite incidents such as with my knee, it has usually worked to my advantage.

Neurotypical brains set up sensory limitations. Most people know when they are getting close to reaching their physical limits as their bodies send the right signals to their brains. My brain lets me stretch them and create new ones.

This has evolved into a "She'll be right, mate" attitude. I haven't died yet, although while I always used to recover quickly, I am getting older. In the Pilbara I knew I was having blister problems because I could smell something rotten. Stopping beside a waterhole I removed my shoes and socks to dip my tired feet into the water and saw that a stack of heel blisters were more red than usual. Lifting the foot onto the knee I had a closer look and could smell it, not the usual stinky foot odour, but rotting foot. I pulled out the first aid kit and cut away three blisters stacked on top of each other to reach the deepest one. It was the fourth layer of the blisters which had become infected. I cut it open, washed it clean with saline solution and doused it with alcohol spray. After letting it dry, I packed it with gauze and kept walking. It was fine after that, healing up in three days. I have come to take pain tolerance and recovery for granted. It is one of the superpowers which helped me walk around Australia.

Attention-deficit/hyperactivity does not always mean doing everything at once or nothing at all and being easily distracted, it also means being able to hyperfocus, or fixate. Deep diving into something of interest is an ability shared by most people on the spectrum. This is how I planned the walk, focussing on maps, gear, meteorology and wild foods for 18 hours at a time, day after day, sitting at the computer, head in books, coming out of the room only for food and snacks, going straight back in to keep researching until I couldn't hold my eyes open. Hyperfocus is also part of my suite of superpowers.

A few people out there asked if it was boring, walking through the same landscapes, day after day. Having super senses kept me distracted from the perceived boredom of repetition. If I smelt a flower on the breeze, it was time for a break so I could find it. Any peripheral movement on the horizon caught my attention and I would focus my long sightedness on it, watching and projecting my imagination to its location, seeing myself through its eyes. Birds filled every day with their sounds and flight; I could pick up their patterns of calls and daily routines. Pretty little wildflowers were a major distraction, each new find requiring at least quarter of an hour to study their detail and smell and take photos. Feeling the landscape and its history was second nature, another superpower, making each day a new adventure.

Sheer stubborn bullheadedness is my strongest superpower. I feed off negativity, turning it into motivation. When told it couldn't be done, I would respond with, "Watch me". I have a memory from when I was 13: a heap of steel pylons with cement bases had been pulled out after we demolished a row of old chicken sheds in the paddock. A guy who had his horse in agistment in our paddock said, "I bet you can't move those." The next day I was down there, lifting and moving all of them into a tidy pile against the pottery shed.

When we moved to Kosciuszko National Park, I made some pocket money putting firewood in bags for campers. After school I would split wood for hours, sometimes as the snow fell and settled around me, until Dad came out to tell me to stop and get ready for dinner. Once I have my mind set on something, I do it with all my energy. If someone tells me I can't, I take it as a challenge.

Not having an autism diagnosis when I was young and when autism was seen as a disability or disorder set me up for being a successful adventurer. I knew I was different, learnt differently, responded and reacted in ways only I could understand, saw the world through different eyes, lived an alternative lifestyle. Not being able to do what everyone else does wasn't a part of my education, I just had to work harder and find my special niche.

We think, behave, respond and solve problems in ways not everyone understands. It can be challenging for us at times, and challenging for others trying to understand where we are coming from or why we are doing something 'the wrong way'. I say stick with it, don't give up, follow your heart and your head in the direction you feel is right. Some of the greatest achievements in the history of this planet, and beyond, have been made by people on the spectrum.

Never let someone else tell you what you can and cannot do. Do it! Do it differently. Only you know what your limitations are. Autism and neurodivergence is a new way of thinking and interacting with the world. We are strong and bring new skills and ideas with our strengths. Watch us change this world and do the impossible.

CHAPTER 23

SUPERPOWERS

On the way up the west coast something quite remarkable happened. I was given an extra superpower.

Yes, that's right, I have joined the multiverse. Unfortunately, it was not as an air bender with control of the wind, or any other weather. No invisibility powers or hammers or making things out of the elements. I could not read minds or fly.

I learnt how to fold time and distance.

Before you think I completely lost my mind out there or an alien abduction sent me back with a gift, let me explain.

I used meditation.

Each leg of the walk was for four to six months in the cooler part of the year and each summer I repaired my body and put on spare weight ready for the next. Each leg of the walk started slowly with short 20-kilometre days and over weeks and months I increased the speed and distance to suit my strength and stamina. I would usually get up to comfortable 50-kilometre days in the fourth month of walking and throw in a few 60-kilometre days if there was an incentive of food, shower and a rest day at the end of it.

At the beginning of each leg, I was in the habit of counting the five-kilometre distance markers beside the road and setting distances for taking breaks throughout the day. For example, when I reached the third marker post it was time for morning tea, the fifth was lunch and the seventh was afternoon tea or make camp, and so on. The more remotely I walked the more kilometre posts were missing or they marked out 10-kilometre intervals instead of five kilometres. When the markers were unreliable, I had to watch the time. Breaks were important, a time to rest and refuel. If I missed one, or walked too far between them, it affected my body later in the day.

Further into each leg, as my daily distance increased, I could walk longer between breaks; around 20 kilometres before morning tea, give or take, the same again before lunch and a small break in the afternoon. Or I could keep walking through, eating as I went. Some days felt longer than others, some very long.

During one of the summer breaks, I studied Thích Nhất Hạnh (1926-2022), a Vietnamese Buddhist monk, peace activist and author, who had/has a very big influence on Western mindfulness and guided walking meditations. He had a way with words, making peace feel easy. “Walk as if you are kissing the Earth with your feet”, “Feelings come and go like clouds in a windy sky”, “Because you are alive, everything is possible.”

Visiting the shop in Nan Tien Temple, Illawarra, I stocked up on his books and read as many as I could find that summer. I also downloaded all his podcast interviews and Plum Village meditations, readying myself to make the longest leg of the walk, the west coast, as easy as possible.

I had the barrow freighted with Toll across to Deb, a friend in Boorloo, and at the end of summer I flew over and began walking north along the coastline. Slowly to start with, 20- to 25-kilometre days. Such short days went fast, but even so I was tormented by heat blisters from the burning hot road surface. North of Geraldton I hit my 40-kilometre groove and began practising the walking meditations of Thích Nhất Hanh, using the above quotes as mantras, quietly chanting as I gently trod the Earth. I saved Oṃ maṇi padme hūṃ for chanting through discomfort and after getting a scare.

The secret to good chanting is to find your resonance, the right vibrations to calm your mind or lift your energy. For me, the vibration and pitch, need to be low, a deep bass, coming from the lower chest and belly, but it is different for different people. The human body vibrates with energy, we each have our own vibration. It is one of the major things other animals use to sense us, it is how dogs and cats know what kind of person we are when they meet us. Even we can do that when attuned to it. Many species of animals and trees communicate using resonance. Essentially, it is what our vocal cords do and why the easiest radio voices to listen to are those with a low pitched, smooth resonance.

When I began walking meditations, everything became easier, there was less muscle fatigue, more stamina and I was not as reactionary to every hill, headwind and hot day. The most amazing thing was how fast the day went by—it was as if I reached my morning tea stop only moments after starting the day.

As I walked in meditation it felt like I was folding time and distance. I made a game of it and pictured the road ahead, all its curves and hills. I created a portal in my mind through to where I wanted to be and before I knew it I was there. I walked every step of the way, but meditation took that chunk of time and road away. I was fully there, aware of everything around, the traffic, animals, plants, clouds, the ground beneath my feet, but I was not aware of the hard work my body was doing. Walking meditation eased my body into its daily routine and eased me out of it when it was time to rest. It also helped prioritise memories needing attention.

Now I'm a time bender and master of portals, you can call me "The Roamer".

CHAPTER 24

HEALTH BENEFITS OF NATURE

By now you should have a pretty good idea how immersing myself in nature has helped me. It is difficult to put into a succinct chapter as it has always been part of my life. To describe it to others requires analysing how it has helped me through different periods of mental health and illness. I'll have a go at being more specific about how it helps all of us.

Being in nature helps so many people recover from stress, anxiety, depression, trauma and physical illness. There are several reasons for this effect on our minds and bodies. I'll start with some chemistry.

Negative ions in the atmosphere are created when are air molecules are broken down by cosmic rays and lightning or by being pounded by water, such as in rainstorms, rivers, waterfalls or surf. There is some evidence that our biochemistry responds to these negative ions when we breathe them in. Many people with depression feel lighter and clearer headed after exposure to negative ions. Real science is still out on this one, but I tested it for 30 years and it worked for me. I thought it was a bit woo woo when I first heard of it, but I was curious, thankfully.

You might have heard of 'forest bathing' and 'shinrin-yoku': going into the forest to soak in its atmosphere. This is one of the simplest ways to meditate. You can walk, sit, lie down, sleep even, as your senses tune into the sounds, smells and feel of your natural outdoor setting. Listen to the birds and the rustle of leaves, smell the earth, crushed leaves and wildflowers, feel the coolness of the shade, warmth of the sun, see the breeze in the tree canopy and light filtering through to the forest floor. Focus only on what is immediately around you and absorb it into your mind. It is relaxing and takes your mind off other things.

Although I had spent most of my life in nature, I had never intentionally tried this until reading *The Celestine Prophecy*, by James Redfield, and completing the companion workbook. Again, curiosity. It prompted me to try out intentional sensory immersion, to sit and become one with nature. One quiet day, in Adelaide Hills botanic garden, I sat in a small hollow of an old oak tree, leaned my back against its bark and placed the soles of my bare feet flat on the cool earth. Closing my eyes, I began tuning my senses into the tree. What happened next was life changing. It felt like my body disappeared, melting into the tree, my consciousness floating up into the branches where I could hear the birds clearly and even see into a nest; I kept going until I reached the top and looked back down and saw myself below. Then I entered the tree trunk and flowed down into the ground, amongst the tree roots, worms, centipedes, mycelium. The further I went, the more my mind dispersed to the feathery ends of the roots. I could smell the earth and feel the moisture, it was like being in a womb, only cool and peaceful. Languidly, I rested for a while until it was time to return to my body and mind. That was extreme forest bathing; all anyone needs to do is go into nature and listen, for the mental health benefits of intentional immersion.

Mindful movement, or walking meditation, combines forest bathing and meditation with mindfulness.

Thích Nhất Hanh puts it best: "Most of us walk without chains, yet we aren't free. We're tethered to regret and sorrow from the past. We return to the past and continue to suffer. The past is a prison. But now you have the key to unlock the door and arrive in the present moment. You breathe in, you bring your mind home to your body, you make a step, and you arrive in the here and the now."

Be aware of each breath, feel your heartbeat, sense each muscle and tendon working as you move. When you are focusing on how your body is doing this simple thing, you are not aware of the past or the future, or even the people around you. After a while feeling your movement, you can begin to reach your mind out to your senses. Can you feel the temperature in your fingertips, the sun on your face, the breeze in your hair, the grass under your feet and soil between your toes? Bask in the feelings of your body moving through the sanctuary of nature. In these moments you are nowhere else, nothing else matters, stay present and let your mind and body relax and heal.

If meditation and mindfulness are not your jam, exercise in nature instead of the gym. Exercise is an excellent serotonin boost. Take a brisk walk, run, ride, paddle, stretch, squat. You're only limited by your personal fitness and accessibility. When we get our heart pumping, our nerve system makes more of the chemical serotonin, which in turn helps send messages to the nerve system. Not only does it help control muscles and the bowels, but it also helps control moods and regulates sleep. Too little and we feel depressed and anxious. Too much serotonin is very rare.* Dopamine is also boosted during exercise—this is a neurotransmitter regulating motivation and reward. Not much is known about exactly how it works, but research has found it to be beneficial for mental health, and what's not to love about that.

Sunshine, or Vitamin D, is an essential nutrient for our body and mind, and the most natural source is our own star, the Sun. It is believed that when you are exposed to vitamin D it helps alleviate some of the symptoms of depression, including fatigue, sore muscles and joints and weakness. Natural vitamin D is created by a chemical process (activated by UV-B) in the skin, so when you are outdoors, enjoying nature, you are also getting a good dose of it (but make sure you don't get too much sun and burn, cover up when you've had enough).

Besides all these reasons to immerse in nature, it feels good to be outside, trekking in the mountains, pottering about in your garden, surfing in the ocean or strolling through the park. It is far more important to look after your mental health and make time to be in nature than prolonged exposure to the situations which are causing illness. Put your health first.

When I trek through the mountains and ride through the countryside I get a buzz, my body might feel tired from all

* Too much serotonin is also dangerous, needing hospital care. Too much is usually caused by overdosing depression medication, contradicting natural medicines or abusing recreational drugs.

the exercise, but my mind is alert and excited by the physical stimulus, plus all the wonderful things I notice along the way. At the end of the day, as I lie in my tent or hammock, I reflect on the beauty I just travelled through and feel lucky.

CHAPTER 25

IS IT ALWAYS A HAPPY WALK?

The Happy Walk was named for the happiness I found through therapy and walking in nature: a representation of the feelings I found on the journey to recovery and those I could not name but became important to recognise as part of the healing process. Also, it needed to be catchy, easy to remember and find on social media. Happiness was trending at the time, so I decided to ride the wave and use my recovery story to help people find their way back to happiness.

If I'm to be totally honest with you (and as this book recounts), it was not always happy. There were hard days and dark days, days when I wanted to quit but these were few and far between. Most days were just days, another day walking and talking to people on the way. Then there were the days of soaring happiness, joy, even euphoria.

Euphoria and joy were feelings I had lost in my childhood, perhaps I had never experienced them. The memories of these extraordinary moments while walking around Australia will stay with me forever, their impact on my heart and mind are so immense that the very thought of them evokes the same feelings as I experienced the first time they happened.

The most euphoric day was walking down the west coast from Perth to Cape Leeuwin. As I was walking through bushland, past various endangered trees, the locals pointed out the critically endangered peppermint bush (*Agonis flexuosa*), which had been heavily cleared for housing and farms. I was very lucky to see these as it is likely they will become extinct soon. That night I camped between them and the next morning, waking with the birds, I began walking in a dew laden atmosphere, peppermint bushes fading into the mist, glowing softly as the sun rose. The dew was cool and crisp, the smell of leaves, bark and dirt was heavy. It felt like I was floating as every sense responded to being surrounded by a most sublime beauty. I stopped and stood still, silently absorbing everything in those precious moments. Every muscle in my body and face softened, every part of my brain switched on, tears ran down my face. This was the purest happiness I had ever felt.

There were breathtaking moments: standing beside the road, alone, watching the sunset over the Channel Country in the Northern Territory, lighting up the ochre red outcrops with palms and pandanus clinging to their sides, coolamon trees flanking the river as it turned into gold, the Evening Star shining bright in the purple-green sky as our own star sank below the horizon. Moments like these were made all the more poignant as I wished they were shared with the people I love.

Other magical moments were meant just for me, when nature wrapped me in her majesty, gently holding me in a place of timeless beauty and immeasurable greatness. As though I no longer existed as an individual, melting into a universal energy, where nothing mattered, my existence ethereal. These were new experiences and feelings, but I felt safe, allowing nature to probe my mind, disperse thought and breakdown any concept of self. These were the moments I really began to understand our connection to Earth. Nature was reminding me of my greater purpose and how I fit into the collective consciousness of society.

'Alone and solitude' are different from 'lonely and isolated'. Personally, I crave being alone and in solitude, I seek them out, they are my comfort zone; that is the wandering dingo in me. I love being with friends and family, catching up, caring for them and enjoying their companionship, and sharing ideas and laughs. But it was not until the nights when I felt the most fatigued, mentally and physically, did I miss them. On those nights, usually when I was on rations and hungry or the day was too hot and windy, I would climb into my tent and cry. Big salty tears I could not afford to waste, because I was on strict water rations and needed all my spare electrolytes to stay inside my body. Realising this would make me cry even more for self pity, then even more from anger at being weak enough to pity myself. Those nights I wished for someone to give me a big comforting hug*, put my life back into perspective and tell me everything would be alright tomorrow. And it usually was. I would wake the next day, rested and recovered, ready to go.

On the really bad nights, out of phone range and unable to phone my sister to share our woes, I would fall asleep thinking about ending the walk where I was and hitching a ride to the closest city the next morning. The next morning, I would wake

* I'm not normally a huggy person, I shirk from human touch, but some hugs are good for the soul.

feeling physically ready but still tired mentally and emotionally anguished. I needed to park the idea of finishing and wait to see how I felt that evening. As it turned out, on those days the first person to stop on the road had always heard of The Happy Walk, was a suicide survivor and shared a story about a loved one lost to suicide. Some had pictures of them on their mirror, in their glove box or wallet. For some it was still too soon, and their tears touched my heart as they reminisced the good times when their lost one was still with us.

They bolstered my resolve to keep going. Not only to share my story and raise awareness about suicide prevention, but also to be there for those who struggled after losing someone close, a friend, a family member, the precious young life of someone in their community.

I loved being out there, meeting the people of Australia, travellers from home and abroad, members of the many nations I passed through. I loved the deep connection I had with the land and being in tune with everything around me. It made me happy, which was part of the reason I embarked on this expedition, it was my own walk to happiness. Having a purpose, a goal, and doing what I loved was fulfilling.

There was another reason the walk filled me with happiness. In 2002-03 I travelled in Africa and Europe. On the way out of Africa, sitting in a small café in the centre of Melilla, waiting for their five-hour siesta to finish, I watched the Spanish news. It was all about a large oil spill off the Galician coast where a tanker had foundered and sunk, splitting in two. There were pictures of volunteers and veterinarians working, and they were requesting more volunteers, so I decided that was my next stop.

In a big International Youth Hostel near the northern Portuguese/Spanish border I spotted a group of four men dressed in what looked like park ranger uniforms—they are rather uniform across the globe, the patches on their shoulders of animals or plants being the giveaway. I approached them and they confirmed they were from the Portuguese Instituto da Conservacau da Natureza (Nature Conservancy Institute) and had just been seconded to help a Portuguese bird rescue program for two weeks. I asked if I could help. Long story short, I spent three months as a volunteer, saving, washing, rehabilitating and releasing migratory birds caught in the oil spill and washed up on the beaches.

The incredible people I worked alongside, community volunteers, veterinarians, university students and park rangers, asked many questions about Australia. They had been taught Australia's black history and knew more than I did about massacres, stolen generations and slavery. I was ashamed of how whitewashed our education system was and my own lack of knowledge. They also asked about many places in Australia I had never been to. One night, during the many deep philosophical conversations we had after work, I was challenged on this, "Why are you travelling around the world when you haven't seen your own country yet?"

Good question. I had seen more of Portugal than most Portuguese, so why not my own country?

When my money ran out, I came home and decided to see more of my own country AND learn as much as possible about Aboriginal and Torres Strait Islander history. This was a big motivator in walking around Australia. To walk would provide me with a myriad of opportunities to see and learn, while helping the wellbeing of *all* Australians at the same time. There is still so much to see but it makes me happy knowing that next time I'm quizzed about Australia I will not be as ignorant as I was then. Knowledge and experience, the good kind accumulated by travelling, brings great life satisfaction and new perspectives.

Let's get serious about happiness now. How important is happiness? We need happiness in our lives, but to recognise it we also need to experience other emotions and feelings. We don't need to be happy all the time, and that is how many of us, seeking happiness, get caught up feeling as though we are doing something wrong, not trying hard enough or wonder if it is an imbalance in the chemistry of our minds. I can only speak from my personal journey in search of happiness and what I learnt on the way. Different aspects of this might feel familiar to you and I hope it can help you feel like you are not alone and balance can be found.

As a child I struggled with undiagnosed autism. Like many children on the spectrum, I had depression and anxiety from an early age, and was vulnerable to abuse resulting in post-traumatic stress disorder (PTSD) from the time I started school. I was not abused by my parents, apart from the occasional smack for insolence. I was born with an angry anti-authoritarian nature. It was definitely not nurtured; in fact, many of those smacks were to try to get it out of me, but it didn't work.

School was hard, with a lot of bullying from kids and one particular teacher—if she liked you she treated you well, if you were a 'problem student', i.e. neurodivergent or arty, she targeted you. Also, an adult male staff member of the school, a groundsman or janitor, sexually abused me from five years of age, grooming and touching. These were some of the things I had to process, box away and leave behind while walking.

Throughout my adult life, from my late teens, I have been involved in emergency first response in one way or another: mountain search and rescue, maritime search and rescue, firefighting, police, animal rescue, remote first aid, terrorism, floods, volunteer frontline work in war zones and shanty towns, stopping human trafficking of young girls and slavery in the Persian Gulf. Having already trained my brain to lock away the trauma, it appeared to anyone I worked with that I had very good coping mechanisms. It was far from the truth. My nights were ravaged by night terrors and when the floodgate of locked trauma broke it was a mess, with anxiety triggers everywhere, but by then I was nearly finished with that kind of volunteer work. These were more of the things needing attention while walking.

Some of the more serious trauma processed and left behind on the road are mentioned in the appendix. Processing it and going through the motions of leaving it behind didn't fully work with everything. There is still the residue of pain and anger. I still have triggers which can set off anxiety and night terrors. Walking alone around Australia avoided most of the triggers: not many crowds or loud noises, no men gave me sexual attention, only a handful mentioned a god, there was resounding support for walking on the autism spectrum, and with mental illness.

Travelling has always been my lifestyle. I have lived a minimalist, itinerant life for most of the last 33 years, working on ships, moving between seasonal work, taking up volunteer roles in Australia and overseas. I wasn't intentionally running away or escaping at the time, at least not until I began therapy. It was then I realised that being a vagabond protected me from the worst of depression, anxiety and PTSD. By the time I unconsciously began to fatigue, I was consciously planning where to go next. Between these I usually went bush for a few weeks or months to rest and feel like myself again, walking long tracks or base camping off track, alone and in solitude, or I stayed with family who generously opened their homes for me to unwind, decompress and feel safe.

Despite all the safe places and spending so much time in nature, I felt melancholy; happiness seemed just out of reach. I loved being in the bush and with family, but my mind was heavy, weighed down with depression and the trauma I saw in the world around me: human rights violations, inequality, destruction of nature and global warming.

At school I had a brilliant geography teacher who taught more than just the school curriculum. As well as survival skills, navigation and our alpine ecology, he spoke to us of global warming, anthropology and social sciences. It was impossible to be ignorant of the big issues. I took them to heart, building on that knowledge, spending my life learning about environmental conservation, world cultures and social problems closer to home. I found happiness when out in nature, connecting with and helping nurture communities of animals and plants who didn't judge me. Freedom.

Anxiety has played a big part in my life. Despite all the volunteer work, I reached a point where I needed to take more visible action to stop environmental destruction, action which would reach a wider audience, something which would start conversations and engage people in the cause. One of my life mottos is "Action is the best antidote to anxiety." This was also introduced to my young sponge-like mind by my geography teacher, and he encouraged us to be proactive in protecting the natural environment. I knew how to walk long distances, so that has become my modus operandi. I began to feel better once the conservation walks were engaging with hundreds of people, then thousands through the news media. Through one person taking the leap into campaigning for something they are passionate about, many more people became aware of the same issue.

It helped until one particular walk. The Shark Walk for conservation in southwest Australia attracted abusive and violent followers. I had glass bottles thrown at me, I was stalked and received death threats for two years from shark fishermen and their families. The one thing that made me feel good and useful was suddenly ripped away and became a nightmare which plummeted me into fear, isolation and suicide attempts, locking myself inside and rarely venturing into the outside world.

That's when my therapy began: the good memory/bad memory timeline, learning about mental health, diving deep into everything I could find and fully understanding how autism influenced my wellbeing. With the help of my sister, Linda, and therapist, Bronnie, I left an abusive partner during this time of recovery. I had to find the courage to walk outside every day and face crippling anxiety triggers. It was not easy, but in the process I found something precious and elusive.

Happiness! Pure joy!

I clearly remember that morning in the peppermint grove, as a new and alien feeling rose up through my belly and chest, filling my head with a chemical cocktail of unadulterated love of life. Later I would wonder, "Is this what everyone with healthy minds feels when they talk about happiness, or is it something everyone seeks, regardless of their state of mind?" Do we use the word "happiness" like we use the word "love". We can love people, things, places, books, art, activities...are there as many layers to happiness as there are love?

That morning changed my life. After 43 rough years, full of pain and mental anguish, anger and just trying to survive, I felt like every step back to mental health was worth it, to find happiness. If I had lived a charmed life, without hardships, I would not have recognised happiness for what it is. If I had died when trying to take my own life, I would never have experienced joy and euphoria. I saw the world as a different place and engaged with people and nature differently. It wasn't a one-off experience. Many more times during the walk around Australia, and since, happiness has welled up to remind me of how lucky I am to be alive, enriched by the beauty of the landscapes and discovering a deeper, more genuine connection with people.

After the walk around Australia, in 2020 during the pandemic, I hit another low point in my mental health. I became suicidal while being professionally attacked while leading a climate action expedition, locked out of my home state and in quarantine. I used the memories of finding happiness to hold on until I was safe again, remembering, all the while, that dark moments don't last forever, and the path to recovery is well trodden by my own feet as well as millions of others. Soon after quarantine I began therapeutic medication for anxiety, PTSD and anger. Until then I managed mental illness through a healthy lifestyle, diet, sleep, meditation, exercise, goal setting and nature. Medication helped a lot when I didn't have the energy left to manage it myself, when the cause of my suicidal ideations and barely suppressed rage made me catatonic and was outside my control. I used the abuse I received to learn more about the human ego, how to ask for help, how to dig deep into the soul for answers and find a way forward.

CHAPTER 26

K'GARI

K'gari, the gem of islands.
Home of the Butchulla Nation.
Where dingos roam the dunes
And whales breach offshore.

For the entire walk around Australia, I had been looking forward to reaching the Great Sandy National Park and traversing the length of K'gari. It is a World Heritage Listed area, declared to protect its rare dune rainforests and bushland. At 223 kilometres long, give or take moving sand banks, it's the world's largest sand island, and has half of the planet's perched water stored in lakes.

Perched lakes are freshwater reservoirs formed over millions of years of dune formation and vegetation. Rainwater is naturally filtered through the sand, into the freshwater lakes. The dark brown coffee rock, cemented decomposed organic matter, stops the freshwater sinking back into the dunes. If you like geology, you'll love K'gari.

The Butchulla people, the traditional owners, have lived and used K'gari for tens of thousands of years. Their own stories and lives are in the sand and tall rainforests, the whales and dugongs, the sea eagles and osprey. One of the first things I tried to find out was the traditional name for the island. It wasn't easy to get this information in 2017, nobody knew it, not even the park ranger I asked. Near the end of my K'gari walk, staying with the caretakers at Dilli Village, they were able to share what they knew of the Aboriginal name and Butchulla history. For over a hundred years it has been called Fraser Island, named after a white woman who was rescued from a shipwreck in 1836, then fed, clothed and sheltered by the Butchulla people, only to turn on them when her story gained notoriety, starting international rumours, calling them savages and cannibals. The recent renaming was long overdue. So many placenames in Australia have terrible European origins which haunt the traditional owners. I celebrated when the island was recently given back its rightful name.

In 1998 a partner and I visited the sand island for a camping long weekend. We took his short wheelbase land cruiser, which was light enough to tackle most of the trickier parts of the link tracks over headlands, between beaches. On that trip to K'gari with Pip, the beauty and diversity of K'gari, the brief moments spent passing through diverse ecosystems I had never seen before, titillated my senses. Four days was not enough, and I swore I would return and give it all the time it deserved.

Weaving through the tall rainforest,
Every shade of green you can imagine,
Glowing, luminescent, reflecting the light.
Sweating skin shining gold and emerald,
I became a creature of the forest floor.

In the rainforest, the most majestic trees grow tall through the dense canopy, winning the slow race reaching up for the best sunlight. Fruit doves coo at each other, monitors and pythons rustle the leaf litter. The air is still and humid at ground level, although the canopyhoughs in the breeze, dropping flowers and fruit. The narrow dirt track wanders through, tree roots form steps and creeper vines swing across the path. Some of the oldest and tallest trees are held up by a scaffold of vines reaching from their crowns in a maypole of living tension wires anchored to the ground. Valley of the Giants has satinays and tallowwoods more than 1000 years old, with trunks over four metres in diameter and buttressed roots wide enough to hide a sasquatch. In other habitats the kauris and hoop pines soar overhead.

For an island only 223 kilometres long, K'gari has an exceptional diversity of ecosystems. The rainforest and perched lakes are only a part of the attraction. Just as magnificent are the dry eucalyptus forest where the bark foams like soap in torrential rain, grass-covered dunes replete with shore birds, casuarina forests along the western sheltered coast, melaleuca and tea trees congregating around swamps full of frogs, reeds and banksias, freshwater creeks lined with arches of pandanus palms and saltwater estuaries feeding sharks and stingrays. To experience all of it you need the time, water carrying capacity and trekking gear to wander beyond the tourist attractions and venture further than the walking track.

There are two types of dingos living on K'gari, the ones who are too curious for their own good, who hang around the periphery of camps and villages, and the ones who know better, who live further into the centre and northern reaches of the island, away from human contact. They don't mix, keeping to their own family groups and territories. It is amazing to see a dingo in the wild on K'gari, but they should never come into camp for food. This group of dingos have learnt to associate humans with food, digging up buried food scraps and being fed. There are signs everywhere warning people not to feed them and to store food in their cars or in the secure boxes available at campgrounds. Dingos have become so bold around camps and villages that they have attacked people, usually children, when they want food. Most people who try to interact with the dingos forget these ones will be caught and shot, to prevent more attacks. It is a sad truth that can be easily avoided.

It was disconcerting seeing crowds of people visiting popular Instagram locations, the damage they cause and their disrespect of sacred Butchulla sites. Lake Wabby was a place I looked forward to seeing and I met the team from the long running children's education program, *Totally Wild*, who were doing a story there. A park ranger had earlier advised me of its imminent closure due to litter, erosion and toxic algae, so I didn't take the detour with the film crew. It is a beautiful freshwater swimming hole, thick forest on one shore and a tall sand dune falling steeply into the other side, pretty as a picture. Lake Wabby is also a sacred Aboriginal men's only place for ceremony and initiation. I stood on the platform at the lookout, built for the walking track, and appreciated the lake formation and significance from a distance. It is shrinking and one day this lake will be swallowed up by the moving dune.

I love that the outdoors is so popular, but it has come at a hefty price, which nature is paying. It is our responsibility, as travellers visiting someone else's land, to ask if it is okay for us to go to sacred places and assess whether our visit is sustainable or will add unnecessary pressure to the environment. We come to witness K'gari's natural beauty and are killing it with love and Instagram likes.

An intriguing phenomenon I noticed on the island was the way the freshwater creeks run out over the beach. Creeks over beaches isn't strange, it was the way the water pulsed out of the island: it was as if the island was breathing. It took me a long time to walk down the beaches as I had to stop at every creek and rivulet to watch, to convince myself it wasn't my imagination. I followed a few up into the dunes and vegetation to see if there were any natural dams or spills made from tree roots or congested reeds causing this to happen. There were not. The freshwater, filtering out of the sand and flowing out to sea, created its own rhythm, the heartbeat of the island. When I stood there, mesmerised by this wonder, my own breathing and heartbeat synced with K'gari.

Slow down, stop, sit,
Don't miss a beat,
The sway of the goanna's tail,
Wind ripples across the dunes,
Rain falling and filling
This reservoir of life.
K'gari

CHAPTER 27

THE EAST

It can be frustrating walking down the Far North Queensland coast, along the white and gold sandy beaches, gazing out at the turquoise blue water and islands, not being able to cool off. Even wading in these waters is dangerous. North of the Tropic of Capricorn is saltwater crocodile territory, but if you speak to the locals, they can give you directions to safe waterholes and waterfalls in the hills. Tiny tropical oases, enveloped in palms, arched with fragrant blooming melaleucas full of chatty rosellas, lorikeets and honey eaters, surrounded by tiny ferns and flowers, with lizards sunning themselves in the speckled shade on the bank. The water tumbles over rocks, so clear its depth to the sand bed cannot be judged without getting in.

I was surprised how many of these sanctuaries I had to myself. Most people go to the ones in the travel guides and social media, and these secret swimming holes will stay safe with me. High visitor numbers change the water quality, adding bacteria, chemicals from sunscreen and soaps that feed algae, causing erosion on the embankments; there are also the inevitable broken tree branches and loss of small soil protecting plants. It was special finding the undisturbed gems.

On the way down the east coast, to avoid the highway and main roads, I zigzagged between the coastal beaches and back roads of the hinterlands and Great Dividing Range. Queensland National Parks has designed 'Great Walks' through places with significant natural and cultural value. Rail Trails Australia has converted many old disused rail corridors into shared walking and riding tracks. The National Bicentennial Trail is a 6,000-kilometre walking/riding route through parks, reserves, private land and back roads from the bottom of Victoria to Cooktown. Using these, I was able to link beaches and coast tracks with mountain trails, most of the way from Agnes Water to the border with NSW and beyond.

Cooloola Great Walk is through the country of Gubbi Gubbi/Kabi Kabi traditional owners and signs of their continuous use of the land can be seen throughout the coastal ecosystem that the walk weaves through: in the names of places, tree markings, ancient stories, middens, artefacts and special places. It is thought that 'cooloola' means whispering cypress, the pine which was later extensively logged and cleared for farming. Starting at Rainbow Beach there is a small sand patch to cross, Carlo Sandblow, where the track entering the bush on the other side can be seen across the sand, unlike the big one later, Cooloola Sandpatch, which requires basic navigation using a compass and map (I always use these anyway). Friends in Rainbow Beach recommended some detours to special Gubbi Gubbi places: gorgeous small, perched lakes, off the main track, with few visitors apart from locals. I was also advised of a place where I should not stop because it was a Gubbi Gubbi men's place, and it felt that way as I walked past.

On the sand patches many animal tracks can be followed. These animals are mostly nocturnal because of the dual threats from burning temperatures and exposure to birds of prey.

Dunes slowly travel over a long period of time, moved by the wind, swallowing up bushland, bones, camps and middens. As they travel, they can also reveal what they hid hundreds of years before: calcified and oxidised shells of trees, Gubbi Gubbi artefacts from their homes, hearths and hunting, extensive shell middens. It is a fabulous insight into their lives if you know what you are looking at. I found some cutting stones and knapping chips, a grinding bowl and a darkened patch of charred sand with oyster shells where there may have been a cooking fire; I took a couple of photos and then left them where I found them; these artefacts don't belong to us. I believe in karma, so I prefer to satiate my curiosity by filling in the details with my imagination, based on what I have learnt about Aboriginal history, while leaving the belongings of the ancestors in situ.

In the rainforests, I saw those ghostly spaces where strangler vines had climbed up and surrounded a tree in a net, killing the tree but standing with the perfect support built around their host, now rotted away. Some of the trees are humongous, with buttresses spreading across the damp rainforest floor (great places to take a break, drink some water and eat a snack). If you're really quiet, the sound of the rainforest comes alive. If you wear insect repellent for mozzies and leeches, it will be even more relaxing. Cooloola

Great Walk isn't only a rainforest walk. You also meander through dry eucalyptus, xanthorrhoea, plains of wildflowers and along the river through banksias, grevilleas, casuarinas and melaleuca. There are so many sanctuaries for different groups of wildlife, with a lot of infrastructure built by the parks service so that humans can enjoy it without hurting it. And you can swim in the river!

The Gondwana rainforests... now they were the most spellbinding of all. On the Queensland and New South Wales border sits Lamington National Park, on Wangerriburras and Nerangballum country. It is part of the Great Dividing Range and the Scenic Rim, the remains of volcanic cores and vents of a massive 23-million-year-old volcano. Besides its natural heritage, the area has a rich history of activism; farmers pioneered protected parks to save old-growth forests from logging and land clearing so we can all enjoy it for recreation.

One of the most beautiful and accessible multi day walks in Australia is the Gold Coast Hinterland Great Walk, between Green Mountain and Springbrook. It doesn't matter which end you start from, you will have lots of mountains to walk up and down and around, with steep hill traverses. It isn't for the faint hearted, but it can be broken down into overnight and day walks. In late August, I began at O'Reilly's Rainforest Retreat, where I had had a rest day, to walk to eleven waterfalls on some of their day walking tracks. I put in a full day to reach Binna Burra Lodge where I had another rest day for more waterfall walks.

The next day I set off for Numinbah Valley but only made it as far as a very steep slippery section of a disused 4WD service road. Halfway down I slipped and somehow managed to get the walking pole under my ankle, shattering the tibia and dislocating the fibula. There was a little bit of phone range in patches along the walk and I was lucky to fall in one. Six months later, my brother Steve and I returned. We visited the volunteer ambulance officer, Guy, in Springbrook, and I caught up with one of the paramedics, Drew, as I continued from the other end of the track, walking back to where I fell.

From the side of Green Mountain, you enter the Gondwana rainforests; this is much as it is thought to have been like before Australia split from New Zealand and India. The 'Antarctic' trees, hoop pines, ferns, moss and lichen, clinging vines, and rare flowering plants are found nowhere else on Earth, and many appear much as their ancestors would have done back in Gondwana times.

Starting In Springbrook you enter tall ash and stringybark forest and head straight down the steepest section of the walk, through hillside covered in xanthorrhoea and into swamps and old reclaimed farms before heading into the rainforest again. With crystal clear creeks, waterfalls and cliff top views, you really can feel like you are a time traveller, walking through a portal into an age before humans roamed the Earth.

Between Naarm/Melbourne and Mulubinba/Newcastle, I have followed the coastline on foot and by bicycle, and crossed the mountains along the Great Dividing Range many times. The coastal route is probably the most arduous with a lot of river crossings and off-track in parts. On the big walk, I headed south from Tathra on the Sapphire Coast, linking the Kianinny Track with the Light to Light, then the Wilderness Coast Track and on via Croajingalong, following beaches and rail trails the rest of the way south through the Victorian

Gippsland. Much of my route was necessarily self-designed as most tracks did not go where I wanted. Across rivers and around headlands were especially troublesome. I was able to hitch a ride across some rivers on fishing dinghies. For one river with a great white shark in it I had to detour 18 kilometres around; at another swift deep crossing, where there were no fisherfolk to flag down, I detoured 45 kilometres. Most rivers were crossable on slack low tides. For the ones I had to swim, I carried a $5 pool donut and towed the pack on it.* For extra waterproofing, I used a garbage bag as a liner inside. Always looking for the cheapest solutions to problems kept the budget down—without sponsorship, brand name gear was usually out of the question.

Nadgee Nature Reserve and Croajingalong National Park was the most remote coastal region I have ever walked. It was wild, stormy and incredibly beautiful. These are the lands of the Bidawal and Gunai Kurnai people, and as you walk through you will see many middens and cross significant and sacred places. The ranger at Womboyn, where I logged in, told me of a black waterhole which was used for traditional lore/law. If someone had broken a law punishable by death they were sent to sit for a number of days beside this hole. If they deserved to die the bunyip would rise out of the water and take their life, if they didn't deserve death they survived. I sat beside the waterhole to get a feel for the place, with the confidence of a clear conscience, and understood how and why this worked. If you truly believed you deserved your

* I backpacked most of the east coast and Tasmania. I used the barrow for about 12,000 kilometres but used the backpack where water and food were accessible most days.

punishment, and bunyips are a very real part of your culture and lore, you could either die of fright or be taken away in the night.

It was a particularly wet and temperamental summer when I walked through but there were enough clear sunny days to allow me to immerse into the landscape. I watched the dingos looking for yabbies in the creeks and walking along the beaches, and the big white sea eagles gliding above, diving for fish and snakes. I tried eating some of the native bush plant foods: banksia seeds, flax lily berries and fringe lily roots. One day, after a swim in the sea, I had a snooze under the tarp in the shade. I woke a few hours later with a big goanna flicking its tongue on my face. I don't know who scared who more! Away from the official campsites, there were more animals to see and hear at night: owls, possums, gliders, micro bats. Between the beaches and the bushland were headlands covered in stunted coastal heath, where the rough weather and salt spray kept the vegetation low, blown over from constant strong winds. The heathlands were predominantly leptospermum, dwarf banksia, hakea, orchids, lomandra, christmas bells, xanthorrhoea, casuarina, lilies, egg and bacon pea flowers, and pink coral heath. There were so many colours of flowers and textures of leaves and bark (beware of the spikey ones) to experience, and surprise snakes lying on the track sunning themselves. Passing the border of New South Wales and Victoria around the rocks and across the dunes, I saw seals hauled out on the rocks to sleep and preen, and so many middens I lost count. The wind was strong, sand blasting me, but sea and shore birds stood together, resolutely, against the weather.

One of the reasons I recommend travellers not to rush, even on the Northern Territory's open speed limit highways, is for all the interesting side trips on the way. Take your time, it might be the only trip to a particular place you make. See as much as you can while you can. Even in the 'middle of nowhere' there are cultural experiences, museums, fossicking centres, wildlife and wetlands tours, caves, eccentric cafés and eclectic pubs, art galleries, hot springs, farm stays, dinosaurs, lighthouses, nature walks and national parks. When someone starts a sentence with "Have you seen..." or "You should go to..." take notes and put it on your itinerary. Make your travel a journey of discovery.

There is also a serious side to travelling around this continent and seeing it change over years, decades. It is not only the different landscapes you pass through; it is how these landscapes are changing with our climate, droughts, floods, fires, warming oceans, mining, logging and tourism saturation. Some of the things I saw have gone and will never be seen again. Animals and plants are being driven to extinction, ecosystems are degrading, culture is being lost because of greedy resource grabbing, even human habitats are under threat due to bad environmental management. Although I walked through some of the most magnificent and precious places on Earth, I also saw the human impact.

Even my walk had an impact on the Earth. I was using roads cut through rare habitats, wearing synthetic textiles, cooking on a stove fuelled with gas, flying across the country to continue the walk each autumn, eating single use plastic-wrapped foods. I try to reduce and offset my environmental footprint as much as is practical, but I still have one. I think this makes me even more aware of what big companies, magnates and governments are doing to our planet.

Even as I write, activists from many diverse cultures are fighting side by side to protect land and water, trying to stop the destruction of sacred places, protecting the plants, animals, water catchments and oceans which provided sustenance and sanctuary for many thousands of years, the places where ancestors live, where stories are alive. I had to mentally see these incredible landscapes through both the eyes of a tourist for the first time and to try to understand them from an Aboriginal perspective of livelihood, ancestry, creation, healing and home. Memories which will last forever continue to motivate my instincts to protect and conserve, not only for myself but for every traveller in the future and to honour those who have been before. Travel is deeper than reaching a destination, it is connecting to a place and carrying it with you forever.

CHAPTER 28

WHAT IS YOUR FAVOURITE PLACE?

"What is your favourite place?" is a really hard question to answer when you have seen so much of Australia. I prefer being asked, "What are some of your favourite places?"

Then we can have a longer conversation about all the most remarkable places we've been, swap recommendations for bakeries and backpacker lodges, secret campsites, bushwalks and experiences with the best value for money.

I'll start with my three favourite areas for training.

The Australian Alps is top of the list for beauty, solitude and hills. You could say I spent my life training for this big walk and most of that was in the mountains. I would even still head up there each year to put in a month of walking before returning for the next long leg. By the time my body had recovered from the previous leg, I had lost some fitness; this was evident by how stuffed I felt on the first mountain, huffing and puffing, sweating and swearing my way up, loaded with a full pack, lots of food and, of course, a small library of books. Within a week, mountain muscle memory kicked in and I could feel my body growing stronger each day. It became even more enjoyable as the pack lightened with each meal. As I progressed through the big walk, it was apparent how much my mind was recovering. Each visit into the mountains became more meaningful as I revisited places, sensing them through a healthier mind and lighter heart.

Growing up around Mulubinba and on Worimi land, I loved that stretch of coastline, especially from Burrinbingon/Stockton to Minimbah/Forster. I could catch the train down to Mulubinba, take the ferry across to Burrinbingon and walk up the long beaches, sweeping away into the distance, and through the coastal banksia bushland, alive with birds. It is an area full of Aboriginal heritage, middens, camps, fishing grounds, food and medicine. Wildlife is prolific, both on land and at sea: dingoes, echidnas, emus, cockatoos, koalas, goannas, pelicans, sea eagles, dolphins, stingrays, turtles, whales. Soft sand is great for strength and stamina training, especially with the extra pack weight. I would always add to this weight by picking up bags of rubbish on the way.

My parents live near Guruk/Port Macquarie, on Birpai land. This is where I usually go between adventures, I call it 'Hotel Mum and Dad'. I drop in for some quality time, until they're sick of me eating all their food, then I go through the three boxes of camping, trekking and cycling gear stored in the guest room cupboard, swapping in what I need according to season and activity. From their place I would walk north to gorgeous Crescent Head, hands down the most beautiful stretch of coastline in the world. This is the land of the Dunghatti nation, and you can feel it. The traditional owners have always had a strong continuous connection to this country and their culture is alive. The best part of this country is the water, its moods, colours, surf, the calm days, dramatic storms and swimming in the cooling water on a hot summer day. On the days I have trouble finding the dangerous rip tides I look for a small gutter in the sand banks and lie there, letting the waves rock me about. It was near here, on a family summer holiday, Dad taught me to count sets of waves. He was a surfer in his younger days and enjoyed watching the ocean. We stood on a headland and watched the waves build in size, and the surfers below getting ready to ride the big three at the back of the set. I still do this whenever I'm by the ocean. I count the sets of sets; it is a meditation.

The big walk took me through all my favourite places and showed me new wonders, but those which stand out from the walk have a community connection.

Eucla, on the Eyre Highway, just west of the Western and South Australia border is an oasis of delightful surprises. It's a tiny town of about 20 homes. The physical and mental relief of reaching it at night after a 67-kilometre day of walking was a contributor to my fondness for this place, as was the generosity of the hotel owners. What hit me most about Eucla was the sense of community and how relaxed everyone was. They took pride in their homes and yards and welcomed travellers. While there I spotted a poster for the Eucla Dog Show! Funny joke. But it wasn't a joke. It is sad but not unusual for people to dump their cats and dogs out there when they're moving house from one side of the continent to the other. If they can't get an animal-friendly rental, and can't rehome their beloved pet, they sometimes release them into the wild on the way over, instead of sending them to the pound where they will most likely be euthanised.

It is irresponsible, but so are landlords refusing companion animals. The lucky among these abandoned and frightened dogs see the lights of Eucla, on the top of the escarpment—lights mean humans and safety, so they gravitate towards them and are adopted into the friendly community. Once a year Eucla holds a Dog Show for them.

There was a telegraph station at Eucla, built in 1898. Having once been a caretaker of Eyre Bird Observatory Telegraph Station, a beautifully restored example of the old limestone telegraph stations between Adelaide and Perth, I was interested to see what they look like in ruins. Most of them are ruins now, and Eucla's had almost been swallowed by the sand dunes. There are remains of battered and eroded stone and doorways, rooms filled with huge drifts of sand, a wall slowly tilting over with the weight of nature building against it. It was eerie, fascinating and joyous at the same time: imagining how busy it was 100 years ago, witnessing the speed of erosion and seeing nature taking back the stone and timber, eventually to bury it for another 200 years.

It is a short walk down the escarpment to the Great Australian Bight and Southern Ocean. Here you'll find a long beach covered in treasures from the sea, the occasional seal and sea lion and broken banks of kelp drying black in the desiccating wind and heat. A little further along is the ruin of an old jetty, tall wind carved support posts angling high above the water. Channelling the Nullarbor Nymph, I took a quick skinny dip in the icy cold surf, briefly joining the famous great white sharks and whales. The winter wind was warmer than the water.

On the way back, at golden hour, I wandered over the dunes,

swept clean and rippling like churning cream. I followed the tracks of insects, reptiles and small marsupials, and played with my long shadow on the plain below. As the sun set, I wandered back up the escarpment to the restaurant, filling my belly with homemade vegetarian lasagne. Eucla Hotel also makes the best veggie burger in Australia.

Next stop on the favourite places tour is Karratha. This is where I met Leah and Julie and the Pilbara Motorcycle Sisters (PMS) who welcomed me into their community with open arms. They do a lot of work in the community for suicide prevention and domestic violence. Leah and Julie had been following my progress up the west coast and had already sent a message to make sure I knew they would look after me in Karratha. They became my rescue team when, about 100 kilometres south of town, my knee refused to take any weight without buckling. They drove out, at night after work, with the motorcycle trailer, loaded up the barrow and drove me back to Karratha where I had two weeks of very painful, but effective, physio, rest and recuperation.

I must admit that I had misjudged Karratha as "just another mining town". I had no idea how pleasant it would be until arriving. Being a mining town, a lot of money had poured into the community in the way of beautification projects, and sports and recreation facilities. Walking and running tracks had been developed around the growing town and up Stove Hill, a favourite track for exercise at sunrise.

Leah, Julie and their kids took me on a tour of the coastal towns, up to Point Samson and down to Dampier. I met the bronze likeness of Red Dog, whose adventures are recounted in Louis de Bernières' book and its film adaptation. I read this book to my Ooma in 2006, after she went blind, so it was a special moment. We visited the historic town of Cossack and had lunch at the Point Samson Pub, looking over the turquoise blue Indian Ocean. If you can ignore the colonial impacts on the traditional owners, it is a gorgeous place. The more time I spent in remote parts of Australia, the more I became aware of how far reaching and generational these impacts were. I try to focus on the natural beauty of these places, nature as it has been for millions of years. We stopped to admire a magnificent sea eagle soaring over us, landing in a tree, watching us. Red kangaroos bounced over the red rocky landscape. A marlin leapt out of the water in front of us while we ate lunch. All reminders of the incredible country I was passing through.

One day we visited Hearson's Cove on world heritage listed Murujuga/Burrup Peninsula for a picnic. Murujuga is home of the petroglyphs depicting thylacines and other animals, carved thousands of years ago by the Yaburara people. It was something I will never forget.

I can't believe I have a mining town on my favourites list, being a staunch tree hugger and all.

One last place is Capricorn Caves, just north of Yipun/ Yeppoon, Queensland. On the way down the coast, I was unaware of this tourist attraction until reading the road sign. It immediately became the next detour. I love caves! The owner was super supportive of the walk and donated an eco-cabin for two nights. I was going to camp, but being exhausted, the offer was too good to refuse. The little range of adjacent hills, protected as Mount Etna Caves National Park, was full of rainforest wildlife. I could sit on the veranda and watch wallabies, goannas and all sorts of birdlife, going about their busy lives. On my rest day I joined the Cathedral Cave tour, and saw stalagmites, stalactites, veils, pillars and crystals everywhere. The highlight of the tour is the cathedral cave. There is an opening in the ceiling which lets in a bright shaft of sunlight at midday. The cave had perfect resonance. Two of the women in our tour group were from a choir and they sang a couple of songs which made our skin tingle. It was so moving I cried. In fact, I've just had tingles run all over my head remembering how glorious it was.

This is hard. I wanted to limit this list to only three places, but my head is now filling with hundreds of them.

Special mentions from the big walk:

- Bridport, Binalong Bay, Bruny Island – lutruwita
- Broken Head, Pebbly Beach, Darlington Point – New South Wales
- Wingan Inlet, Waterloo Bay, Robinvale – Victoria
- Laura, Streaky Bay, Fowlers Bay – South Australia
- Esperance, Echo Beach, Wyndham – Western Australia
- Timber Creek, Bitter Springs – Northern Territory
- Bowen, Clairview, K'Gari, Binna Burra – Queensland

Ultimately though, my recommendation is for you to travel around and find your own favourite places; your list will be different to mine.

CHAPTER 29

MAD MATS

Everyone expects a female adventurer to have a romance. If you are, then I'm pleased to say I will disappoint you. Personally, I think romance and intimate relationships are irksome and avoid them at all costs. Kissing is gross! Hands up all the four-year-olds who agree with me.

However, there was a guy who helped me work out some confusing feelings. Long story short, I thought I had fallen in love with him when in actual fact I had fallen in love with his lifestyle. You see, the problem with me and romance is that I have no idea what it is; my concept of love is limited to the familial kind: mateship, places, activities and things. I do not have the capacity for intimate love.

So when I met Mats I was confused. Here was a human that I had these weird foreign uncomfortable strong feelings for. Thankfully, Mats is a chilled-out Swede, and as I processed this confusion, sharing it with him, I could sort out exactly what it was I was in love with. He was, no doubt, relieved when I came to the conclusion it wasn't him.

Mats is also a superhuman.

We met at Edith Creek on the Stuart Highway, during

his 22,000-kilometre walk across the planet from Stockholm, Sweden, to Sydney, Australia, with extra adventures by bike and kick bike.

I had left Katherine that morning and walked 43 kilometres to the free campsite. As I pulled into the camping area, just before sunset, I glanced up the highway and spotted the strangest thing. I wasn't sure what I was looking at, as the sun was in my eyes, but it looked like some nutter pushing a barrow down the highway. I stood there a moment while my brain caught up and then headed up the road to meet them.

Mats had walked 48 kilometres from Pine Creek that day, he was heading across to the east coast via Mt Isa and Rockhampton. At this point in his journey, he had already walked 18,000 kilometres. His footwear of choice was thongs. I couldn't believe it! Thongs?! His feet looked strong and gnarly but none the worse for it; in fact, they were probably healthier than mine, being cramped up inside shoes and boots for the last 12,000 kilometres.

It was the first time I had met, in person, another extreme long-distance walker. After running through the usual chatter—"Where have you come from?" "Where are you going?" "Why are you doing this?"—my conversation skills were lost for a while as I thought to myself, what do we have to talk about? We were, after all, living the same life, so we were only going to have the same answers to all the usual questions. We camped together and compared gear, music vs podcasts, motivation, thongs vs trail runners. Eventually we settled in to share stories of encounters, our longest days, our hardest days. When he passed muster, when I decided he was an okay human and could be a good friend, my interest in his lifestyle was piqued. I needed to know more.

Mad Mats the Minimalist introduced me to minimalism. Until meeting him, I had never heard of it. It is a choice to reduce your worldly possessions to only what you need. I had mine in the barrow and he had his in a big insulated toolbox bolted onto a four wheel baby buggy chassis.* It is surprising just how much stuff we don't need. It was harder for Mats to become a minimalist. I think he's a bit of a hoarder of bikes and camera gear. He had a house and double garage full of stuff to get rid of before beginning his walk. I had already lived the life of a minimalist for most of my adult years, without knowing what it was.

I was excited to learn my lifestyle was now trending (the minimalist part, not the walking around Australia part). He was proud of achieving minimalism, but it must have been difficult for Mats to pare down everything he had collected over the last 50 years. Some of it must have been painful to let go of, but the motivation to prepare for the walk was stronger. The process of letting go is freeing for the mind and a passive form of rebellion against the consumerist society. Without all that property to care for, you can step away and walk across the world.

I thought of all the happy grey nomads I had met, who had sold up, bought a home on wheels and travelled. They had been through the same process of lightening their worldly belongings to be free to roam where and when they wished. No more mortgages†, council fees, home insurance,

* We both had a few boxes of gear in storage.

† Have you ever thought about the word 'mortgage'? In Latin mort means death. Just saying...

lawn mowing. Sounds good, huh? I remembered when I was married, briefly, we had an apartment, briefly, and filled it with a bed, sofa, dining set, washing machine, fridge, cutlery, crockery and utensils. When we divorced, after a very brief marriage, I had to find new owners for all our stuff. It was a real headache. I made that mistake only once. My freedom is too valuable to tie down with stuff. I was so ahead of the minimalist trend.

Mats also used the term 'vagabond', discussing his choice to walk across the planet. I had been calling myself a wanderer, wayfarer, vagrant and homeless for a while. Vagabonding was also trending, like minimalism, and definitely sounded better than homeless. It's funny how terminology can change our attitude to something or someone. What if we all thought of the homeless as wayfarers and vagabonds? Would we treat each other better if it sounds like there is an engaging story behind living without a home? Would we be more generous in showing kindness?

The writings of Walt Whitman, Robert Louis Stevenson and Ralph Waldo Emerson, played a part in Mats' decision to become a vagabond, following his natural instinct to travel on foot.

"Nor I, nor anyone else can travel that road for you. You must travel it by yourself. It is not far. It is within reach. Perhaps you have been on it since you were born, and did not know. Perhaps it is everywhere – on water and land."
— Walt Whitman

"I travel not to go anywhere, but to go. I travel for travel's sake. The great affair is to move."
— Robert Louis Stevenson

"Few people know how to take a walk. The qualifications are endurance, plain clothes, old shoes, an eye for nature, good humour, vast curiosity, good speech, good silence and nothing too much."
— Ralph Waldo Emerson

Exactly why Mats chose to walk is his own story, which started with a drunken oath in a pub on his 50th birthday. Was it an existential crisis, did he seek a transcendental reality to be found only through connecting with creeds and cultures of the world as an unpretentious traveller? I picture Mats as a modern-day Walt Whitman, walking through the countryside, learning, sharing, living simply and peacefully, at one with the people and world around him.

Thanks to Mats, I had to do a deep dive into existentialism and transcendentalism, two great things to distract your mind with philosophical worm holes while walking all day. Existentialism is the idea of being free, having control of your own destination and free will. Transcendentalism is about the self-reliance of goodness and spirituality. They are far more than my short definitions; philosophers and writers have spent their entire lives studying them. Applying them to my life was akin to learning Buddhism, taking both the philosophies and my life ethos back to basics, looking at where I already use them and how they might enrich other parts of my life. Another piece of thought to put in my mental health toolbox. Being an atheist, I'm allowed to pick and choose what works for me and what doesn't; I pick up concepts, try them out and discard them if they don't feel right. I'm still a student of existentialism and transcendentalism; it makes the world less intense when I see it through another lens.

Mats was one of those people I was meant to meet in this life. He is a decade older than me and had walked almost twice as far. The week after we met, I sent him an email asking if he would be my mentor, teacher, sensei. I have been grateful ever since for his acceptance of this role.

For more than a year I flipped between seeing him as a teacher, a mate and that confusing feeling I could not name. Many quiet moments of meditation were filled analysing what that feeling was. I knew it wasn't love, lust or whatever the icky message brain chemicals send when you fall in love. So what was it then? I had very strong feelings. One of the possibilities was the feeling of overwhelming relief finding someone on this planet who might understand me, thinks like me, does weird shit like me. It could have been the yearning for him to live on the same continent so we could hang out, drink whisky and share our crazy adventure plans. Over time, I came to realise that I saw in him a reflection of myself, the person I wanted to be, the person I actually was: a minimalist vagabond travelling my own path, through nature, experiencing the common goodness of the human spirit.

Writing this has now shown me a new revelation. I was in love with *myself*, he was an affirmation of my *own* life. Sorry mate. Trust me to make it all about myself!

After reaching Darwin, the barrow went into storage and

I flew back to the east coast to rest. During that time Mats reached Sydney and was celebrated by family and friends. I made it down to watch him finish. There was a piece of my walk across the bottom of Australia missing. Mats called his buggy The Mule. Leading up to his finish, I asked if I could borrow it for a few months. Mats was happy that The Mule would be continuing its journey. I put my own insulated toolbox on top of the chassis and spent March and April walking the Riverina, River Lands and across Flinders Ranges, from Canberra to Port Pirie. Mats' Mule has been handed on twice to others planning walks for mental health.

We've stayed in touch and will hopefully get to take a crazy adventure together, before he's an old man.

On a side note, when I was 14 or 15, I wrote a list of the attributes the person I wanted to meet would have. Tall, fair hair, loves camping, building bikes and bushwalking, kind, not racist, Norwegian. Mats is Swedish, so that sucks.

CHAPTER 30

HOW MANY SHOES DID YOU WEAR OUT?

Six pairs of boots, nine pairs of runners and five pairs of thongs.*

From the beginning, Columbia came onboard with a factory discount of 50 percent, so almost all my clothing and boots were from them. When I trek through the mountains I wear high ankle, rigid sole, waterproof boots, so I bought four pairs of their best. Even with a good sole they wore out every 1,000 kilometres. I wore each longer than I should. I had a strange little right foot roll and always wore down the outside of that heel faster than the rest of the boot. By 1,200 kilometres the roll became too accentuated, causing ligament strain and a new pair would be sent out to a roadhouse.

They were also very heavy. After walking across the Nullarbor and down Eyre Peninsula to Balinyala/Port Lincoln the weight began straining my Sartorius tendons and muscles. This is the longest muscle/tendon group in

* In Australia we call them thongs, not flip flops.

the body, running from the inside of the knee to the outside of the hip, and they hurt with every step. I had to extend my rest days and stretch a lot. When the heatwaves started rolling across South Australia it was time to stop, spend the summer recovering and look at lighter shoes.

During the break I tried out shoes trail runner friends recommended and settled on a couple of brands of light runners which felt comfortable on the tracks around my parents' home. They were expensive, and having thinner soles they would need to be replaced more often.

I could not get any reply from the companies when requesting sponsorship, so I began with two pairs in the barrow and hoped I would have enough money for more when they wore out. Unfortunately, the soles were too thin for the melting bitumen road surface, and the soles of my feet blistered badly. At their worst I stopped for three days to let them completely heal and collected a new pair of shoes, men's Salomon X-Trail. These came highly recommended by friends at Wilderness Sports Jindabyne, who also donated my first pair. They felt great, like walking on clouds, compared to what I had been using. The foot box of the men's shoe was a little bit too narrow and rubbed for a week with each new pair, but my feet stopped blistering. I was put in touch with the importer who declined to sponsor but provided a few more pairs with a 30 percent discount. The soles on these lasted 700 kilometres before the right outside heel wore down. Every few weeks I phoned up to buy a new pair, all the way to Garramilla/Darwin. Shoes really stretched my budget and I always needed to sacrifice something else, food or accommodation, to afford them.

When I could no longer afford shoes and could find no shoe sponsors, my friend Denise, in Garramilla, heard the trouble I was having and came to the rescue with Slappas! Denise designed Slappas, the original Australian orthotic thongs. A big supporter of suicide prevention, she donated as many as I needed.

The year before, I had met Mats on the Stuart Highway, walking in thongs, so when Denise offered to sponsor my walk, I didn't hesitate to accept. That summer, while recovering from some foot injuries, Achilles tendonitis and plantar fasciitis, I wore Slappas everywhere. The heel and arch support helped my feet recover faster.

For the next 2,500 kilometres I walked in Slappas, some days I even had enough excess energy to run in them. The EVA sole lasted about 500 kilometres before I could feel the coarser abrasive blue-metal bitumen and thorns began sticking through. I still wear them everywhere: as I write this, I'm section riding my pushbike around Australia in Slappas.

When it was time to switch to the backpack and walk off road, I needed something more supportive and protective than thongs. Barefootinc donated two pairs of men's ultralight Inov8 Roclite GTX boots. The rest of the walk was on softer ground and the two pairs lasted the final 3,000 kilometres. They were an excellent boot, especially going from thongs to a barefoot designed sole, wide, soft, light and comfortable.

I suspect the reason why so many shoe manufacturers refused to sponsor—many never replied—was because they knew their brand would not be up to what I was putting them through, and I am a brutally honest field tester and critique. It is different when walking with a support crew: you are not pushing, pulling or carrying the extra weight of your gear, so the wear and tear on your shoes is not as extreme, you can wear whatever feels comfortable. If sponsors take you seriously, it makes a world of difference to your budget, freeing you up to walk with more confidence and afford to fuel properly. Good shoes cost a lot.

CHAPTER 31

WHO SPONSORS YOU?

I have a lot to say about this but first of all THANK YOU to the individuals, community groups and businesses who helped me carry the message of suicide prevention around Australia.

I would have thought that businesses, particularly the big ones, would see philanthropy as a way of expanding their presence and increase market exposure, but it didn't always seem to be the case. I was very disappointed by the majority's lack of interest and even rudeness while I sought support.

Unfortunately, we now live in a world full of online egos, who drown out the greater achievements of others. There are many people doing incredible things who go unnoticed without strong community support. I was lucky to build an organic community of over 8,000 people during the walk. It was hard work and stressful. I eventually deleted all my social media when someone attacked me during a climate action expedition. One of the difficult things for female and non-male adventurists is the lack of sponsorship support and recognition. This comes down to two main reasons. Sponsors don't take female adventurers seriously and men get more media attention and awards. This is a problem perpetuated by Australian news, adventure media platforms and elite adventure societies. I not only speak from experience, but I have watched this happen to other female adventurers who have gone above and beyond, without support, then been ignored while male peers receive accolades for achieving less with huge sponsorship. Anyone, regardless of their gender, should be celebrated equally for setting and breaking expedition records, finding new routes and beating the odds. Expeditions are not a 'boys' club'.

Once you realise that most sponsors, media and elite societies are only interested in using people who are already popular or well known as a platform to generate more interest in themselves, you begin to understand why you are left in the cold. So, in order to be seen, believed and supported you need to know how to sell yourself. To do this you need to think like a male, let everyone know how great you and all your achievements are, do it 'for the boys'. Women don't support each other like men do. We need to pick up our act. This will upset some of you, but it is the truth.

Unless you, or someone in your support network, knows how to use social media effectively you will be lost in the algorithms. I highly recommend having someone do this side of your campaign for you; it can be exhausting on top of all you are already doing, and you may not have phone range every day to update your followers. Some adventurers can even afford to employ a marketing company to do it for them.

Don't be disappointed by the lack of engagement. You might have thousands of people watching you but until you do something wrong or something terrible happens, most of them won't like, dislike, comment or share. Don't take it personally; online is its own world with its own rules, and one of them is an ingrained hesitancy to show support. There is also the 'tall poppy syndrome' online in Australia: don't grow too big or you'll be cut down. I think we're getting past this as more of us enjoy living vicariously through others' adventures.

That environment has improved a lot since my walk, and I am impressed by the support other adventurers are now getting from their communities. Supporting and acknowledging female adventurers became almost as big a campaign for me as suicide prevention. I was invisible, ignored and rejected. It made me angry, not only for myself but for the adventure arena, the greater community. For females to be treated equally they must succeed in far more gruelling, dangerous and longer challenges than the males who dominate awards and media. If it isn't better than a male's achievement, it isn't good enough. I carried around a lot of bitterness until I realised the best thing to do was improve the situation for future female adventurers. If I made enough noise about it, engaged with the people who can change it and supported females in their endeavours by sharing their achievements, things might get better. I had a good platform and used it. In the last year of my expedition, I could see the tide turning, people were listening. It was too late for me, but it has helped other females since. Campaigning for equality in the adventure community was hard work, but today I can see the fruits of my efforts, and of other female expeditioners of our time, in the incredible journeys of younger female adventurers. Their strong support and celebrated success are the result of women, non-binary and the trans community speaking up and holding media and societies accountable. Today, social media plays a greater role in bringing inclusive and diverse outdoor communities together where we are seen and heard.

Rejection was the hardest part of the walk for me to handle. I sent out hundreds of emails, made hundreds of phone calls, requesting sponsorship and support from businesses, philanthropists and the media. Most of the emails were ignored. If my phone call was answered I was either rejected on the spot, put through to a number which never picked up or given an email address which was rarely replied to. It was not until I had nearly finished walking around Australia that people began to believe I could do it. By then it was too late to support me. I was jaded and became selective in which media I would speak to when I finished—definitely not the ones who never bothered replying when I asked them for help at the beginning.

For potential sponsors there were many missed opportunities. I had a barrow with a lot of room for sponsor signage and generated a lot of interest via my social media, website and blog: all 'free' additional advertising. I made all that clear when asking for their support, and even had a four-tier system set up, starting at $100 and up to $10,000. Many people asked who my sponsors were. I was very proud of the few small businesses who were supporting me but also embarrassed when admitting I had failed to get funding or a big gear sponsor.

I applied to be an ambassador for a few companies, but they expected far too much in return for a small amount of gear or funding. When out on an expedition, you just don't have the spare energy, phone range or spare battery power to meet an ambassador's contractual requirements. They don't only ride your coattails, they crack the whip too. The exclusivity clause stopping you from requesting or receiving support from competitive branding is asking too much in a country with a small adventure marketplace. I was an ambassador after the walk for one great company, Adventure Junky, a real-life outdoor adventure game and travel guide. They were fabulous to work with. Another company, an adventure gear store kept asking more from me, and it ended up being too much. Working only from a phone while out on multi-week treks, mostly out of phone range, I was not able to send them files and the ones I did send were not in the correct format. When I needed their sponsorship for a record-setting expedition for climate action, they were not interested so we haven't been in touch since. I would like to see them sponsor more females.

Most of my support came from small, Australian, family-owned businesses, some producing cottage industry handmade gear. I knew that these people couldn't really afford to be giving away what makes them money and in return I supported them as much as possible, generating more business online, write ups on the blog, word of mouth recommendations, showing people the quality of the gear and with my continued loyalty.

It was always the people with the least to give who gave the most.

I was fundraising for a non-profit crisis hotline and eventually sought fundraising support for myself to finish the walk. The entire way, Australians displayed the same pattern as businesses. The ones who supported me the most gave out of compassion for the cause because they had life experience in mental health and suicide prevention. They gave out of empathy, understanding what it is like to live hand to mouth, rationing food when you have no money, panicking because you can't afford shoes, wholly reliant on the generosity of strangers. This is the side of awareness and fundraising campaigns most people never see because we are trying to look strong, confident and successful, while prioritising our message and helping others. We put the needs of others before ourselves until someone reminds us with a cash donation to spend on your own needs, a meal or shelter. A few times kind-hearted people gave me $20 and made it very clear, "This is for you, not the fundraiser."

As I've made clear in this chapter, I believe sexism is as ingrained in adventure and expedition sponsorship as it is in most of Australian society. We are known globally as a sexist nation. I am not non-binary because of this, but I can understand women who write books, scientific papers and produce art under male names, just so they are taken seriously and can make money. Sexism was often in my face while walking around Australia, not only while seeking sponsorship and recognition. Some of it was unintended, as in old ways of thinking handed down through generations, some of it was simply blatant and inappropriate misogyny. How can we raise younger generations to treat each other equally when sexism is inbuilt into our society through nurtured behaviour, conversation and jokes?

Some readers will be uncomfortable with this, some

of you will be angry enough to contact me. You can, if it helps you process your feelings around the issue. Most male, female, trans and non-binary friends and acquaintances of mine are inclusive, actively promote equality and make the outdoors accessible for everyone. Most men know our society is sexist and most men in the adventure community know sexism is rife in clubs, training, employment, expeditions, literature, recognition, accolades and especially clothing. Mostly, it is passive traditional sexism but go online and read some of the criminally offensive things men say about female adventurers, survivalists and leaders. In the safety of their social media groups and 'for the boys' pages, you see another side of adventure misogyny. Australians need to be held accountable for sexism and we must do more to support women who work harder, longer and more persistently than men to achieve equal recognition. This can start with sponsorship, support and celebration, equally, of all genders. In the last 20 years a major Australian adventure society has given achievement awards to 23 women and 69 men. Equality here would be a great place to start.

If you sponsor a female, you can be guaranteed they will do their utmost and push through limits men baulk at, because they have extra motivation. Women get less funding, gear sponsors and online community support. When they set out to do something extraordinary, like walk alone around Australia, they are usually doing it with less money and face the insecurities of not having enough food or gear or needing to ration and make compromises They also often do it without the moral support of a large community cheering them on. Not only are they motivated to prove to themselves and the adventure community it can be done, but they face greater hardships than their male peers. They will do it, and they will do it better, with more strength of will and greater determination.

CHAPTER 32

MOTHER GOANNA AND HER EGGS

WARNING Aboriginal and Torres Strait Islanders mentioned in this chapter may be deceased.

Until 1998 I was shamefully ignorant of Aboriginal cultures, nations, dreamtime stories and massacres, but that year was the beginning of a journey of learning and ever-increasing respect.

When I had my Queensland coxswain ticket, I ran water taxis on the Gold Coast Broadwater for an island resort. The resort was relatively new and after my last taxi run, I did security until the first run the next morning, 12-hour shifts, six days a week. It was a great job and I was good at it. At night I began noticing strange things happening, which were also experienced by other staff and guests: ghostly apparitions, scary energies and poltergeists. One in particular bothered me more than the others. There was a loop road I needed to drive, in the electric buggy, to check half a dozen cabins each night. I was always given that section because the other big brave security guards didn't like it. It began as I came around the bend in the banksia bush, with a feeling of being watched. As I turned into the first cul-de-sac to drive by a cluster of cabins, I could feel something behind me. By the time I entered the other cul-de-sac my hair was standing on end, I felt a chill down my back and felt I was being chased out to the main access track. Honestly, it felt as if I was going to die if I stopped or looked over my shoulder, the buggy couldn't go fast enough.

That happened every night.

As well as this, I had started having strange dreams in sets of threes, warning of things which were about to go wrong on the island, like the water table or storm surges, or letting me know the season to collect a particular seed.

After a month I decided to find an elder of the Aboriginal people from Minjerrabah/(South) Stradbroke Island. Phoning around, I was told by traditional owners that they knew of no elders, or any living descendants of the Quandamooka/Bundjalung/Yuggera nations who had used south Minjerrabah. I was put in touch with a Bundjalung elder living on Minjerrabah/(North) Stradbroke who told me stories from when the islands were one, connected. After explaining what I was experiencing, he evinced surprised I was not Aboriginal, as the spirits traditionally only reached out to the people of their nation. He told me the scary energy was a very angry spirit, angry at the resort for desecrating sacred and significant sites. The spirit felt that I was receptive and was trying to communicate. The elder taught me about the spirits of the land and the ancestors, this one sounded like a protective spirit of the land.

The elder offered me very important advice: "When you meet the spirit, stop, introduce yourself, let it know you mean no harm and are only passing through."

For the dreams, I needed to pay more attention—I wouldn't be getting them unless they were urgent—and let the environment staff know their messages. The water table dreams ended up helping them avoid running their surface tanks dry, and after I pointed out the seeds from the dreams, they were collected to rehabilitate the damaged land around the resort.

As for the spirit who haunted us each night, it became a companion spirit, only for that loop, but I made a point of visiting more regularly to say hello and talk about the Bundjalung history I was learning.

Throughout the years since I have had connections with both spirits of the land and ancestors, always when out alone in wild places, usually through dreams or visions. I became a conduit.

My favourites were in the Alps, walking through Ngarigo, Ngunawal, Jaitmatang and Taungurung country where Wiradjuri, Yuin and Bidwell nations visited and traded during summer. I would find artefacts on the tree line, like grinding stones, in places perfect for camping. Naturally, I would stop, ask permission of the spirits, and make camp, enjoying the same shelter under snow gums, views across the valleys and air infused with the scent of alpine tundra, as the Aboriginal people enjoyed for perhaps 60,000 years, until less than 100 years ago.

As I slept under the tarp or in the tent the most beautiful dreams would visit me through the night. I was allowed to watch as families went about their business making food and textiles, women would come and go with bags of yams, berries and grubs, men came down from the peaks with bogong moths, men and women cleaned possum and kangaroo skins. Emu feathers were woven into their hair, clothes and harvest bags. On occasion I saw huge corroborees, some were during the day and smaller ones were at night. I watched, mesmerised, from a distance, feeling the rhythms, watching their feet dance, flashes of white, yellow and red ochre, sweat reflecting the sun or fire light.

Twice, during rests as I walked along ridgelines, I saw men and boys sitting on granite outcrops and beside navigational tors, holding spears and gazing across the valley to the opposite ridge. I could barely breathe, not wanting them to turn around and see me or break the spell. Only once I dreamt of a war between the Ngarigo tribes and settlers, in Crackenback Valley. In that dream a settler woman rescued injured Ngarigo warriors and sheltered them in her cabin.

There were places I could not walk or camp, such as men's places and those used for sacred lore or significant dreamtime places. This is why I make a habit of asking first. Being attuned to these things certainly makes it easier. At times I could feel when I wasn't welcome and change direction. Each evening, before making camp, I asked the spirits of the land and ancestors if I could camp. If I had a bad feeling in my gut, I moved on; if it felt good or I felt nothing I was allowed to stay. This kept me safe; it protected me.

It was the same for passages through sections of tracks. If an unsettling energy made its presence known I would stop and follow the instructions given by the Bundjalung elder, introducing myself, letting it know I was just passing through and meant it no harm. Every time, that energy immediately changed, feeling like a force opening up in front of me to clear the way.

Knowing these things, being able to feel them, see them, imposed on me the responsibility to walk around Australia with greater care and respect for the traditional owners and their sovereignty.

Circumnavigating Australia took me through at least 130 nations, each of which have their own languages, place names, traditions, food and medicine, taboos, dreamtime stories, sacred plants, animals and places, rites of passage, ancestors, spirits of the land and other sacred knowledge, which as a white I was not permitted to learn.

It was a unique opportunity to learn as much as possible when meeting Aboriginal people on country, to meet them with an open mind and heart, ready to learn and share stories. Many of them loved what I was doing but thought I was crazy. There is a tradition of 'walkabout' in some nations, where an individual will leave home and walk, for many reasons including to clear their mind, find answers, get away from stress, connect to country and/or talk to ancestors. I met a couple of men who regularly do walkabout and we completely understood and respected each other. It is an ideal way to learn more about yourself, your place on this planet, and safely process the big emotions weighing down the heart.

One of the most disappointing aspects of the walk was racism; meeting people who couldn't help themselves from warning me about places or had an offensive opinion to share. I'm not one for letting these things go, but one thing racists share is protecting their ignorance and refusing to engage in challenging civil discussions which contradict them.

The place the most racists warned me about was Yirramugardu/Roebourne, on the west coast near Karratha.

One thing I have learnt is never take someone else's word but go into a new experience with curiosity and openness. We are all influenced by our own biases, therefore our experiences will be different. On my way up the coast, Tangiora Hinaki, a Yirramugardu resident and Maori warrior of the airwaves, interviewed me for ABC Pilbara radio. Tangiora, now with Ngaarda Media, invited me to stay in the family donga out the back of their home when I reached Yirramugardu. A donga is a portable room, usually with a small ensuite and fridge, great for roadhouse accommodation and when your family needs an overflow living space or guest room. Her family were lovely, curious and gave me a warm welcome.

The next day I walked around town, having a bit of a tourist look, before stopping for coffee and a toasted sandwich with local aboriginal women at the café. Aunty Marion Cheedy came across the road from Ngaarda Radio Station. She was due to start her community news program in five minutes and invited me to join her for a chat, live. We didn't have much time, a spontaneous moment. I left the barrow at the café for the women to look after, we ran to the production room and began pretty much straight away. This was a very special interview.

Youth suicide in the Australian Aboriginal population is the worst in the world. I had already met mothers and aunties who had lost their young ones in this way. There is a tragic pattern in communities, one youth suicide will often be followed by others in the following twelve months. Just one young person lost to suicide tears the hearts of the community apart. The further north I walked, the more I would meet local Aboriginal people and listen to their stories of loss. Our interview about suicide prevention was very important; a message of hope, letting people know I was out there walking for them. Ngaarda broadcasts in 30 languages, and Aunty Marion made sure as many people as possible heard the message. As a result of the radio interviews, I was invited to share my story with community centres and medical clinics. It was not easy, and I would get choked up sharing my experience of all the people who helped on my own path to recovery. I could feel the pain amongst these groups, their own struggles with mental health and loss.

In Katherine I spoke at the PCYC for their youth group. They were a great crowd, a mix of Aboriginal and white kids, enthusiastic for their weekly basketball games, movies, dinner and cordial. For a quick 15 minutes, before they grew impatient, I spoke about walking around Australia, mental health, suicide prevention and supporting each other. Afterwards most of them came up to chat, and many of them wanted to talk privately about their family and how to help them. Everyone went home with mental health cards in their pockets. I only wished I had the time to visit every community.

The first time I walked onto Wirangu country in 2004 I tried to request walking passage. I spoke with a white representative of the land council who refused me entry, no questions or negotiations. The second time, in 2014, I spoke with a woman from the Wirangu nation. After explaining how the land is used, where I was permitted to walk and camp, she welcomed me and wished me luck. I turned off the phone, packed it away, and picked up the barrow handles. As I walked onto country I could see and feel the spirits gather around and welcome me. They had traditional body paint, head dress, attire, clapping sticks, carrying smoking branches, coolamons, some were dancing, and they were all smiling. This was the most special welcome to country I have ever experienced. When I close my eyes I can still see them.

Mother goanna and her eggs
As I walked through ancient Purnululu
Surrounded by ancient monuments
Stone carved by aeons of rivers and wind
Deep gorges cut through mountains
Giant boulders sitting on plateaus
Three red eggs perched high above the landscape
There must be a story...

I asked the spirit of the land and she answered. There was a great flood and mother goanna carried her eggs to the highest point to save them. She was carried away by the water as she rescued her babies. They stayed high, dry and safe.

Reaching the next town, I asked about the three boulders on the plateau. The dreamtime story given to me was the same as that belonging to women of Purnululu.

CHAPTER 33

WHAT DO YOU THINK ABOUT?

"What do you think about?"
"Do you meditate?"
"What kinds of music help you walk?"
"Do you listen to books or podcasts?"
"I bet you have lots of time to get to know yourself."

I have often been asked how I kept myself entertained while walking around Australia. It's a good question. At first, I only carried books to read at night. I didn't listen to music, so I could listen to the birds and hear when vehicles were approaching. It was lovely listening to the animals and later, when I did have things to listen to, I often went days without any other noise apart from those of nature. It was the loud traffic which finally convinced me to begin plugging into music.

I reached a point in the walk where I was able to identify the type of vehicle by the sound of the engine before I saw it. I knew what tyres they had, and how many motorcycles were travelling together. Only the caravans stumped me. The sound of the caravan on tow made the engines and tyres sound different. 'Guess The Car' became a game which filled a lot of the road days.

I picked up a cheap $5 two-way radio, with a two-kilometre line-of-sight range and started chatting to truckies. It was only a quick one-minute chat unless it was a long flat plateau and we sometimes had three minutes to talk. On some long stretches of highway, with the right atmospheric conditions at night, we could get five minutes, and every few days we could continue our conversations as the truckies passed by on their regular run between cities. It was a great way to check in on each other. Some truckies would pull over as I reached the end of the highway, knowing it was the last time we'd see each other and wanted to meet face to face.

There was a stage of the walk I almost threw it out because of some of the things I heard the rougher truckies saying to each other and, of course, I could not help but say something in response.

As I left one roadhouse, I met two young female backpackers who had been working there and were heading off to a new job. They were hitchhiking; it was a hot day and they weren't wearing much. From my own years of hitchhiking, I knew it was safest to dress conservatively so as not to attract the wrong kind of lift. We chatted beside the road, about their work, plans and hitchhiking. They were typically friendly and sweet backpackers, and I wished them luck getting a good ride to the city. A few kilometres up the road, as I stopped for morning tea, I tuned in to the radio chatter and was shocked by what I heard. Truckies were talking about the women hitchhiking, and what they would do to them if they had picked them up. I was sitting in the shade, just off the highway in the scrubby bush, out of sight.

Stepping out of the bush I held my radio up to my mouth; as the three trucks approached, I interrupted their abuse and asked them if they would let someone talk about their sisters and daughters like that. Radio silence ensued...

Music also became good company. I had an old iPod loaded with almost every genre of music (no country though, yuck: if you want to torture me, just play country music). Growing up a Countdown fan, I loved Aussie rock and pop. I'm a diehard early Whitlams fan, so some days I listened to them on loop. Aboriginal, world music and funk were also played regularly, anything with a good beat for walking. The days of reminiscing past world travels were spent playing traditional and modern music from countries I had visited.

On the way through some spectacularly rugged landscape in the West Kimberley Ranges, I was really getting into a funk album, dancing and singing as I pushed the barrow beside the highway. As a carload of people and kids drove past, I waved and kept dancing. A moment later they came back, rolled down their windows and asked if I was okay.

"I feel great! How amazing is this place!" I replied, sweeping my hand towards the colourful rock formations and outcrops.

"That's good, we thought you were having a fit."

Is that what my dancing looks like?! With that, I danced with even more vivre. But I toned it down to a bop when other cars passed so nobody else needed to check in on my wellbeing.

After meeting Mats, I loaded up the spare space on my 164GB iPod with every adventure podcast I could find, and many more which explored the sciences, nature, ethics, spirituality and other big ideas. It felt like meeting hundreds of people who I would never have crossed paths with otherwise. I have also now done my own share of podcast interviews about this walk.* When I started the walk, audio books were only available in cassette and CD form, not downloadable. On some highways the roadhouses had audio book swaps for truckies, like community street libraries. It was a well-used service.

I love dinosaurs and megafauna! These would fill my mind on many days while walking through this ancient continent. Crossing the Nullarbor Highway I would imagine the inland sea on one side of me and the Southern Ocean on the other. I could see *Diprotodons* and sabre-toothed tigers, giant kangaroos, rainbow serpents, *Austrosaurus*, *Imperobators*, pterosaurs, even megalodons swimming along the coast. The landscape lent itself to rich daydreams.

There were always more serious things to think about. I solved the world's problems while out there. I didn't read the news much, mostly the local papers, but I wasn't isolated from it. Roadside conversations usually kept me up to date with what was happening around the world and in Australia. I had my social media algorithms tweaked so I only saw good stuff and not news, which meant most of what I heard were major events that had an impact on the people who shared them.

Usually, the news which travellers shared was about gas projects, logging, mines, the latest atrocity by a mining magnate or politician, racism, drugs, poverty, domestic violence, homelessness, extinctions, global warming, mental

* These can be found on my website.

health: the big things as far as I'm concerned. As travellers, we see what is really happening out here and the impacts it has on the environment and communities; it is not only news but is being played out in front of our eyes, in the real world where a cityscape cannot protect and distract us. I was able to report to investigative journalists some of the illegal resource activities of big energy and mining companies and the exploitation of Aboriginal communities, happening out of the public eye. I could have spent weeks, months, stewing over the things I saw and heard but I have made it a habit to act on human injustices and environmental destruction. If I can, I do something about it; if I can't, I hand it to others with more clout.

The wide-open spaces were the most perfect places to process pain, trauma, anger and bad memories. It was a safe space to yell, scream, cry, gesticulate, throw rocks at psychological nemeses, to physically and emotionally let go of it all. I could dump my barrow beside the road, storm off into the bush, release a primal scream from the pit of my belly and then continue walking, feeling lighter and brighter. If therapy had taught me anything, it was to process the trauma and not lock it away, only for it to emerge again later. It was a painful process, the memories sometimes hurt almost more than I could bear, but it was also a healing process. I found answers and strength, learnt where the fault was mine, recognised my mistakes, where I'd ignored warning signs; also where the fault was *not* mine, the situations I had no control over but had to pay the consequences of someone else's actions. I took responsibility where it was mine, made a clear division where it was not, and accepted when it was shared or when it was simply bad luck (wrong place, wrong time) for everyone involved. After doing that, I physically made an imaginary box with my hands, opening it I neatly coiled the memory into the box, like a ship's rope, and put it down on the ground, leaving it behind and walking on.

It was not mentally sustainable to do this every day or for every messy memory that arose. Somewhere on the west coast I learnt to say "no" to the memories if I didn't have the energy to work through them. The memory would pop into my head, and I could acknowledge it and make a written note in my notebook to address it the next day. Then I let it go, emptying my mind by singing the Buddhist chant Oṃ maṇi padme hūṃ until my mind cleared, calmed and I could walk in meditation.

I had many daydreams about meeting Keanu Reeves again*, he always had a hot margherita pizza on the back of his motorbike. I wondered if cats could be allergic to humans. I would make up words, my favourite were groups of animals and things, a group of thongs is a throng. I learnt morse code and tried to design my own code. Most importantly, I chose who would join my zombie apocalypse team.

---

* I used to workout at the gym with him while he filmed the first matrix film. We both went while it was quietest, he went so as not to be bothered, I went when all the machines and weights were free. At the time I had no idea who he was, just a gym buddy.

EPILOGUE

WHAT'S NEXT?

Finishing the walk around Australia felt strange. It was exciting, with lots of radio and TV interviews as I walked down the dunes to the ferry. I met friends and family on both sides of the ferry who walked the last few kilometres with me to Nobbys Beach, chatting all the way. It was a special moment, and I was glad to share them with my biggest supporters. At the end, when the film crews arrived, they peeled off so I was alone again for the final few hundred metres.

Up ahead, on the beach steps the rest of the family were waiting, with a huge banner and, wrapping me in it, we all hugged, joked and laughed.

I didn't know what emotions would surface that day; would I cry or want to escape the crowd or feel euphoric? The day before, after leaving Monique's home, I had a moment sitting on top of the biggest dune for lunch (packed by Monique). A moment of reflection, thinking of all the people who helped and donated, making the walk possible, carrying me with their kindness all the way to the end. The Williamtown RAAF jets flew by as I ate lunch and I waved to the pilots who were so close I saw them waving back. That feeling I would get as a kid, the excitement the noisy jet engines would elicit in me, rose and became a flash of excitement about my own accomplishment.

I knew when I started, I would finish it, no matter how long it took, so it wasn't a surprise for me. The whole way I knew there would be a successful end one day. I guess I had been preparing mentally for it for a long time.

Every interview that day was a celebration of the completion of an epic adventure; the end was being pre-played through our conversations before I reached it. Any emotion which could have built up in those last 25 kilometres was dispersed by the time I reached Nobbys, arriving with a clear head and prepared for more TV and radio.

Pride was probably the strongest feeling I had. Proud of my own achievement and proud to have my family there with me. Relief was another strong feeling: relief that I wasn't finishing alone, that there were people to share the biggest moment of my life with. I was worried it would be only Mum and Dad there to pick me up, as they had often done at the end of smaller adventures. It was a big deal to see a crowd of excited familiar faces.

In the last 100 metres I fleetingly wondered if I was expected to cry and why I didn't feel tears coming, before remembering I'm autistic, I don't need to do what is expected of me. Inside my head, this was the same as finishing any other trek, but with a big banner, family and friends and news crews. I was very practical about it all: hug everyone, take photos, pose for newspapers, chat live on the radio and quickly walk back and forth for the TV so they could get their stories onto the 6pm local news. My 20 minutes of fame: I had to milk it!

Nearing the end, the most common question became, "What will you do next?"

Stopping at Nobbys Beach didn't feel right. I wasn't mentally prepared to finish and was at a loss as to what came the next day, week, month. I finished with a strong body and mind, there was no need to rest and recuperate from injuries or exhaustion. It only made sense to keep walking, so I kept going on the Great North Walk, as a 'cool down', until I decided it was time to stop.

And after that? For five years I have been promising this book. I was approached by four publishers for the story but no matter how many times I tried I couldn't get past the sixth chapter. I was also asked for the book to be adapted into a film (call me).

Instead of writing a book I did a lot of public speaking, podcast interviews, more expeditions and have begun a slow section bicycle tour around Australia which will probably take a few more years to complete. I have dabbled in making short films and my own podcast. There are so many things I want to do but this lifestyle limits my ability to keep gear charged, get to the places I need to be and find the spare energy needed for these goals. Many will need to wait until I can afford a reliable vehicle for remote travel; realistically, this will not be anytime soon with so many other expeditions lined up for the next nine years.

During the walk I met a lot of cyclists, riding their bicycles across or around Australia. It was these encounters which prompted my own ride around Australia. A few months after finishing the walk I bought a touring bike, a Surly Disc Trucker named Eva Jean, after my grandmother, and rode my first 1000 kilometres from Adelaide, down and around Kangaroo Island and across to Mount Gambier, close to the Victorian border. I was still experiencing some PTSD from the Barkly Highway incident and had to stop for a while before a 600-kilometre ride up the coast to see Steve, Sil and Linda. I have since ridden 7,000 kilometres between Melbourne and Cape York and the outback.

Over the next few years, I will ride more sections in the cooler months until completing another lap of Australia. On the bike I can travel places I could not walk, it's faster, and I'll do most sections in the opposite direction, so I can see the views which were behind me on the walk (and there will be more tailwind than headwind). In the winter of 2026, there will be a hiatus from the ride for something a little bit different. I'll be tapping into my Norse Viking heritage, going a little berserk and embarking on a raid, conquering a goal I have failed to achieve in the last two attempts: the full traverse of the Australian Alps in winter. My last winter attempt was 610 kilometres with fire closures and a pandemic; it set a new snowshoe record, but my personal goal is still waiting to be claimed. The next traverse will raise awareness about chronic traumatic encephalopathy (CTE). It will be filmed and there will be beards.

Adventures are starting to feel urgent, and I regularly need to slow down, relax and be mindful. I have had eight concussions from sports and accidents, and I have all the signs of chronic traumatic encephalopathy, including memory loss, aggression, cognitive dysfunction, involuntary shakes and apathy. This is dementia from multiple concussions, which can't be diagnosed from scans on a living brain; my brain will go to the Sports Brain Bank if I die in a controlled environment. I am starting to feel time running out for what I want to write, and for further adventures. Where this takes me over the next five years I do not know. It is a little bit scary: not the dying part but losing my hard-earned freedom. Riding around Australia, completing a full winter snowshoe traverse of the Australian Alps, sailing around Australia and hopefully a few more books are waiting for me, if my brain holds on for another ten years.

THANK YOU!

I must first acknowledge all the people, literally thousands of you, who helped me along the way with food, water and shelter; many of you were strangers when we met, but you invited me into your homes and we separated as friends. My online community gave me the moral support I needed to keep going, and sharing the walk with friends who were able to help was invaluable. I would not have been able to do this without you.

Thank you to my Patreon patrons and the people who contributed to my fundraisers, for both the suicide hotline non-profit and for myself. Your contribution helped phone counsellors listen to people in crisis and allowed this walk to keep going when I ran out of funds.

ABC regional radio stations, newspapers and local TV not only helped me but uncountable thousands more who were able to find their own paths to recovery and therapy by listening to stories of, reading about and watching my walk. Many of them came out to talk to me, as their first step in seeking help. I cannot overstate how vital media support is for suicide campaigns. Programmers and presenters don't see the results of their interviews, but I can assure you, hundreds of lives were saved sharing my story with your audiences. Big shout out to Totally Wild who filmed some bushwalking safety with me in Meanjin. The message is still helping many people struggling with mental health through a score of podcast interviews and Oliver Pelling's Red Bull interview.

Slappas, Tier Gear, Terra Rosa Gear, Wilderness Threadworks, Mont, Toll Ipec, Blue Dinosaur, Shotz, Power Super Foods, Hemp Foods Australia, Honest to Goodness, Loving Earth, Strive Food, Wilderness Sports Jindabyne, Columbia, Barefoot Inc Australia, YHA Thredbo, Dockside Food and Coffee, Bridport Backpackers, The Gladstone, Binalong Bungalows, St Helens Community Newsletter, Beachfront Bicheno, Waves Holiday House, Orford Blue Waters, Hamilton Inn, Derwent Bridge Chalets and Studios, Queenstown Motor Lodge, Hanlon Guest House, Penguin Seaside, Bannockburn Station, Creswick Holiday Park, Dunsborough Lakes Holiday Park, Cape to Cape Tours, Prevelly Caravan park, Hamelin Bay Holiday Park, Flinders Bay Caravan Park, Blackwood Mead, Pemberton Caravan Park, Northcliffe Hotel, Green Haven Tourist Park, Gibson Soak, Salmon Gums, The Railway Motel and Woodlands Guesthouse, Kalgoorlie Quality Inn, Kambalda Hotel, Caiguna Roadhouse, Cocklebiddy Roadhouse, Eucla Motel, Head of Bight Whale Watching, Penong Ampol, Streaky Bay Motel and Villas, Calypso Star Shark Cage Diving, Whyalla Sundowner Hotel, Motel Poinsettia, Bosons at Port Germein, Travelway Port Pirie, Lifeline Port Pirie, The Marina Hotel, YHA Lancelin Lodge, Lancelin IGA, Jurien Bay Tourist Park, Leeman Caravan Park, Dongara Denison Beach Holiday Park, S Bend Caravan Park, Billabong Roadhouse, Hamelin Pool Caravan Park, Wooramel Roadhouse, Carnarvon Motel, Nanutarra Roadhouse, Pilbara Motorcycle Sisters, Whim

Creek Hotel, Port Haven Village, Sandfire Roadhouse, Shelamar Station, Eco beach Resort, Roebuck Roadhouse, Stoked, Matsos Brewery, Roebuck Bay Hotel Fundraiser, Broome Time Resort, Willare Roadhouse, Spinifex Hotel, Kimberley Hotel, Doon Doon Station, Kimberleyland Waterfront Holiday Park, Wirib Tourism park, Victoria River Roadhouse, Hayes Creek Wayside Inn, Oasis Tourist park, Crocosaurus Cove Cage of Death, Value Inn, Lifeline Darwin, Bowning Hotel, Darlington Point Riverside Caravan Park, Balranald Motor Inn, Euston Riverfront Caravan Park, The Shouse BnB, Burra Bon Accord, Spalding Hotel, Fleur de Lis BnB, Beagle Motor Inn, Cutta Cutta Caves, Bitter Springs Cabins and Camping, Larrimah Pink Panther, Maryfield Station, Daly Waters Pub, Elliot General Store, Threeways Roadhouse, Barkly Homestead, Avon Downs Police, Babinda Quarters, Innisfail Woolworths, Tully Motel, Cardwell Beachfront, Ayr Traveller's Motel, Bowen Senior Citizens, Scott Martin Acupuncture, MacKay Lifeline, BarraCrab Caravan Park, Royal Oak Hotel, Capricorn Caves, The Coast Motel, The Links Camping, Quest Rockhampton, Mantra Gladstone, 1770 Lagoons Central Apartment Resort, Baffle Creek Nomad Caravan Park, Burrum Heads Beachfront Tourist Park, K'gari Beach Resort, Dilli Village Campsite, The Spotted Chook Ferme Auberge and Amelies Petite Maison, Landsborough Holiday Park, Glasshouse Mountains Ecolodge, Woodford Hotel, Dag Pub, Cabins @ The View, Bearded Dragon Hotel, Mountain Brew Coffee, O'Reilly's Rainforest Retreat, Binna Burra Lodge, Log Cabin Camp, The Happy Herb Shop Uki, Main Arm General Store, The Brunswick, YHA Byron Bay, Red Rock Reflections Holiday Park, Hat

Head Holiday Park, Crescent Head Beauty and the Beach, Waves Campground, Port Macquarie Lifeline, Travel Play Live, Blueys Motel, Reflections Hawks Nest Holiday Park. I can't remember every business who helped on this journey, there were so many, thank you.

Loyalty Beach Campground friends, Patsy, Sue, Moon, Thalma, Lea, Eli, Louma, Austin, Camil, Matt, Luke, Zac, Ellie May, Andy, Maribel, Rami, Froggy, 22, have been very generous these last two months as I've camped in the hammock by the beach, doing a little cleaning for pocket money, drinking lots of coffee, watching the crocodiles cruise past. It has been the most perfect location, sitting here on Gudang Yadhaykenu Atambaya Angkamuthi land, under the verandah, in the cool breeze, looking out over Torres Strait. It took five years to seriously knuckle down and write this promised book, but this was the right time and place.

My family and friends, thanks for putting up with me, helping during this and many other expeditions before and since, and during several earlier attempts to write this, and all your messages of support. I might not show my gratitude enough, but I remember you all and everything you do for me.

Last, but not least, my friend, adventure buddy and editor, Wendy Bruere, who responded to an open invitation to join my alpine snowshoe expedition during the pandemic in 2020, arriving in the midst of a team dynamics crisis and sticking by me since. This book would never have happened without your encouragement, guidance and support. Thank you.

APPENDIX I

WRONG GEAR

As mentioned in Snow Falling on Waratahs, the beginning of the shakedown section walking around lutruwita/Tasmania was an example of taking too much (so as to be beyond criticism). I knew from 20-odd years of solo trekking experience that it was too much but had to prove to myself and supporters that most of what we think we need isn't always necessary. After lugging all this gear around for 400 kilometres I changed to an ultralight kit.

I won't mention brands as I had no sponsorship for lutruwita. Where a brand offered support by way of a discount, I will mention them.

This is what I started with:

- 80lt backpack
- 20lt day pack
- 2 backpack rain covers
- 2-person tent
- Tent footprint/ground sheet
- Large inflatable down sleeping mat
- Alpine winter rated sleeping bag (it was the only one I owned at the time)

- Large silk sleeping bag liner
- Small inflatable down pillow
- Pillow slip
- Spirit burner, pressure pump, 1.5lt white spirits in 2 steel canisters, wind break
- Cooking pot, pan, mug, utensils
- Walking poles
- Topographic and road touring maps
- Photocopied sheets from the Camping Australia guide (the days before apps)
- Letter of authority to fundraise for selected charity and police clearance to work with kids
- Compass
- Large map case
- GPS
- Emergency beacon
- Notebook, pens, drawing pencils
- 2 reading books
- Pack of cards
- Laptop and bubble wrap bag
- Phone
- Camera
- Headlamp
- Batteries, power banks, cables, wall charger
- Tissues, toilet paper, baby wipes, trowel, female standing urination funnel
- Soap, deodorant, toothbrush, paste, nail clippers, tweezers, comb
- Essential relaxing oil, teatree oil, clove oil, foot balm, muscle rub

- Swamp strength insect repellent
- Teatree antimicrobial foot talc
- Trekking sandals
- High ankle rigid hiking boots (Colorado)
- 7 pairs merino hiking socks
- 7 pairs merino sock liners
- 7 sets merino sports bras and undies
- 2 sets of thermal l/s shirts and leggings (Colorado)
- 1 set of silk thermals
- 3 pairs of hiking trousers
- 5 airflow fishing shirts (Colorado)
- 1 polarfleece jumper
- 1 Gortex rain jacket
- 1 pair Gortex rain pants
- 1 pair Gortex gaiters
- 2 beanies, 2 pairs of gloves, 2 neck socks, 1 balaclava
- 1 comprehensive first aid kit
- Sunscreen, wide brim sun hat, sunglasses
- Nutritional supplements
- Maximum 10 days of food, snacks, coffee and powdered milk between resupplies
- Capacity for 8lt of water in bottles and bladders
- Straw water filtration device
- An occasional bottle of local cider or beer.
- Folding tripod stool
- Repair kit
- Laundry bag, soap, pegs, line and laundromat coins
- Good luck talismans and other gifts
- Various water-resistant stuff sacks for compartmentalising.

APPENDIX II

ULTRALIGHT GEAR

After 400 kilometres carrying more than 40 kilograms of gear in two packs, back and front, it was time to switch almost everything out and replace it with ultralight and lightweight gear. The new kit weighed only 15 kilograms with food and water and made the last 800 kilometres of walking around lutruwita much more enjoyable.

This is the list:

- 65lt pack (included two 2.5lt front pouches)
- Light summer weight sleeping bag
- Light inflatable bed mat
- Nylon ground sheet
- Sil-nylon 2x3m tarp, 6 pegs and small gauge cordage
- Spirit burner, 600ml fuel bottle, wind break
- 600ml pot/mug
- 1 spork
- Topographic maps
- Compass
- Small map case
- Emergency beacon

- 1 reading book
- Small notebook and 1 pen
- Phone
- Camera
- Charger
- Headlamp and batteries
- Pocket tissues, small pouch baby wipes, toilet trowel
- Soap, toothbrush (cut in half), nail clippers, tweezers
- Swamp strength insect repellent
- Thongs/flipflops
- High ankle rigid sole hiking boots
- 3 pairs socks and liners
- 3 sets of underwear
- 1 set of silk thermals
- 3 trousers
- 3 shirts
- 1 polarfleece
- 1 rain jacket
- 1 rain pants
- 1 beanie, 1 gloves, 1 neck sock
- 1 solo first aid kit
- Sunscreen, sun hat, sun glasses
- 4 days of food and snacks
- 6lt water
- Straw water filtration
- Repair kit
- Laundry soap and pegs
- Various stuff sacks

APPENDIX III

WHAT'S IN THE BARROW?

Using a barrow or trailer was essential for the long remote distances, traversing the continent a few times. Many people who traverse continents push a baby trolley or pull a converted bike trailer. I pushed a barrow designed from my previous trek experience using trollies and trailers. The barrow had a lot of room to carry more than the basic necessities and it was much easier pushing than pulling or carrying.

Here is the final barrow design. The original, a pea pod shape with rolled alloy was going to cost at least $10,000 and a fibreglass mould would cost much more, so I had to forget about aesthetics and be practical.

The Barrow

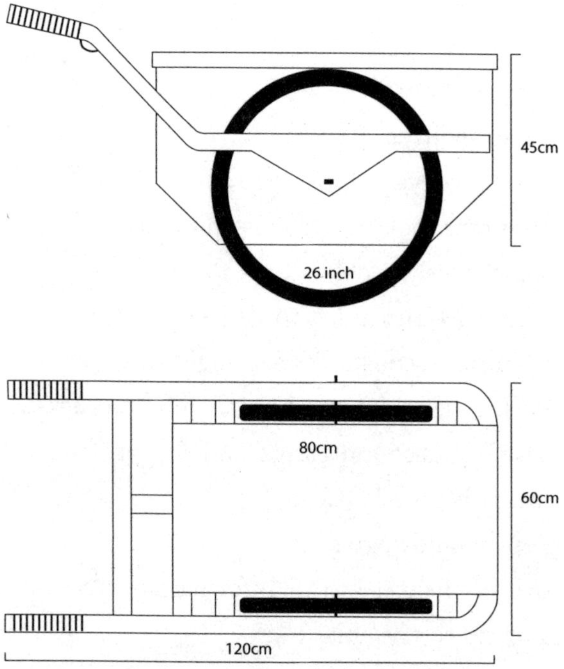

With a greater carrying capacity, about 200 litres, I packed more comforts. I didn't tell anyone this during the walk, but the barrow was really easy to push, even fully loaded, on flat hard surfaces. Gear was switched around a lot according to seasons, distance between food and water, distraction hobbies and size of my personal library.

- One person tent and ground sheet
- Sleeping mat
- Small pillow and slip
- Sleeping bag and liner
- Blanket
- Books
- Laptop

- Music
- Craft hobbies
- Yoga mat
- Playing cards
- Up to 50 litres of water
- Up to 10 days of food
- Different cooking systems and fuels, sometimes no cooker
- First aid kit to assist roadside emergency response
- Wildlife rescue kit for overnight care
- Basic toiletry kit, toothbrush, mini toothpaste, soap bar, deodorant stick, nail clippers, tweezers, foot rub, muscle rub
- Repairs and spares kit
- Bag of mental health information cards, flyers and stickers to give out
- Bag of fun gifts, badges, stickers, toys to give out
- Hiking boots, changed to trail runners, changed to thongs, changed to ultralight barefoot boots
- Fresh food for two days out of each town—bananas, avocados, oranges, tomato, cucumber, hommus, flat bread
- Rations – turmeric porridge, nutritional supplements, electrolytes, fruit powders, energy bars, peanut butter, dried fruits, lots of nuts and seeds.

APPENDIX IV

TRAUMA BACKSTORY

Here is a true "appendix": a small part of the bowel, the shitty backstory, the parts of life which sometimes need removing because they cause so much pain we want to die.

I did not want to write too much of this into the book. There are too many mental health triggers for readers. For those of you curious about why I live with PTSD, depression, anxiety and have tried taking my life several times, this appendix will give more insight. Please remember as you read that I am still recovering, and managing my safe space is a lifelong commitment.

My birth, in 1972, was traumatic. I can't remember, but I was facing the wrong way, pulled out with forceps, badly bruised and in intensive care for two days.

For more than three years I was deaf, only hearing loud sounds like yelling, but loud sounds also hurt. The small bones in my ears had not developed. It was difficult for my parents, needing to yell to communicate. It was not the best foundation for a relationship with their first child, taking a toll on all three of us. Imagine being yelled at all through your formative years. Imagine needing to yell at your child every time you needed to communicate. I imagine a great deal of those years were silent, to reduce the stress. They were silent for me.

I was an escapist from the moment I could crawl. Our neighbour found me crawling down the road before I could walk. No matter how much mum child-proofed the house I always found a way to get out and go exploring, usually down the road. As soon as my sister could walk, I would take her too.

My parents could tell I was different to other kids. Parties were bad, alone time was good. Especially my own parties, which normally ended up with me losing my shit and running away to hide. These were much later identified as autism meltdowns. It was the noise and crowds. they physically hurt my sensory system.

One of my earliest memories is of being three years old, inside the children's hearing clinic. I remember the glass windows, reception desk, bright walls, lots of toys. I was placed into a booth with a window facing into the clinic; a lady put my headphones on and pointed to a panel of bulbs and buttons in front of me. If I could hear a beep in my ears, I had to press the button. I remember the first time I heard something and pressed the button. It was exciting, it felt like I had finally done something right.

In another memory, I was standing outside under the Hills Hoist clothesline while mum put out the laundry. I was four years old. I had had a buzzing in my ears, like tinnitus, for a few weeks, but it was impossible for me to explain this to mum as I didn't have the vocabulary. I have had it ever since, for half a century, never a moment without the buzzing inside my head. Sometimes it hurts, especially in crowds and enclosed spaces, or where the noise of machinery such as garden tools, mowers, blowers or jet skis, cause the buzz to go static and send piercing pain through my head. The higher the pitch, timbre, frequency, the more it hurts.

Around this time, I was diagnosed with ADD and given Ritalin. I was one of the first children in Australia to get it. My parents were alarmed by what it did to me: apparently it dulled me so much that I had no energy or interest in anything, like an empty shell of a child. They took me off it within a few months.

The summer before I began school, dad took me to the school grounds to show me around. It was the same state school he went to. During that walk around I saw some boys riding bikes down the stairs. It impressed me so much I went home and tried doing the same with my Trinky Dink trike bike, down the back stairs of the house. I remember it, riding over the first step, bouncing to the edge and falling. There is a memory gap between falling and waking up on the lawn amidst flashing lights then being carried away. It is all a blank again after that. I didn't even know until years later that I had a broken nose and smashed lip which needed surgery.

School was hell. So much so I tried getting a class action together to take them to court after I tried suiciding in my 30s. This section will be difficult to read if you are a victim of child sex abuse, bullying and teacher bullying.

That is a WARNING

I went to school at four years old. My hearing was then about 50 percent. I remember kindy lessons, having no idea what the classes were about. The square counting blocks were great for building things, but during story book time I could only hear mumbling and would get in trouble for squirming and not being able to cross my legs properly. There were times it was easier for the teacher to just let me go outside and wander around the playground, playing hop skip jump or following the snakes and ladders painted on the concrete. If I was lucky, another teacher had left a ball, Hoola Hoop or spring plank out.

This only set me up to be a target for a groomer. It was either the gardener or cleaner who tried making friends with me. Over the next two years he groomed me to keep secrets, meeting after school, touching me inappropriately and wanting me to kiss his penis. My memory has blocked some things, but I have been scared of public toilets ever since. I still have PTSD school toilet night terrors. The school completely denied all my claims. I also have dreams of walking through the abandoned school grounds with a crowbar, looking for the child abuser and enablers.

In 1st class, when I was only five, one teacher decided early in the year that she didn't like me or two boys, Sean and Shane. Sean and Shane's parents were able to pull them out of that school and send them to another. My parents had no idea of what was happening because I was too scared to tell them. The teacher picked on us relentlessly. In almost every recess and lunch we did something wrong: we were too quiet, too talkative, laughing too loud, sitting on the wrong seat. She confiscated the boys' tennis balls, crayons and toys, which we would steal back by sneaking into the classroom during lunch and getting them out of her desk. This was also a reason for her to hit us. When Sean and Shane left, I was on my own. In class, if I needed to go to the toilet, I would be punished by being made to stand in front of everyone and recite the days of the week, months of the year or planets in the solar system. She didn't do this only to me: anyone who needed the toilet was treated like this; five-year-olds were expected to remember to go during recess or lunch. I was not the only one who peed their pants in front of the class, or in our seats because we were too scared to ask. I remember trying to tell her about the man behind the classroom who asked me to kiss his penis. She told me I was a liar.

In 2nd class I broke my leg during lunch, playing horse chases and being hit from the side by a boy doing sprint races. Guess who was on playground patrol? I was lying on the ground, unable to get up, probably crying from pain or fear or both. She insisted I stand up, but I couldn't, so she grabbed my arm, yelling. Violently yanking me to my feet, she hit me. Luckily, my 2nd class teacher, Miss Harris, and the school mistress had been told I needed help. They came running down, scooped me up and ran back to the sick bay.

Many years later, I told the school about the abusive teacher, and how many other students I had been in touch with had confirmed they had also been bullied by her. They denied all of it, saying she was one of their favourite and most respected teachers. I still have PTSD night terrors of her: being trapped under a desk, peeing myself in front of people, locked in a storage room, forgetting the months of the year, being hit.

In 3rd class the student bullying began: wrist burns, name calling, being spat at, being called retard and spastic. I was a loner with transient friends who quickly rejected me or preferred to keep our friendship secret and out of school; some of the latter were friends only because our parents were church friends, so we had to play together. The worst incident was just after school one day. I was about to leave to walk home when a bunch of big boys grabbed me. Four of them pinned me to the ground while two others rode their bikes over my stomach. When I reported it I was called a liar. I once threw a handful of rocks at the boy who had spat on my back: I had had enough. The boy told the principal I was lying about the spitting and the principal believed him. I was caned, had to say sorry and be nice to him, and burned with the injustice of it.

My first memories of obvious behaviours pointing at depression and PTSD were as early as eight, when I developed a comfort eating disorder. I would steal whole frozen cheesecakes, tubs of ice cream, packets of biscuits, then hide under the house and eat until sick. I still lapse back into this unhealthy coping mechanism. I also spent a lot of time alone in the yard crying. The only time I felt safe was alone in the bushland and later with a horse called Joe.

Signs of learning difficulty, developmental issues and anxiety were there from the beginning.

Another WARNING: this one is about cult church abuse

I was raised in a conservative fundamentalist Baptist reformed family. It didn't start that way; we first went to a normal Baptist church full of young families. I was real friends with some of the kids, until the church split and my parents went with the extreme crowd who formed the 'reformed' church. It was awful! Not just being unable to see my real friends anymore, but the change in pious religious practice: the control of young minds and their behaviour, door knocking, loss of freedoms, the guilt tripping and the consequences of that control.

Thankfully, as a neurodivergent child it was not easy to control me or mold my mind. I was born wilful, rebellious and with a different basic grasp of right and wrong. When they did try to control my mind I fought against it, within my disciplinary tolerance. I could not memorise scripture verses or catechism lessons, and they all eventually gave up on me. I hated going to church, not just disliking it. It made me angry, sad and sick. Weekly morning and evening church, Bible study, prayer meetings, youth group and weekend door knocking were the worst things in my life. I dreaded every church event and tried every way of getting out of them. I hated church to the core of my being. Hate is a strong word; my feelings and memories are still strong too.

Because I would not conform, I was rewarded with a continuous guilt trip from my parents, church leaders and peers until I was 16 years old. Door knocking in neighbourhoods where kids from my school lived was humiliating. The worst was their control of our education and entertainment. The pastor and his wife would read books and watch films before they were approved or banned for church youth. When the school introduced personal development classes about puberty, dating, sex, drugs and consent, the pastor told our parents we were not to attend. This was one of the worst decisions and had one of the greatest consequences for my later life. I have trouble writing about it: my heart rate is up, breathing has shallowed, scalp is tingling and all the hate for the church is bubbling up again.

Was it a cult? Yes. I had refused to be baptised and my behaviour was noticed by the church leaders, so two females, the pastor's daughter who was my age and the youngest elder's wife, took me to my favourite picnic spot (which I loved because of the memories it held of my grandpa). We had a picnic and went for a walk before they sat me down and had a hard chat about how my rebelliousness and refusal to give my soul to their god was holding my dad back from becoming an elder. That was the last straw for me; my head and heart would never be Christian, but I physically had to go through the motions to save face for my parents.

When we moved away, I was 16 years old and aware enough to know what was happening. The church tried to tell us where we could worship. They gave us an ultimatum: if we didn't worship there, they would disown us. We moved somewhere not on their prescribed list and the church cut us off, instructing members to have nothing to do with us, including the youth. Other cult signs, if you need more evidence, were picking and choosing extra beliefs like mansions in heaven, believing the Bible is literally the words of a god (to be followed to the letter), a secret magazine and tape-recording mail-order catalogue, and beliefs such as the dinosaurs didn't exist and the Earth is only 9,000 years old.

WARNING: sexual crimes, abuse and rapes

Being different, on the autism spectrum, made me a vulnerable target for predators outside of school. As explained above, I was banned from school lessons about sex and consent. The day after finishing senior high school I was on a bus to a town called Young where I spent a month picking cherries. I enjoyed the job. On the final night we all went into town for an end-of-season party. I did the right thing and stuck with soft drinks, I had never used alcohol or drugs and at the time had no intention of trying them. The club closed after the taxis had stopped running so I had to walk a few kilometres back to the caravan I rented. One of the guys, a pom called Andy, kindly offered to walk me home. At the caravan he asked for a drink, so I made us two glasses of cordial. Then my body began to go numb. I was paralysed but fully conscious as he raped me.

For seven years I thought it was my fault: I had asked for it by letting him walk me home. Then sitting in a café, eavesdropping on two women's conversation, I learned I was drugged and raped. My first adult sexual experience was rape, which I had to keep secret because I was supposed to be a virgin bride.

While backpacking through southeast Asia, a Bima local on Sumbawa, Indonesia, tried molesting or possibly raping me while I was sleeping. I had fallen asleep while waiting on a bus and woke to find a man with his arm up my culturally appropriate ankle length skirt. I grabbed his arm and broke it over the back of a bus seat. I was in shock for days afterwards. The ex-husband I was travelling with didn't know what to do but took no responsibility for having left me alone to have a drink.

In Darwin in 2006, on New Years night, walking back to the backpackers from a friend's home, I was raped from behind with a knife held against my throat. The attacker said they knew me and would kill me if I told anyone. I quit my job and moved. Three months later I had an abortion.

Only a few years ago I learned about another rape which happened to me in 2005. The company ship I worked on at the time had shore leave in Broome, so we all went out and partied. I was drunk but one of the crew and I were keen on each other, so we went back to his room in a share house. Until 2019, I thought it was him I had sex with, but apparently he fell asleep making us a cuppa and someone else entered his room and raped me. I tried following it up with the company but was stonewalled and threatened.

Basically, if anyone tries touching me these days I want to punch their throat.

WARNING: Emergency First Responder PTSD

Some complex trauma timelines are not tidy. While life went on, I pushed everything down and locked it away, a bad survival technique learned in childhood.

An emergency first responder is any professionally trained individual or team who arrives first on scene in an emergency situation, such as natural disasters, accidents, search and rescue and domestic violence, to save humans, animals and property.

Over the last 35 years I have been involved in this work in both professional and volunteer roles. In Venturers we assisted the alpine search and rescue teams, being trained in the process. I have been able to apply this training many times since. One time I led a team of police into the mountains at dusk to rescue two small children left on the track by their parents. It left us, the police and I, flabbergasted when the parents explained how they took their family of six down the track hoping to find a hill to watch the sunset. The early darkness and rapid temperature drop caught them unprepared. To get the two babies back to the cabin quickly, the other two children (who "would have slowed them down") were left waiting beside the track for the father to return for them, trusting them to stay put. The children were frightened and began walking, ending up off the track and lost, on the wrong side of the valley. We found them alive just on last light. The parents never bothered to thank me, but the police gave me an award.

Not all rescues have good endings. During my years in maritime search and rescue, I was on call-out and attended many incidents, usually breakdowns or sinking boats. I occasionally performed resuscitation or retrieved drowned bodies. But one jet ski accident stands out more than the rest. It happened on the weekend, right in front of our rescue base during lunch, with the entire crew watching. We were able to respond immediately: in the water and at the scene within three minutes. When our rapid response team reached the injured jet skier, I had to hold his head steady to stabilise his spine while another volunteer positioned themselves on the jet ski to apply first aid until paramedics arrived. He had been hit by another jet ski from behind, his skull was smashed into three pieces and his brain was coming out between my fingers. Unbelievably, he survived massive head and spine trauma and came back six months later to thank us.

For seven years, across three states, I volunteered in

rural fire brigades, twice through devastating fires. Being young, a fast runner and switched on, I was often sent to the front or ran a backburn through a gully or around homes. I enjoyed the job, the adrenaline and the genuine gratitude from people. On Karta Pintingga/Kangaroo Island I joined the Kingscote Fire Brigade in 2004. We trained twice every week and attended a few small grass fires. At 10pm one night my pager went off and the phone rang; there was a fire on Cape Hart, a very remote part of the island. Within half an hour a crew of us were dressed and leaving the station to navigate our truck across the island, through national park and sandy 4WD tracks to save a farmstead. The crew from Penneshaw were about to run out of water when we arrived, and another crew arrived soon after us.

The hot dry summer night was dangerous and windy, and the fire began generating its own wind. As we contained this one, others were spreading across the island. We saved the house using foam spray, but the fire jumped our line soon after sunrise. We had to retreat when we ran out of water. As the wind increased, the fire moved across the island faster, cutting off roads. We took the most direct route out to Wilson River Road. The sandy road was rough, but we had to go as fast as possible with the fire closing in behind us. The cabin was full and I rode on the back with one other crew member. We had the hoses and used the last of our water to stop the fire overtaking us. Our spare water ran out and the fire began to engulf us, licking at the tyres, blistering paint. We thought we were going to die. At that moment the bush to our right opened up into a sheep property. Our driver left the track, smashed through the fence and saved us.

We were sent to Penneshaw where the Red Cross emergency response team treated us for smoke inhalation, sore eyes and offered debriefing. We had been out for more than 12 hours and we all fell asleep in our chairs or lying on the ground. Twenty-four hours later we were back out there chasing spot fires around American River, Pelican Reserve and Brown Beach. The following day I joined a crew mopping up, wetting down and cooling off hot spots where the fire had been through.

It was too soon for me and I had trouble with immediate PTSD; I could still do my job, but it was the last fire I attended. That fire burnt almost half the island although thankfully no human lives were lost. Since then every fire season puts me on alert and when it's bad I can become catatonic, paralysed with fear.

Note, there were a few bad fire seasons at the start of this century where volunteer firefighters were not as lucky as us. Certain rules and training have been made mandatory to try and prevent this happening again, including more systems fitted to the trucks to protect crews and a reserve tank of water for emergencies. Comms and satellite imaging has improved a lot in 20 years.

Let's move onto a lighter trauma, one which might have increasing impacts as I get older. Eight concussions have resulted in possible chronic traumatic encephalopathy, as mentioned previously. Most of them were sports concussions, but not football. Some were from bike riding, roller skating, horse riding, sailing and yoga. The worst was on a ship, hitting my head on the top bunk and then falling unconscious for 15 hours before anyone checked on me to see why I had missed my watch. After vomiting over the side of the ship and losing my balance, I was evacuated to hospital. It took 12 years before I could stand on the deck of a ship without falling to my knees from vertigo. I still cannot stand on solid ground with my eyes closed without falling.

When I travelled around the world in my 20s and 30s it was mostly independently and off the beaten path. This took me to war torn countries, disputed borders and slums – I witnessed acts of terrorism. At the time I was trying to learn as much as possible and how I could help. It wasn't until later I realised the mark these experiences had on my suppressed memories, especially watching a bus with passengers being blown up by Moaist terrorists in Kathmandu, Nepal. I have been robbed, caught in landslides and floods, had people shoot at me, almost died from blood poisoning and malaria; but none of that compared to watching the bus explode.

The final thing I want to add is the impact of living on the autism spectrum. As mentioned earlier, I was diagnosed with ADD as an infant. My parents and grandparents knew I was different and some of my teachers helped with learning difficulties. In my earliest memories I already had gender dysphoria. I thought I was a boy, then prayed I wouldn't reach puberty or would wake up a boy. For 27 years I have been trying to get gender affirming surgery but can't afford it. I have never felt comfortable in this female body. It took until my 40s to learn about being non-binary, which is what I now identify as. I have synaesthesia, where numbers, words, colours and objects have sensory stimulus; for example, the colour pink makes me angry, the number 6 is green and smells like fruit. Numbers with colours and smells didn't help my dyscalculia, a number dyslexia where I write numerals and sequences backwards or the wrong way around. It's easier as an adult but requires a lot of mental energy and concentration.

At 40 years old I was clinically diagnosed with Asperger's. My clinical psychologist said there was no question about it, and my mum and I already knew. Having an official diagnosis helped understand how it affected each stage of development and caused depression and anxiety. It also helps me feel like I am not alone, that my neurodivergent traits are super strengths, and it is nothing to be ashamed of. Every decade until my 40s was hard; I was targeted by bullies at school and in the workplace, predators in relationships, misunderstood by many and falsely accused by others.

Despite all the hardships and trauma throughout my life I have tried to live it as fully as possible. In the last decade I have learned effective ways to manage my mental health and autism triggers, and to live an alternative lifestyle which allows me to control what I am exposed to and avoid upsetting encounters.

GLOSSARY OF ABORIGINAL DUAL PLACE NAMES USED IN THE BOOK

On my way around Australia, I tried to learn the traditional names of places and use them. Dual Aboriginal and colonial names were not being used in many places at that stage, it was a small way to support the nations I walked through by acknowledging their sovereignty and history. And an act of activism against places named for the people responsible for genocides, slavery and stolen generations.

Over the last decade many more clans are stepping up and speaking out for their rights and sovereignty, languages are being saved and original names are being used in the media. The colonial reins are still tight, and racists are always making a noise against acknowledgement, respect and treaty. As a nation, we still have a lot of work ahead of us, to work together for equality, recognition and repairing the wrongs of the past.

This is obviously not a definitive list of place names, but I have tried to include all the names I learnt during the walk and since from the places I passed through. Some places are the traditional land of more than one clan group and share traditional names from their local dialects, in these cases I have chosen the one used the most. Some cities, Boorloo for example, the city recognises and also uses traditional names for many places within its centre and suburbs.

Awaba – Lake Macquarie
Balinyala – Port Lincoln
Birpai – around Port Macquarie
Boorloo – Perth
Garramilla – Darwin

Goordnada – Port Augusta
K'gari – Fraser Island
Kanamaluka – River Tamar
Karta Pintingga – Kangaroo Island
Kunanyi – Mount Wellington
Larapuna – Binalong Bay
Limilinaturi – Devonport
Lunawuni – Bruny Island
lutruwita – Tasmania
Mayaluwarana – Freycinet Peninsula
Mardoowarra – Fitzroy Crossing
Minjerrabah – Stradbroke Islands
Mulubinba – Newcastle
Murujuga – Burrup Peninsula
Naarm – Melbourne
Nipaluna – Hobart
Karta Pintingga – Kangaroo Island
Putalina – Oyster Cove
Puthimiluna – Anna Bay
Rubibi – Broome
Takayna – Tarkine
Targungal – Mt Kosciuszko or Mt Townsend*
Tarparrie – Port Pirie
Truwana – Cape Barron Island
Yipun – Yeppoon
Yirramugardu – Roebourne

* Targungal is the Ngarigo name for the Main Range peak which looks the highest, which is Townsend (Kosciuszko didn't actually have a name).

OTHER BOOKS FROM WOODSLANE PRESS

Go to **www.woodslanepress.com.au** for details of dozens of inspirational books, all written to help empower you to better understand and explore Australia.

Road Trips Australia

Backroads and Byways

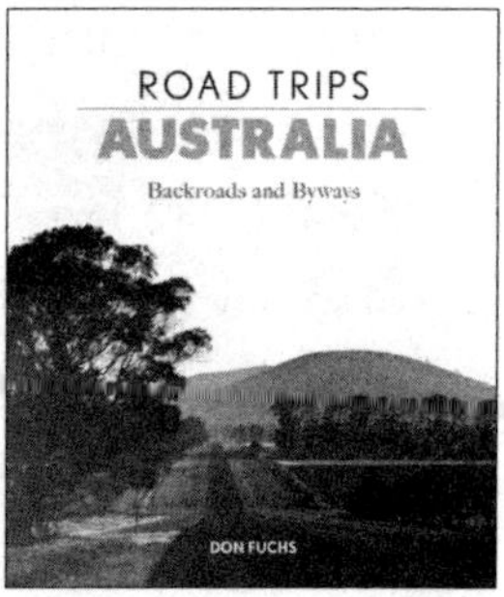

Australia is the ideal country for adventurous driving trips. A gigantic network of roads, many unpaved or back roads, runs through the almost endless expanse. Fascinating national parks are connected with country towns; long stretches of coastline, vast forests and large tracts of the outback are accessible. All you need is a sturdy (SUV or 4WD) vehicle, camping gear, navigation skills and a good dose of common sense.

$44.99 | ISBN: 9781922800046

Adventures in Climate Science

Scientists' tales from the frontiers of climate change

These tales of adventure from remote and remarkable parts of the Earth explore a multitude of ways the world is changing and explain the science behind exactly what those few degrees mean.

Afterword by Terra Roam

$24.99 | ISBN: 9781922800282